THE LIFE AND TIMES

OF

WENDELL PHILLIPS

BY

GEORGE LOWELL AUSTIN

AUTHOR OF A "HISTORY OF MASSACHUSETTS," "LONGFELLOW: HIS
LIFE, WORKS, AND FRIENDSHIPS," ETC.

"A public man is often under the necessity of consenting to measures he dislikes, to save others he thinks important. But the historian is under no such necessity." — LORD MACAULAY.

"In God's world there are no majorities, no minorities; one, on God's side, is a majority." — WENDELL PHILLIPS.

NEW EDITION

BOSTON
LEE AND SHEPARD, PUBLISHERS
1901

Copyright, 1884,
By GEORGE LOWELL AUSTIN.

All rights reserved.

TO

THE COLORED CITIZENS OF THIS LAND,

TO WHOM WENDELL PHILLIPS WAS ALWAYS A FRIEND;

TO WIVES AND DAUGHTERS,

OF WHOSE NATURAL RIGHTS HE WAS ALWAYS A FEARLESS

ADVOCATE;

TO YOUNG MEN AND WOMEN,

TO WHOM HIS UNSTAINED LIFE WAS ALWAYS AN EXAMPLE,

HIS WORDS AN ADMONITION FOR GOOD AND RIGHT,

THESE PAGES

ARE RESPECTFULLY INSCRIBED

BY THE AUTHOR.

PREFACE.

I HAVE entitled the following pages, "The Life and Times of Wendell Phillips." Hence a few words, in the form of a preface, would seem to be necessary.

Mr. Phillips came prominently before the public in the year 1837. From that time onward, he was, in a large sense, a public man. At no time in his career was he regarded as a statesman: he never cast a vote at the polls, and never played the *rôle* of a politician, so-called. Notwithstanding all this, he was, in a very great measure, a public man. During the period in which the slavery question was agitated, — that is, from the year 1837 until the adding of the Thirteenth Amendment to the Constitution, — his name, his utterances, his acts, were constantly recorded in the newspapers. He was an acknowledged leader in the movement, and the part which he played tended to shape the course of American history. With the Woman's Rights Movement, with the causes of Temperance, of the Irish nation, of Labor Reform, of Prison Reform, and indeed with every effort seeking the good of humanity, Mr. Phillips was closely identified.

It would be impossible to write the life of such a man without also writing, however briefly, the history of his times. Public events, and his connection with them, alone give prominence to any individual: eliminate them, and all interest in him is lost save to his family. What Wendell Phillips was in his own home belongs exclusively to that home, and to the beloved companion who was the centre of that home and of his life. I have not wished to invade its sacredness.

But what Wendell Phillips was to the world belongs to the world; and by his acts among men he has bequeathed a record which belongs to humanity, and which, in these pages, I have endeavored to recall in a permanent form. If I have erred in my judgments, I trust that the error will be attributed to that sincere admiration for the great agitator and orator which I cherished from earliest years.

In the preparation of these chapters, I have sought information far and wide. Every person, to whom I have applied, has freely offered his or her assistance. They already have, individually, my expressed thanks.

G. L. A.

CAMBRIDGE, April 1, 1884.

CONTENTS.

CHAPTER I.

ANCESTRY AND PARENTAGE.

PAGE

Memorials of the Phillips Family. — Rev. George Phillips. — Arrival in America. — Death of his Wife. — Life at Watertown, Mass. — Rev. Samuel Phillips of Rowley. — His Marriage. — His Sons. — John Phillips the Merchant. — William Phillips. — His Marriage to Margaret Wendell. — Their Son, John Phillips, the Father of Wendell Phillips. — His Schooldays at Andover, Mass. — Enters Harvard College. — Studies Law. — His Marriage to Sally Walley. — Public Honors. — Chosen the First Mayor of Boston. — His Death. — Character. — His Children 17

CHAPTER II.

THE PERIOD OF YOUTH.

The Phillips Mansion. — Birth of Wendell Phillips. — His Early Training. — Enters the Boston Latin-School. — The Boys of that Period. — Reminiscences of Schoolmates. — Death of Adams and Jefferson. — Lafayette. — Webster's Address at Bunker Hill. — Phillips's First Impressions of Politics. — Mr. Appleton's Recollections. — Phillips enters Harvard College. — Motley and Sumner. — The Faculty. — Life at College. — Opposes Temperance. — Courses of Reading. — Favorite Authors. — Enters the Junior Class at the Law School. — Methods of Instruction. — Cherishes no Fondness for the

Law. — Graduation. — Admitted to the Bar. — At Lowell, Mass. — Benjamin F. Butler. — Practice 27

CHAPTER III.

THE EARLY ANTI-SLAVERY MOVEMENT.

Garrison establishes "The Liberator." — The First Number. — A Dingy Office. — Mr. Garrison's Supporters. — Dr. Lyman Beecher. — Jeremiah Evarts. — Oliver Johnson's Testimony. — "The Liberator" creates a Stir in the South. — The Might of King Cotton. — Garrison's Appeal to his Countrymen. — The New-England Anti-Slavery Society. — Story of its Organization. — Preachers and Politics. — The Rise of the American Anti-Slavery Society. — Growth of the Movement. — The Reign of Terror dawning. — The Charleston Riot. — Faneuil Hall pays a Tribute to Slavery, and the New-England Pulpit Dumb! 45

CHAPTER IV.

THE GARRISON MOB, AND ITS RESULTS.

Where was Wendell Phillips ? — The Female Anti-Slavery Society hold a Meeting, October, 1835. — Inflammatory Handbills. — "The Commercial Gazette" excites the Mobocracy. — The Ladies assemble at the Hall. — The Opening Exercises. — The Mob gain Possession of the Hall. — Mayor Lyman counsels Adjournment. — Mr. Garrison seized by the Rioters. — Dragged through Boston's Streets. — At City Hall. — Conveyed to Jail. — The Outcome. — Phillips views the Spectacle. — Learns a Lesson. — Foresees his Future. — His Speech on the Twentieth Anniversary of the Mob 58

CHAPTER V.

THE DÉBUT OF WENDELL PHILLIPS.

The Year 1837. — Slavery the Dominant Power of the Country. — Earnestness of the Abolitionists. — The Lovejoy Tragedy.

— Story of the Alton Riots. — The Tidings reach Boston. — Faneuil Hall refused to the Indignant Abolitionists. — Dr. Channing appeals to the Citizens of Boston. — The Hall opened at Last. — A Packed Audience. — Resolutions. — Harangue of Attorney-Gen. Austin. — Its Effect. — Reply of Wendell Phillips. — Great Uproar and Excitement. — The Result 68

CHAPTER VI.

PHILLIPS AN ABOLITIONIST. — MARRIAGE.

Phillips's Aspirations. — The Lyceum-Lecture System. — Phillips delivers his First Lecture. — "The Lost Arts." — Joins the New-England Anti-Slavery Society. — Status of the Colored People. — The Chapmans. — Ann Terry Greene. — Phillips falls in Love. — Marriage. — His Domestic Life. — The Faithful Wife. — Phillips's First Anti-Slavery Lecture. — Recollections of Edwin Thompson 82

CHAPTER VII.

THE WORLD'S ANTI-SLAVERY CONVENTION.

Begins its Sessions June 12, 1840. — The Rights of Women discussed in the American Anti-Slavery Society. — David Lee Child's Resolutions. — Prominent Delegates. — Freemasons' Hall, London. — Debate on the Admission of Women. — Speech of Mr. Phillips. — The Women rejected. — Adverse Criticism, and Wisdom of Mr. Phillips 93

CHAPTER VIII.

PROGRESS OF THE ANTI-SLAVERY CAUSE.

Phillips arrives Home from Europe. — Limited Acquaintanceship. — Letter to George Thompson. — The "Remond Case." — A Petition to the Legislature, and its Result. — Arrest of George Latimer. — The Action of the Legislature. — A Voice in Congress. — Phillips argues for Disunion. — Discussion. — An Interesting Letter. — Mobs 102

CHAPTER IX.

ERA OF THE FUGITIVE-SLAVE ACT.

James K. Polk becomes President of the United States. — The Annexation of Texas. — Origin of the "Liberty Party." — The Massachusetts Legislature of 1846. — The "Free-Soil Party." — Fleeing from Slavery. — An Outrage in Boston. — Election of Gen. Taylor. — Growth of the Free-Soil Party. — The Fugitive-Slave Bill proposed in Congress. — Debates. — Apostasy of Daniel Webster. — The 7th of March Speech. — Indignation Meetings. — The Act signed by the President. — Faneuil Hall speaks. — Charles Sumner chosen Senator. — The "Shadrach Case." — The "Sims Case." — Public Meetings. — Election of Franklin Pierce. — The Darkest Day in the History of the American Republic . . . 121

CHAPTER X.

A YEAR OF MOBS AND CONVENTIONS.

Friends of Temperance assemble in New York, 1853. — Women excluded from the Convention. — A Busy Autumn. — Comments of "The Tribune." — Rev. Antoinette L. Brown. — Her Experience at the Temperance Convention. — Exclusion of Miss Brown and Mr. Phillips. — The Woman's Rights Convention. — Riotous Disturbances. — Madame Annekè. — Phillips's Bitter Invective. — The Convention forced to adjourn *sine die* 143

CHAPTER XI.

PHILLIPS AND THE WOMAN'S RIGHTS MOVEMENT.

A Plan for Action first proposed. — The Call. — Responses. — The Worcester Convention of 1850. — Outline of the Proceedings. — Attitude of the Press. — The Convention of 1851. —

Mr. Phillips's Address. — Harriet Martineau. — The Legislature. — The Boston Convention of 1854. — Resolutions. — The Convention of 1855. — Donations. — Assembling of the Seventh National Woman's Rights Convention in New York, 1856. — Mr. Phillips's Speech. — Indifference of Political Parties towards the Movement. — The National Convention of 1858. — The Convention of 1859. — Mr. Phillips makes a Stirring Address. — The Legislatures Memorialized. — The New-England Convention. — Mr. Phillips again. — The "Drawing-Room" Convention. — Mrs. Dall's Lectures. — The Tenth National Convention, 1860. — Marriage and Divorce discussed. — Mr. Phillips opposes Discussion. — The Woman Question laid aside. — "After the Slave — then the Woman," 152

CHAPTER XII.

THE PREPARATION FOR WAR.

The Politics of 1853. — Franklin Pierce President. — The "Kansas and Nebraska Bill." — The Repeal of the Missouri Compromise. — Sumner foresees the "Beginning of the End." — A Convention of the Free-Soil Party. — The Republican Party. — Workings of the Fugitive-Slave Act. — Arrest of Anthony Burns. — A Famous Meeting. — Indictments found against Phillips, Parker, and Others. — The Result. — A Petition for the Removal of "Slave Commissioner" Loring. — Mr. Phillips's Argument. — "The Crime against Kansas." — Assault on Charles Sumner. — Election of James Buchanan. — The Signs of the Times. — The John Brown Raid. — Mr. Phillips's Eulogy. — His Lecture in Brooklyn. — Mr. Slack's Recollections. — Riotous Feeling in New York. — Anniversary Meeting in Boston. — A Riot prevented 170

CHAPTER XIII.

PHILLIPS DURING WAR-TIME.

The Outbreak of Rebellion. — Winter of 1860–61. — The Fight for Free Speech in Boston. — The Personal-Liberty Act. —

Status of the Press. — The Virginia Peace Commission. — President Lincoln inaugurated. — The First Gun. — The Country aroused. — Phillips at New Bedford. — The Call for Troops. — The Patriotism of the Press. — The Memorable April Twenty-first. — A Morning Meeting in State Street. — Wendell Phillips in Music Hall. — " Under the Flag." — State Conventions. — The Question of Slavery ignored. — The Year 1862. — The Emancipation Proclamation. — Ratification Meeting. — Phillips favors arming the Colored Men. — The " July Riot." — Progress of the War. — The Thirteenth Amendment. — Peace. — Return of Troops. — Woman Suffrage. — Conventions of 1866-69 193

CHAPTER XIV.
NEARING THE END.

The Fifteenth Amendment. — Phillips nominated for Governor. — Arraigns the Republican Party. — Meeting of the Reform League. — Convention. — A Labor Platform. — The Butler Campaign of 1871. — Phillips at Steinway Hall. — " Courts and Jails." — Phillips supports Grant. — Letter to the Colored Citizens of Boston. — The Days of the White Leaguers. — Opposition Meetings. — Phillips on Finance in 1875. — Phillips on Daniel O'Connell. — Sir Harry Vane. — The Grant-Sumner Controversy. — Phillips on License. — Letter to " the Liberal Clergy." — Phillips *vs.* Crosby. — The Irish Crisis. — Phillips at Cambridge. — Reminiscences of Dr. Clarke. — Letter of Parker Pillsbury. — Declining Years. — Phillips's Last Speech. — Illness. — Death and Burial 257

CHAPTER XV.
PHILLIPS AS A PHILOSOPHER.

Origin of the " Radical Club." — Phillips's Views on Religion. — On the Christian Name. — On Heart in Religion. — Economic Laws. — Phillips on the Boston of To-day. — Phillips's Opinion of Jonathan Edwards 370

CHAPTER XVI.

Eulogies and Tributes 388

LIST OF ILLUSTRATIONS.

PAGE

PORTRAIT OF WENDELL PHILLIPS.
   ENGRAVED ON STEEL EXPRESSLY FOR THIS WORK . *Frontispiece.*

THE RENDITION OF ANTHONY BURNS.
   MARCH DOWN STATE STREET 140

THE PHILLIPS HOMESTEAD.
   THE ESSEX-STREET HOUSE 349

WENDELL PHILLIPS'S LATE RESIDENCE.
   THE COMMON-STREET HOUSE 358

IN FANEUIL HALL.
   THE REMAINS LYING IN STATE 364

LIFE AND TIMES

OF

WENDELL PHILLIPS.

CHAPTER I.

ANCESTRY AND PARENTAGE.

Memorials of the Phillips Family. — Rev. George Phillips. — Arrival in America. — Death of his Wife. — Life at Watertown, Mass. — Rev. Samuel Phillips of Rowley. — His Marriage. — His Sons. — John Phillips the Merchant. — William Phillips. — His Marriage to Margaret Wendell. — Their Son, John Phillips, the Father of Wendell Phillips. — His School-Days at Andover, Mass. — Enters Harvard College. — Studies Law. — His Marriage to Sally Walley. — Public Honors. — Chosen the First Mayor of Boston. — His Death. — Character. — His Children.

> "There is a pedigree of the body and a pedigree of the mind."
> WENDELL PHILLIPS.

FEW names that the history of the commonwealth of Massachusetts has underscored are more worthy of being cherished than that of the Phillips family; and it is a matter for public congratulation, that there exist to-day such worthy monuments for its perpetuation as the two academies of Andover, Mass., and of Exeter, N.H.

We have intimated that these two institutions are monuments to a family. They are so, because they were built up, not by the wisdom and self-denial of one individual of that family, but by the very remarkable unanimity of aim and coincidence of judgment of six members of it, representing three generations. Still more essentially are they so, because they were the outcome of a marked nobleness of spirit and elevation of character, that have not ceased to distinguish representatives of the Phillips family through nine generations.

The progenitor of the Phillips family in America was the Rev. George Phillips, son of Christopher Phillips of Rainham, St. Martin, Norfolk County, England, *mediocris fortunæ*. He entered Gonville and Caius College, Cambridge, April 20, 1610, then aged seventeen years, and received his bachelor's degree in 1613. He gave early indications of deep piety, uncommon talents, and love of learning, and at the university distinguished himself by his remarkable progress in scholarship, especially in theological studies, for which he manifested a partiality.

After his graduation he was settled in the ministry at Boxted, Essex County, England; but his strong attachment to the principles of the nonconformists brought him into difficulties with some of his parishioners; and, as the storm of persecution grew more dark and threatening, he resolved to cast his lot with the Puritans, who were about to depart for the New World. On the 12th of April, 1630, he, with his wife and two children, embarked for America in the "Arbella," as fellow-passenger with Gov. Winthrop, Sir Richard Saltonstall, and other assistants of the Massachusetts Company, and arrived at Salem on the 12th of June, where, shortly afterwards, his wife died, and was buried by the side of Lady Arbella Johnson.

Mr. Phillips was admitted "freeman," May 18, 1631; this being the earliest date of any such admission. For fourteen years he was the pastor of the church at Watertown, a most godly man, and an influential member of the small council that regulated the affairs of the colony. His share in giving form and character to the institutions of New England is believed to have been a very large one. He died on the 1st of July, 1644, aged about fifty-one years.

The son of the foregoing, born in Boxted, England, in 1625, and graduated from Harvard College in 1650, became in 1651 the Rev. Samuel Phillips of Rowley, Mass. He continued as pastor over this parish for a period of forty-five years. He was "highly esteemed for his piety and talents, which were of no common order; and he was eminently useful, both at home and abroad. He officiated repeatedly at the great public anniversaries, which put in requisition the abilities of the first men in the New-England colonies. It is not known that any of his productions were printed; yet it is on record, that, in 1675, he preached the artillery election sermon, and also the election sermon in 1678." [1]

In September, 1687, an information was filed by one Philip Nelson, against the Rev. Samuel Phillips, for calling Randolph "a wicked man;" and for this "crime" (redounding to his honor) he was committed to prison.[2]

He was married in October, 1651, to Sarah Appleton, the daughter of Samuel and Mary (Everhard) Appleton of Ipswich. He died April 22, 1696, greatly beloved and lamented. His inventory amounted to nine hundred and eighty-nine pounds sterling. In November, 1839, a chaste and handsome marble monument was placed over the remains of Mr. Phillips and his wife, in the burial-ground at Rowley, by the Hon. Jonathan Phillips of Boston, their great-great-great-grandson.

He left two sons, the younger of whom, George (1664–1739, Harvard 1686), became an eminent clergyman, the Rev. George Phillips, first of Jamaica, L.I., and afterwards of Brookhaven. The elder son, Samuel, chose the occupation of a goldsmith, and settled in Salem. It is from this Samuel of Salem that the two Boston branches of the Phillips family have descended.

A younger son of Samuel, the Hon. John Phillips,

---

[1] See Gage's History of Rowley.
[2] See Washburn's Judicial History of Massachusetts.

was born June 22, 1701. He became a successful merchant of Boston, was a deacon of Brattle-street Church, a colonel of the Boston Regiment, a justice of the peace and of the quorum, and a representative of Boston for several years in the General Court. He married, in 1723, Mary Buttolph, a daughter of Nicholas Buttolph of Boston. She died in 1742; and he next married Abigail Webb, a daughter of Rev. Mr. Webb of Fairfield, Conn. He died April 19, 1768, and was buried with military honors. According to the records, he was "a man much devoted to works of benevolence."

His son, William Phillips of Boston, was born Aug. 29, 1737, and died June 4, 1772. In 1761 he married Margaret Wendell, the eleventh and youngest child of the Hon. Jacob Wendell, a merchant, and one of the Governor's Council. His widow died in 1823.

John Phillips, the only son of William and Margaret, was born in Boston on the ancient Phillips place, on the 26th of November, 1770. His mother was a woman of uncommon energy of mind as well as of ardent piety, and early instilled into the heart of her son the principles of religion and a love of learning and of his native land. She placed him, at the early age of seven years, in the family of his kinsman, Lieut.-Gov. Samuel Phillips of Andover, where he remained until he entered Harvard College in 1784. In this excellent and pious family, and in the academy under the charge of the learned Dr. Eliphalet Pearson, young Phillips acquired the rudiments of a sound scholarship as well as that urbane and conciliating manner which was so conducive to his success in subsequent life.

Judge Phillips and his excellent lady took a lively interest in the studies of their ward. They examined him from time to time, not only in his catechism, which was then regularly taught, but also in respect to his literary efforts and acquirements. They encouraged him to make strenuous efforts to obtain a high rank as a scholar, speaker, gentleman, and Christian. Their labors were not lost. On leaving Andover, the youth was prepared to take an elevated stand in college, which he maintained to the completion of his course, when the honor of pronouncing the salutatory oration was conferred on him by the college faculty.

Mr. Phillips chose the profession of the law, and soon gained an extensive practice. His popularity became such, that in 1794 he was invited to pronounce the annual Fourth of July oration before the people of Boston. "This production," says a writer, "bears the finest marks of intellectual vigor." Some extracts from it have found their way into the school-books as models of eloquence.

In this same year Mr. Phillips was married to Miss Sally Walley, daughter of Thomas Walley, Esq., a respectable merchant of Boston. On the establishment of the Municipal Court in Boston, in 1800, he was made public prosecutor, and in 1803 was chosen representative to the General Court. The next year he was sent to the Senate, and such was the wisdom of his political measures, and the dignity of his bearing towards all parties, that he continued to hold a seat in this body every successive year until his decease; always discharging his duties, either as a debater or in the chair, to which he was ten times called, most creditably to himself, as well as most acceptably to his constituents and the State.

In 1809 Mr. Phillips was appointed judge of the Court of Common Pleas. Three years later he was elected a member of the corporation of Harvard College, and in 1820 a member of the convention for the revision of the State Constitution. In this able and dignified body he held a conspicuous rank. His remarks upon the various questions which arose were learned, judicious, and sometimes rendered all the more effective by the flashes of his wit. Speaking, for example, on the third article of the Bill of Rights, he said he hoped they would not be like the man whose epitaph was, " I am well, I would be better, and here I am."

The next year the town of Boston, which now contained nearly forty-five thousand inhabitants, began to agitate in good earnest the question of adopting a city government. A committee of twelve, of which Mr. Phillips was chairman, drew up and reported a city charter for the town, which was adopted at a meeting held March 4, 1822, by a vote of 2,797 to 1,881, and the result formally announced on the 7th of the same month by a proclamation from Gov. Brooks.

The two prominent candidates for the office of mayor were Harrison Gray Otis and Josiah Quincy, both men of high accomplishments, and enjoying a large share of public confidence. But after a vote had been taken, resulting in no choice of mayor, the friends of these gentlemen suddenly agreed on Mr. Phillips, who at the town-meeting held on the 16th of April, 1822, received 2,500 out of 2,650 votes, and thus became the first mayor of the city of Boston.

The inauguration occurred at Faneuil Hall on the 1st of May following. The ceremonies of the occasion were unusually impressive; the venerable Dr. Thomas Baldwin invoking the favor of Heaven, and Chief Justice Isaac Parker administering the oath.

In discharging the duties of his office, Mr. Phillips wisely avoided sumptuous display on the one hand, and a parsimonious economy on the other, but observing that *juste milieu* which good sense dictated, and the spirit of our republican institutions demanded, succeeded in overcoming all prejudices against the new form of municipal government, and in establishing a precedent, which, followed by succeeding mayors, has saved the city millions of dollars of needless expense, and has served as a worthy example to many other cities in this country.

Perceiving, towards the expiration of his first term

of service, that his health was beginning to fail, Mr. Phillips declined being a candidate for re-election, and on the twenty-ninth day of May, 1823, was suddenly stricken down by disease of the heart; he being then in the fifty-third year of his age. His death was universally lamented, and public honors were paid by all parties to his memory.

John Phillips was a good man, true as steel, and always trustworthy in the various relations of life. He lived in the fear of God, and from his Word received instruction for the guidance of his conduct. He lived in stormy times; yet such was the consistency and elevation of his character, such the suavity and dignity of his manner, such the kindness of his heart, the clearness of his conceptions, and beauty of his language, that he commanded the respect and admiration of his political opponents, wielding perhaps as great an influence as any public man of the State at that period; and he will ever stand as a worthy model for the incumbents of that high municipal office, which his wisdom, prudence, virtue, integrity, and eloquence adorned.

The following are the names of the children of John and Sally (Walley) Phillips: —

1. Thomas Walley, born Jan. 16, 1797.
2. Sarah Hurd, born April 24, 1799.
3. Samuel, born Feb. 8, 1801.

4. Margaret, born Nov. 29, 1802.
5. Miriam, born Nov. 20, 18—.
6. John Charles, born Nov. 15, 1807.
7. George William, born Jan. 3, 1810.
8. WENDELL, born Nov. 29, 1811.
9. Grenville Tudor, born Aug. 14, 1816.

CHAPTER II.

THE PERIOD OF YOUTH.

The Phillips Mansion. — Birth of Wendell Phillips. — His Early Training. — Enters the Boston Latin School. — The Boys of that Period. — Reminiscences of Schoolmates. — Death of Adams and Jefferson. — Lafayette. — Webster's Address at Bunker Hill. — Phillips's First Impressions of Politics. — Mr. Appleton's Recollections. — Phillips enters Harvard College. — Motley and Sumner. — The Faculty. — Life at College. — Opposes Temperance. — Courses of Reading. — Favorite Authors. — Enters the Junior Class at the Law-School. — Methods of Instruction. — Cherishes no Fondness for the Law. — Graduation. — Admitted to the Bar. — At Lowell, Mass. — Benjamin F. Butler. — Practice.

"The greatest praise government can win is, that its citizens know their rights, and dare to maintain them. The best use of good laws is, to teach men to trample bad laws under their feet.

"On these principles, I am willing to stand before the community in which I was born and brought up, — where I expect to live and die, — where, if I shall ever win any reputation, I expect to earn and to keep it. As a sane man, a Christian man, and a lover of my country, I am willing to be judged by posterity." — PHILLIPS, 1852.

"Whoever sees farther than his neighbor is that neighbor's servant, to lift him to such higher level. Then, power, ability, influence, character, virtue, are only trusts with which to serve our time." — PHILLIPS, 1881.

IN a large mansion, still standing on the lower corner of Beacon and Walnut Streets, Boston, Wendell Phillips, the eighth child of Hon. John and Sally (Walley) Phillips, was born, on the 29th of November, 1811.

In his earliest years, surrounded by all the advantages which the wealth, culture, and social position of his parents afforded, the boy advanced under wise training. To his father, who made this rule for all his children, "Ask no man to do for you any thing that you are not able and willing to do for yourself," he was indebted for those lessons of self-dependence which he invariably practised in after-life. To his mother, who never wearied in searching the Scriptures, and who believed in the value of early religious impressions, he owed that simplicity, that earnest sincerity, and that remarkable disposition to stand by the right, which afterwards developed itself with such force, and produced such important effects.

In August, 1822, he entered the Boston Latin School, which was then located at the corner of Chapman Place and School Street, — a site now occupied by the Parker House. The late B. A. Gould was the headmaster. Those of his schoolmates who survive remember Wendell as at that time a boy of about eleven years of age, finely formed, vigorous, and quite tall for his years. Had Puritan Boston cultivated muscle, he would have excelled in athletic exercises; but muscle was at that time at a discount.

Many of the youths of that period were pale and puny, — forced to be so by the absurd notions of their ancestors, — who walked sedately, with their bundles of books, to and from school, who never loitered by the way, nor snowballed, nor skated, nor kicked foot-ball, nor swam in the harbor of the Charles. They were the heirs to all the promises of intellectual greatness. They were not all as wise, however, as they looked.

But Phillips was neither pale nor puny. He had a fine physique, and his mind was as brilliant as his body was vigorous. "What first led me to observe him," says a fellow-student, "and fixed him in my memory, was his elocution; and I soon came to look forward to declamation day with interest, mainly on his account; though many were admirable speakers. The pieces spoken were mainly such as would excite patriotic feelings and an enthusiasm for freedom.

"I remember distinctly the hot summer day when, the windows of the schoolhouse all open, we heard the tolling of the bells for the death of Adams and Jefferson. We were informed why they were tolling; and, in those days of belief in special providences, it was for us a remarkable providence that they died on that day they had made sacred, and that, in their deaths, they were not divided; and it added to the solemnity of the occasion, that Heaven thus seemed to set the seal of its approbation upon their lives and their work.

"What have since been sneered at as 'glittering generalities,' were to us great truths; and with the men whose 'souls were tried,' and who gave or risked their lives for those truths, many of us claimed a near relationship. Some of us had heard our grandfathers sing that inspired battle-hymn of the Revolution, composed by Judge Niles of Vermont, beginning with the lines, —

> 'Why should vain mortals tremble at the sight of
> Death and destruction on the field of battle?'

— a hymn worthy of the cause it was written to sustain, and worthy of preservation, from its associations, as the battle-hymn of the republic.

"We had heard them tell of that bitter winter encampment in New York, when the snow fell to five feet on a level; when they were short of provisions, without shoes, nearly naked, many of them, and huddled together in heaps under straw for warmth; when officers as well as privates were despondent, and only a belief, stimulated by the eloquent pen of Paine, that those 'glittering generalities' were rights worthy of the effort and the sacrifice, kept them from despair and desertion. We could realize how intense their enthusiasm, how bright their hopes, at the surrender of Burgoyne and Cornwallis.

"We had stood in line on Tremont Street, with ribbons, on which were portraits of Lafayette, pinned to our jackets, when that enthusiast for liberty, then a grand old man, revisited the land to which, in the hot blood of youth, he had given his sword; wondering at the enthusiastic greetings of the crowds, and at the evidences of thrift and prosperity, which, as we were told, led him to inquire, 'Where are your poor?' so unconscious of any great merit for what he had done, that he was disposed to decline the offer of a national ship, and take passage in a private vessel; little dreaming that his journey was to prove a triumphal procession such as the world had never seen.

"And we had walked over the bridge to Charlestown and Bunker Hill, and had heard Webster, then the embodiment of eloquence and patriotism; while before him were the venerable men, among whom Lafayette was seated, the survivors of those who, on that memorable night, had thrown up the breastworks that time had not levelled, — Webster, whose philippic against the slave-trade at Plymouth, in 1820, every school-boy knew by heart: —

"'I hear the sound of the hammer. I see the smoke of the furnaces where manacles and fetters are still forged for human limbs. I see the visages of those who, by stealth and at midnight, labor in this work of hell, foul and dark as may become the artificers of such instruments of misery and torture. If the pulpit be silent whenever or wherever there may be a sinner bloody with this guilt, within the hearing of its voice, the pulpit is false to its trust.'

"Words of fire these that burned into the souls of boys like Phillips those 'prejudices' which Webster in vain begged them to 'conquer,' when he had sold himself to the slave-power for a mere nomination to the presidency that was never made, and, for such a consideration, was not fit to be made."

Educated among such influences, never was pupil

more faithful to the teachings of his master than the thoughtful boy to these burning words of the then foremost man in New England.

The recollections of Mr. Thomas G. Appleton may be given in this connection: —

"Phillips was an old friend of mine. I remember how we used to play together long ago, and the recollection is very pleasant indeed. He was a fine, manly little fellow; and I was very proud of him as a playmate. Wendell Phillips, J. Lothrop Motley, and I used to play together in the garret of the Motley House; and I remember that their favorite pastime used to be, to strut about in any fantastic costume they could find in the corners of the old attic, and shout scraps of poetry and dialogue at each other.

"It was a fine sight to see them, for both were noble-looking fellows; and even then Wendell's voice was a very pleasant one to listen to, and his gestures as graceful as could be.

"After that I knew him at the Latin School, and later at college. I remember at college that we got a notion that Phillips was laboring under some religious excitement; and so, to revive him a little, we got him into the Porcellian; and he soon became our president. He was well liked at college, and his radicalism did not then develop strongly enough to make him in any way unpopular. He was always a fine elocutionist, and elegant in his manner of delivery."

In those days the course at the Latin School was one of five years. According to the years of study, the school was divided into five classes, and each class into three divisions. The curriculum included, — in Greek, Valpy's "Greek Grammar," the "Delectus Sententiarum Græcarum," Jacobs's "Greek Reader," the "Four Gospels," and two books of Homer's "Iliad;" in Latin, Adams's "Latin Grammar," "Liber Primus," "Epitome Historiæ Græcæ," "Viri Romæ," "Phædri Fabulæ," "Cornelius Nepos," Ovid's "Metamorphoses," Sallust's "Catiline," and "Jugurthine War," Cæsar, Virgil, Cicero's "Select Orations," the "Agricola," and "Germania" of Tacitus, and the "Odes" and "Epodes" of Horace; in the study of mythology, Tooke's "Pantheon of the Heathen Gods" served as the text-book; Lacroix was used in arithmetic; and in reading, Lindley Murray's "English Reader."

Having finished a course at the Latin School before he was sixteen, he entered Harvard College, and was graduated, in 1831, in the class with Motley, the future historian of the Netherlands. Phillips and Motley were warm personal friends; and both ranked high among their fellows on account of their beauty, elegant manners, and social position. In the class preceding was Charles Sumner, whom Phillips knew while they were both in the Latin School.

When Phillips entered college, Rev. John T. Kirkland was president; but in 1829 he was succeeded by

Josiah Quincy. Among the professors were Edward T. Channing in rhetoric, George Ticknor in French and Spanish literature, John S. Popkin in Greek, George Otis in Latin, Levi Hodge in logic and metaphysics, and John Farrar in mathematics and natural philosophy. Of the corps of instructors then in service, not one survives.

At college, Phillips was a fair student. He was a daily boxer and fencer, and acquired some skill in both departments of this manly art. He was never in the opposition; never got into trouble on account of his dissent from the opinions of others; and was so far from inclining to radicalism, either in politics or in social life, that, after having been elected president of the "Hasty-Pudding Club," he was made president of another exclusive society, known as the "Gentlemen's Club." He had so little interest in reform, that he succeeded in defeating — or bears the infamy, as he himself phrased it, of having defeated — the first proposition to establish a temperance society at Harvard.

But it was of the man considered so sarcastic and critical and harsh in after-life, that a classmate said, "Whenever we are abusing a fellow, Phillips always finds something good to say of him." To his class, it was the greatest surprise when he joined the anti-slavery movement.

During his college-life, Phillips rarely read speeches, or even had any taste for oratory. But debate, and the arguments which it necessitated, was always his hobby. His favorite study was history, including a lively interest in genealogy, and even in heraldry.

"But," said Mr. Phillips one day, in speaking of his college-life, "if I had followed my own bent, I should have given my time to mechanics or history; and my mother used to say, that, when I became a lawyer, a good carpenter was spoiled."

An intimate friend, writing in 1874 of Phillips's college-life, says,

"Mr. Phillips, when at college, gave a year to the study of the English Revolution of 1640. He studied every thing relating to it, from Clarendon to Godwin, — every memoir, every speech, every novel, every play, that was accessible to him, whether written at the time, or the scene of which was laid in those years.

"He gave another year to the study of biographies and memoirs of the age of George the Third, covering our own Revolution with the same completeness. He next studied Dutch history with equal thoroughness as far as English literature afforded the means of doing so. Proverbs were his especial delight. The character of a young man is best known by a knowledge of his heroes. Those of Mr. Phillips in English history were Sir Walter Raleigh, Andrew Marvell, Pym, Sir Harry Vane, Cromwell, Chesterfield, De Foe, Lady Mary Wortley Montague, John Hunter, James Watt, and Brindley. In American history they were Jay, Franklin, Hamilton, Samuel Adams, and Eli Whitney.

"Among novelists, Richardson was a great favorite; and Scott he knew almost by heart. In Latin literature, Tacitus and Juvenal were his favorites. In French literature, Sully, Rochefoucauld, De Retz, Pascal, Tocqueville, Guizot, and Victor Hugo.

In English, his pets were Swift, Ben Jonson, Jeremy Taylor, Massinger, Milton, Southey (in 'The Doctor'), Lamb, the elder Disraeli, and 'all of Horace Walpole.'

"He was late in opening to Shakspeare. Then he regarded Elizabeth Barrett Browning as the first of modern poets, an opinion that he has not changed. To-day he thinks that George Eliot and Charlotte Brontë see life truer and deeper than either Dickens or Thackeray, though they lack the artistic skill of their more celebrated contemporaries."

We are indebted to Rev. Edgar Buckingham of Deerfield, Mass., a classmate of Mr. Phillips, and for many years the class-secretary of the class of 1831, for the following interesting reminiscences. They begin with the days at the Latin School.

"Any one may be happy in having been the schoolmate of Wendell Phillips. We were in the same class, in school and college, for five years. Comparatively few men can tell of him when he was a boy. But, to my mind then, he was the most beautiful person I had ever seen, — handsome, indeed, in form and feature; but what I mean by his beauty was his grace of character, his kindly, generous manners, his brightness of mind, his perfect purity and whiteness of soul. His face was very fair, though it could not have been called pale; and it had a radiance from which shone forth the soul that dwelt within. He was a good scholar, and the happiest and most charming of companions, either in play or talk. I shall never forget when, in our play around the houses in Montgomery Place, then unfinished, I tumbled down an open cellar-way, he was down first to see if I was hurt. In school-time, besides Horace and Homer, the boys did a great deal of talking. We drew pictures. We carved alabaster into shapes to stamp letters with, in days when letters for the mail were sealed with wax or wafers. The seats on which we sat during our last year were so placed in regard to the desk of the teacher, that the teacher could not conveniently watch us unless he was particularly anxious to do so; and I think he had a fellow-feeling with us, and allowed us to talk unless we disturbed others by noise. The subject of our conversation at that time — boys fourteen or fifteen years of age — was the trinity, atonement, or some other point of orthodox theology. Dr. Lyman Beecher was at that time reigning as sovereign over the orthodox churches of Boston, and was in the height of his power and influence. Large numbers of persons were attending his church in Hanover Street, to listen to the terrors of his eloquence, — some from the Unitarian connection, among them some of the nearest relations of Wendell; and he himself was drawn in as a convert. I suppose he needed no conversion from the moral education his mother had given him, and from the dispositions he inherited from his ancestors; but he probably obtained clearer ideas of duty and consecration from the instruction he received, and the excitement through which he passed, and became, for the most part, fixed in some ideas of a great, important life. At any rate, his conversion, it is plain, exercised no permanent narrowing influences over him. It did not, by overwhelming views of a future world, make him, as a technical conversion does some, uninterested in people's welfare in the present life, nor, as it often does, make theology superior to philanthropy. I have not learned that he ever changed his theological opinions. It has not been opinion that has made him the man he has shown himself to be, and no sectarian could argue in favor of a special creed from the life and labors Mr. Phillips has pursued. At one time, in his middle life, he renounced the church, as at present constituted or conducted; and to a friend, a minister, who said to him, 'I suppose you think "*laborare est orare*," — " your working is your prayer," or otherwise, "your devotion to duty is your devoutness," — he replied, 'Yes; but I think much of the "*orare*," the praying, too.' But to return to his earlier days. The excitement of the revival gradually passed off in him; that is, in a few years. But his conversion for quite a while made a deep impression on his companions, awakening their reverence — the word is not too strong — for this religious boy, and probably leading some on for a time in interesting views of the religious life.

"His evident religiousness continued for some time after his entrance into college. I remember well his appearance of deep devoutness during morning and evening prayers in the chapel, which so many attended only to save their credit with the government. Doddridge's 'Expositor' Wendell bore to college in his freshman year, — a present, I think, from his mother, a new volume, — to be his help in daily thought and prayer. His interest in his studies was never remitted through his college course: and to the last he stood high in a class, the largest but one that had at that time ever been graduated from Harvard; and its members, however justly or unjustly, believed that their eighth or tenth scholar would have been first in any other class. Motley the historian was also a member of it, and an intimate friend of Phillips. But, out of the first ten scholars, a large proportion died in their youth, and despoiled the class of power to prove by subsequent achievements and by public fame that their self-flattery was really just. Phillips was really handsome, as I have said, in figure and feature a young Apollo. I remember, in his room, measurements we made of him to see how near his proportions came to that example of Grecian ideas of manly beauty.

"He was of a wealthy family; and with manly beauty, with a most attractive face, 'a smile that was a benediction,' with manners of superior elegance, with conversation filled with the charms of literature, with biography and history, full of refined pleasantry, with never a word or thought that the purest might not know and listen to, it was no wonder that his society was courted, and especially by those who had wealth at their command, and still more by those young men that came from the South. It is said that he is proud; that he was a born patrician. In a good sense of the words, he was a born patrician: in the sense of the French expression, '*noblesse oblige,*' he felt the responsibilities of his birth and education, — his responsibility to keep himself pure, upright, and good. I would not say that he never developed at any time any thing of worldly pride also. I believe he did look down with scorn on that vulgarity, that form of professed democracy, whose virtue only was to envy those better and purer than themselves as well as loftier in position. I never knew that he scorned any one who was merely poor. But it happened, as one of the strangest of all human phenomena, that this young man, who, in all his public life, has been the defender of the trodden-down and despised, was the especial pet, in his junior and senior years in college, of the aristocracy in that institution. Indeed, he had the credit of being their leader: they put him up to it. The democracy of the class became excited to the highest degree, — for reasons that I do not now recall, and believe I never knew (and I dare say there were none), — and it was determined to put Phillips and others of his associates down. I think he used some of his fine scorn at that time. We had then a military organization, a great pride of ours, — the Harvard Washington corps; and though our uniform was black coats and white pantaloons, and the officers had golden-appearing buttons on their coats, with the usual feathers, epaulets, and sashes, yet, in my mind then, no company, however richly uniformed, made a handsomer appearance. When the time came for election of officers by the class to which we belonged, a great struggle took place. It ended in a compromise. Phillips was not chosen captain. A young man from the South, yet not of the acknowledged aristocracy, — a young man of herculean stature and proportion, and one who had never taken sides in this social quarrel, and whom the whole college would have said was properly the man for the place, — was chosen; and Phillips became one of the highest officers, — lieutenant, I think. I never asked him what he learned about Southern pride and assumption in those days. But was it not singular, that, from having been the most admired companion and most ardent champion of Southern men in his youth, he should have become in after-years an opponent of Southern principles, — than whom there has been none more powerful in the country? I would like to tell my readers what dear companion as I suppose it has been, — the pride of his heart, his counsellor and his support, — that suggested or brought about the change. But he has a right to keep that secret sacred to himself. But, if he was born a patrician, he had a nature, which, by birth, was ready for the upspringing from within of a true Christian democracy. During the days of his boyhood I should never have imagined that he had any conception of the superiority of one man over another, except as superiority was made by mind and soul. And if laboring-men now who may ever be in his company, while he is ready to give his life for their service, feel, that, while he is with them and for them, he is not of them, that sentiment of theirs is, as the philosophers say, a subjective feeling of their own. Many think he is not of them, because they cannot conceive how such a man, so born, and so accomplished, can possibly have so much goodness as to know a man only for his humanity, and not for his money and his show. However, such considerations venture beyond recollections of school-boy days."

Mr. Buckingham supplements the foregoing facts by the following statements: —

"In an acquaintance that began in 1826, and has now extended over nearly sixty years, I always admired him [Phillips] for purity and goodness. His life was beautiful, if I understood him right. He was beautiful, too, in form and face, in expression of countenance, in tones of voice, in attractiveness of manners and of conversation. Without exercising the arts of fascination, he inspired the confidence, I think, of all who became acquainted with him; and he was admired, and he was loved. His friends were charmed with him: all felt themselves at ease in his presence, as with one who had no secret purposes, whose heart was open to all, — a heart which men might examine, and angels might love to look upon.

"Perhaps it was the natural beauty of his outward manners and appearance, that in early life attracted me; but it was more his moral excellence. He was a faithful student at his books. He spoke often of his mother, and her care over him, and her counsels. He was a lover of outdoor sports: he helped others to enjoy them. He was generous, and even chivalrous, with others at play. I don't think he was ever reproved for any carelessness or other fault in the schoolroom, nor was ever complained of among the boys for any unfairness. I do not mean to exaggerate his excellences. I give you my impressions, and I am willing all the truth should be known. In college-life I knew that he developed some faults; for born of what might be called a patrician family, if there were any such, he was courted by the wealthy and elegant, whose lives were not in all things correct: but I never knew of any vice in him. He resisted the vulgar in their manners, and may have been haughty towards them; but I never knew, or do not recall, an instance of neglect or dislike towards any whose lives and conversation were correct."

The class of 1831, at the time of its graduation, numbered sixty-five members. Of these, several afterwards achieved eminence in different walks in life, as, for example, Francis Gardner, long the beloved headmaster of the Boston Latin-School; John Lothrop Motley, already mentioned; George C. Shattuck, M.D.; Nathaniel Bradstreet Shurtleff, and others.

In September, 1831, Phillips became a member of the junior class in the Harvard Law School.

This school grew out of the royal professorship of law, which was established in 1815. It was organized as a distinct department two years later, but did not begin to show much life until 1829, when Judge Story and John H. Ashmun were appointed professors. At that time the method of teaching was, not only "to illustrate the topic of study by decided or supposed cases, and to comment upon and criticise the text-book, but also to examine most of the students quite closely upon the lesson of the day. The exercise was a recitation rather than a lecture, — a mode of instruction which becomes inconvenient when a professional school is largely attended."

In October, 1832, Dane Hall, which was specially erected for the law-department of the university, was opened for use. Prior to this, instruction had been given in No. 1, College House. At the time of the opening, the school numbered forty students; and these were divided into three classes, — the senior, middle, and junior.

Of Phillips's course at the law-school, many remembrances are cherished by his surviving fellows. It is the testimony of all, that, like his intimate friend Sumner, he had no particular fondness for the law, except as a science, and that he did not much care whether or not he ever entered upon its practice.

In September, 1834, he was graduated from the law-school, and received his professional degree. A few weeks later he was admitted to practice at the Suffolk bar.

Phillips was no longer a boy; from a well-blessed and blooming youth he had now passed into the maturity of manhood. Genius surely he had, united to all the gifts and graces of Boston's most exclusive culture. This college graduate, elegant as Antinous, and as beautiful as Apollo, carried with him everywhere the unmistakable atmosphere of classic training.

After his admission to the bar, Phillips went to Lowell, Mass., and continued his studies in a more practical sort of way in the office of Thomas Hopkinson, a former fellow-student of his at Cambridge. Hopkinson was, on the whole, the ablest man in his class, as he was also the oldest. Immediately after leaving college, he had opened an office at Lowell, and rapidly gained headway. It was while Phillips was associated with Hopkinson, that Benjamin F. Butler, an errand-boy in the adjoining office, first met and became acquainted with him.

Returning to Boston, Phillips hired desk-room in an office on Court Street, and for the first time displayed his sign. Weeks and months crept on; but for him it was the old story of "a good calling, but no clients." But what did he care? To him the law was not the all-absorbing study of his life; and even now, impatient of its details, he sought recreation in the exciting topics of the times.

When Phillips came to sign the roll of the court as a member of the bar of Suffolk, already had he ventured to doubt the Constitution, that threw even a partial protection around the master of a slave. When he wrote his name to the oath to protect the Constitution, he writhed in shame at his own weakness. It was not for a day, nor for a week, that his manly conscience waged war against that deed of honest troth. For him it was a plighted vow to an unloved. He had covenanted with circumstances.

Says one of his friends of early years, — again Mr. Appleton, — "I remember a year or so after we left the university, I met Mr. Phillips on the street; and I asked him if he were getting any clients. He said no, he was not. I told him the case was much the same with me; and added that I was much surprised to hear of his ill-success, knowing what a good orator he was in college.

"'Well,' said he, 'I will wait six months more; and then, if clients do not come, I will not wait for them longer, but will throw myself heart and soul into some good cause, and devote my life to it if necessary.'"

CHAPTER III.

THE EARLY ANTI-SLAVERY MOVEMENT.

Garrison establishes "The Liberator." — The First Number. — A Dingy Office. — Mr. Garrison's Supporters. — Dr. Lyman Beecher. — Jeremiah Evarts. — Oliver Johnson's Testimony. — "The Liberator" creates a Stir in the South. — The Might of King Cotton. — Garrison's Appeal to his Countrymen. — The New-England Anti-Slavery Society. — Story of its Organization. — Preachers and Politics. — The Rise of the American Anti-Slavery Society. — Growth of the Movement. — The Reign of Terror dawning. — The Charleston Riot. — Faneuil Hall pays a Tribute to Slavery, and the New-England Pulpit Dumb!

"When the pulpit preached slave-hunting, and the law bound the victim, and society said, 'Amen! this will make money,' we were 'fanatics,' 'enthusiasts,' 'seditious,' 'disorganizers,' 'scorners of the pulpit,' 'traitors.' Genius of the Past! drop not from thy tablets one of these honorable names. We claim them all as our surest title deeds to the memory and gratitude of mankind. We indeed thought man more than constitutions, humanity and justice of more worth than law. Seal up thy record! If Boston is proud of her part, let her rest assured we are not ashamed of ours."

"The last lesson a man ever learns is, that liberty of thought and speech is the right for all mankind." — PHILLIPS.

IN August, 1830, William Lloyd Garrison issued the prospectus of a weekly paper to be published in Washington, and called "The Liberator." The prospectus created no interest, and the proposition was finally "palsied by public indifference." Having thus made known his project, Mr. Garrison left Washington, and, after looking about him for a while, located in Boston. His object in establishing "The Liberator" was, to fight slavery to the bitter end. He wisely concluded, that "to fight slavery at the South while the North was hostile would be like going into battle in an enemy's country with no base for re-enforcements or supplies."

The first number of the paper appeared in January, 1831; and an exceedingly small folio of four pages it was, too, — so small and insignificant, that nobody, in those days, ventured to think that it would ever be able to exert any influence. If the paper was unattractive in its external appearance, the office of publication, which was in the third story of the building then known as the Merchants' Hall, was even more so. The dingy walls; the small windows, bespattered with printer's ink; the press standing in one corner, and the composing-stands opposite; the long editorial and mailing table, covered with newspapers; the bed of the editor and publisher on the floor, — all these make a picture never to be forgotten. Harrison Gray Otis well described it as "an obscure hole,"

"Yet there the freedom of a race began."

In establishing "The Liberator," Mr. Garrison announced that he should not array himself as the political partisan of any man, and that, in defending the great cause of human rights, he wished to secure "the assistance of all religions and of all parties."

But who were Mr. Garrison's supporters? At this time Dr. Lyman Beecher stood at the head of the orthodox pulpits in Boston. The great controversy which had been going on between orthodoxy and Unitarianism was drawing nigh to its culmination in the complete divorcement of the two parties. Dr. Beecher was a born belligerent: Dr. Channing, on the Unitarian side, was a man of gentle and humane spirit. Mr. Garrison, being a strict orthodox himself, naturally looked for support to Dr. Beecher and his adherents. Garrison approached Beecher on the subject.

"I have too many irons in the fire already," said the doctor.

"Then, you had better let all your irons burn than neglect your duty to the slave," replied Garrison solemnly.

Dr. Beecher, like a good many other people of his day, while not an advocate of slavery, believed in colonization, — in other words, that all the blacks ought to be sent over to Africa. To his mind, immediate emancipation upon American soil suggested a frightful picture, and might prove a curse. "Your zeal," he said to Garrison, "is commendable; but you are misguided. If you will give up your fanatical notions, and be guided by us (the clergy), we will make you the Wilberforce of America."

Disheartened by such indifference on the part of Dr. Beecher, Mr. Garrison next sought Jeremiah Evarts, secretary of the American Board of Commissioners for Foreign Missions, who was an earnest pleader in behalf of the red men of America. But, no: there was a marked difference between red and black; and, with the black, Mr. Evarts would have nothing to do.

To the honor of Boston, however, there were a few friends who dared to stand by Mr. Garrison. "Among those who came to confer with the editor," writes Mr. Oliver Johnson, who was himself a stanch "friend," "I remember Samuel J. May, who combined the courage of Paul with the lovingness of John, and who was ever afterwards a conspicuous figure in the anti-slavery host; Ellis Gray Loring, then a rising young lawyer, with a clear head and a sound conscience, whose death in the prime of his powers left a vacancy that could not be filled; Samuel E. Sewall, of an honored Massachusetts family, a man fitted by his legal attainments and a judicial spirit for a high place on the bench; David Lee Child, the bold editor, and the faithful champion of the oppressed of every nation and clime; John G. Whittier, then almost unknown to fame, but whose flashing eye and intrepid mien foretold the songs of freedom with which he afterward thrilled and stirred the hearts of his countrymen; Joshua Coffin, the antiquarian, Whittier's old schoolmaster, and the subject of one of his characteristic lays; Arnold Buffum, the Quaker hatter, lately returned from England, where he had caught the spirit of Clarkson, Wilberforce, O'Connell, and Buxton, and thus prepared himself to greet the rising liberator of America; Moses Thacher, an orthodox clergyman, one of the first of the profession to welcome the call for immediate emancipation; and Amos A. Phelps, then pastor of the Congregational church in Pine Street."

Ere long "The Liberator" began to make itself felt, not alone in the North, but also in the South, where every effort was made to prevent its circulation. The Vigilance Association of South Carolina (Columbia), on the 4th of October, 1831, "offered a reward of fifteen hundred dollars for the apprehension and prosecution to conviction of any white person who might be detected in distributing or circulating 'The Liberator,' or any other publication of a seditious tendency." In a similar manner the paper was proscribed in other sections of the South.

In the North, a moral stupor rested upon the public and the press. Most people regarded Mr. Garrison and his faithful band of co-workers as so many fanatics, as disturbers of the peace, and as breeders of evil. There were moments when it seemed as if the misguided public opinion of the hour would demand the suppression of "The Liberator;" and it is not easy now to see what it was, except the interposition of

Divine Providence, that prevented the people in their madness from doing all that King Cotton desired.

At an hour when the worst seemed to be culminating, Mr. Garrison addressed the following noble words to his countrymen. They should be read by all who now wish to catch something of the spirit that impelled him in all his endeavors: —

"I appeal to God, whom I fear and serve, and to its patrons, in proof that the real and only purpose of 'The Liberator' is to prevent rebellion, by the application of those preservative principles which breathe peace on earth, good will to men. I advance nothing more. I stand on no other foundation than this: 'Whatsoever ye would that men should do to you, do ye even so to them.' I urge the immediate abolition of slavery, not only because the slaves possess an inalienable right to liberty, but because the system, to borrow the words of Mr. Randolph, is 'a volcano in full operation;' and by its continuance we must expect a national explosion. . . . The present generation cannot appreciate the purity of my motives or the value of my exertions. I look to posterity for a good reputation. The unborn offspring of those who are now living will reverse the condemnatory decision of my contemporaries. Without presuming to rank myself among them, I do not forget that those reformers who were formerly treated as the 'offscouring of the earth' are now lauded beyond measure. I do not forget that Christ and his apostles — harmless, undefiled, and prudent as they were — were buffeted, calumniated, and crucified; and therefore my soul is steady to its pursuit as the needle to the pole. If we would not see our land deluged in blood, we must instantly burst asunder the shackles of the slaves, treat them as rational and injured beings, give them land, to cultivate, and the means of employment, and multiply schools for themselves and their children. We shall then have little to fear. The wildest beasts may be subdued and rendered gentle by kind treatment. Make the slaves free, and every inducement to revolt is taken away. . . . I see the design of the clamor raised against 'The Liberator.' It is to prevent public indignation from resting upon the system of slavery, and to concentrate it upon my own head. That system contains the materials of self-destruction."

The beginning of the year 1831 witnessed the birth of "The Liberator," as we have shown. At the close of the year another step was taken, which was destined to good results.

On the 13th of November fifteen persons assembled in the office of Mr. Samuel E. Sewall, in State Street, to consider the feasibility of establishing an anti-slavery society in New England. Of this little company Mr. Garrison was the moving spirit and the chief figure. All present appreciated Mr. Garrison's motives, but not all approved his plans. Only nine of the number favored immediate emancipation.

Another meeting was held at the same place on the 16th of December. Ten gentlemen were present; and a committee of five was appointed to draft a constitution for an anti-slavery society, to be reported Jan. 1, 1832. The body of the constitution reported by the committee was adopted; but an adjourned meeting was reported to be held Jan. 6, in the schoolroom under the African Baptist Church in Belknap Street. The fellowing preamble was then and there adopted: —

> "We, the undersigned, hold that every person of full age and sane mind, has a right to immediate freedom from personal bondage of whatsoever kind, unless imposed by the sentence of the law for the commission of some crime. We hold that man cannot, consistently with reason, religion, and the eternal and immutable principles of justice, be the property of man. We hold that whoever retains his fellow-man in bondage is guilty of a grievous wrong. We hold that mere difference of complexion is no reason why any man should be deprived of any of his natural rights, or subjected to any political disability. While we advance these opinions as the principles on which we intend to act, we declare that we will not operate on the existing relations of society by other than peaceful and lawful means, and that we will give no countenance to violence or insurrection."

Such was the "fanaticism," the "incendiarism," and the "infidelity" which the American churches scorned and resisted.

The preamble and the constitution were then signed by the following persons. May their memories ever be kept green! —

William Lloyd Garrison, Robert B. Hall, Arnold Buffum, William J. Snelling, John E. Fuller, Moses Thacher, Joshua Coffin, Stilman B. Newcomb, Benjamin C. Bacon, Isaac Knapp, Henry K. Stockton, and Oliver Johnson, — all but the last named dead.

Messrs. David Lee Child, Samuel E. Sewall, and Ellis Gray Loring refused their signatures at the time, but soon afterward joined the society. All of these original members were poor men. Not one of them could have put a hundred dollars into the common treasury without bankrupting himself. But such was the origin of "The New-England Anti-slavery Society," — the first association ever organized on this continent upon the principle of immediate abolition.

As the little company stepped from that schoolhouse out into the storm and darkness of the night, Mr. Garrison impressively remarked, "We have met to-night in this obscure schoolhouse. Our numbers are few, and our influence limited; but, mark my prediction, Faneuil Hall shall ere long echo with the principles we have set forth." We shall see how well the prophecy was fulfilled.

Of the work of the New-England Society we can say but little. The story has often been told, and with what results the whole world now knows. It was earnest work, that told mightily in the end. At times it seemed as if nothing could be accomplished, as if the entire purpose must be given up. But in the darkest hour came cheering tidings from England, that the whole kingdom was shaken by the eloquence of Wilberforce, Brougham, O'Connell, Thompson, and others. The thundering words of Lord Brougham, "It is the law written by the finger of God on the heart of man; and by that law, unchangeable and eternal, while men despise fraud, and loathe rapine, and abhor blood, they shall reject with indignation the wild and guilty fantasy, that man can hold property in man," stirred the hearts of British citizens and Christians. But, alas! the statesmen and divines of America preferred to weave defences and apologies for slavery out of the Bible and the Constitution; while the people, who blindly followed and looked up to them, seemed to care no more for the abolition movement than they did for what was going on in the heart of Africa.

In December, 1833, the American Anti-slavery Society was organized, with its headquarters in New-York City. After its organization, the Society immediately adopted and published a "Declaration of Sentiments," in which they declared, —

"The right to enjoy liberty is inalienable. To invade it is to usurp the prerogative of Jehovah. Every man has a right to his own body, to the products of his own labor, to the protection of law, and to the common advantages of society. It is piracy to buy or steal a native African, and subject him to servitude. Surely the sin is as great to enslave an American as an African. Therefore we believe and affirm, that there is no difference in principle between the African slave-trade and American slavery; that every American citizen who retains a human being in involuntary bondage as his property is, according to Scripture, a man-stealer; that the slaves ought instantly to be set free, and brought under the protection of law; that if they lived from the time of Pharaoh down to the present period, and had been entailed through successive generations, their right to be free could never have been alienated, but their claims would have constantly risen in solemnity; that all those laws which are now in force, admitting the right of slavery, are therefore, before God, utterly null and void, being an audacious usurpation of the divine prerogative, a daring infringement on the law of nature, a base overthrow of the very foundations of the social compact, a complete extinction of all the relations, endearments, and obligations of mankind, and a presumptuous transgression of all the holy commandments; and that therefore they ought instantly to be abrogated. We further believe and affirm, that all persons of color who possess the qualifications which are demanded of others, ought to be admitted forthwith to the enjoyment of the same privileges, and the exercise of the same prerogatives as others; and that the paths of preferment, of wealth, and of intelligence, should be opened as widely to them as to persons of a white complexion."

In regard to the measures by which the Society would seek the accomplishment of its purpose, the declaration asserts, —

"Our principles forbid the doing of evil that good may come, and lead us to reject, and to entreat the oppressed to reject, the use of all carnal weapons for deliverance from bondage; relying solely upon those which are spiritual, and mighty through God to the pulling down of strongholds."

From this time onward the cause grew, and agitation became more and more intense. Agents of the societies were everywhere, and thousands of tracts were sent out to hasten on the good work. Occasionally ministers of the gospel ventured to inveigh against slavery, and whole congregations changed attitudes. The signs of the times all pointed to a victory in the end. People in the Southern States, however, were furious; and their opinion of the new movement was voiced in the following paragraph from "The Richmond Whig:"—

"Let the hell-hounds of the North beware! Let them not feel too much security in their homes, or imagine that they who throw firebrands, although from, as they think, so safe a distance, will be permitted to escape with impunity."

"Let your emissaries," said the Rev. Thomas S. Witherspoon of Alabama, in a letter to the editor of "The Emancipator," "dare to cross the Potomac, and I cannot promise you that your fate will be less than Haman's. Then, beware how you goad an insulted but magnanimous people to deeds of desperation!"

The reign of terror was dawning. In the summer of 1835 great quantities of printed matter, emanating from the anti-slavery societies, were sent through the mails to citizens at the South. Naturally a tremendous excitement followed. In Charleston, S.C., the post-office was broken into by an infuriated populace; and all the anti-slavery publications were taken out, and publicly burned. The example set in Charleston was followed in other cities; and, as a rule, all such action was commended in the North.

In Boston, the abolitionists asked for Faneuil Hall wherein to explain their objects and to defend themselves. The request was rudely denied. But, on the

15th of August, the doors were opened to their enemies. The mayor took the chair; and, by intemperate speeches, Harrison Gray Otis, Richard Fletcher, and Peleg Sprague intensified the public feeling against the abolitionists. In the most abject manner, Boston crouched before the will of slavery.

Shortly afterward Mr. Garrison was hung in effigy, and his life was constantly endangered. In the midst of all these proceedings, which threatened the overthrow of the freedom of speech and of the press, the pulpit of New England was either dumb, or offered an apology to the rule of the slave-power. But, even thus, under Providence the cause of the bondmen was marching on.

CHAPTER IV.

THE GARRISON MOB, AND ITS RESULTS.

Where was Wendell Phillips? — The Female Anti-Slavery Society hold a Meeting, October, 1835. — Inflammatory Handbills. — "The Commercial Gazette" excites the Mobocracy. — The Ladies assemble at the Hall. — The Opening Exercises. — The Mob gain Possession of the Hall. — Mayor Lyman counsels Adjournment. — Mr. Garrison seized by the Rioters. — Dragged through Boston's Streets. — At City Hall. — Conveyed to Jail. — The Outcome. — Phillips views the Spectacle. — Learns a Lesson. — Foresees his Future. — His Speech on the Twentieth Anniversary of the Mob.

"Such was the temper of those times. The ignorant were not aware, and the wise were too corrupt to confess, that the most precious of human rights, free thought, was at stake. These women knew it, felt the momentous character of the issue, and consented to stand in the gap. Those were trial-hours. I never think of them without my shame for my native city being swallowed up in gratitude to those who stood so bravely for the right."

"It is a singular result of our institutions, that we have never had in Boston any but well-dressed mobs." — PHILLIPS.

WHERE was the young Boston aristocrat, the pet of Boston society, the rising and promising lawyer, Wendell Phillips, all this time? How did he view the storm that was pending? What were his emotions, and where were his sympathies? We shall see.

While the events recorded in the previous chapter were fast crowding upon one another, several ladies in

Boston and its vicinity — all ladies of culture, refinement, and social position — themselves formed an anti-slavery society, and entered upon the good work with a courage and zeal truly remarkable. One of the moving spirits of this bond of union was Mrs. Maria Weston Chapman, now of Weymouth, Mass., whose "Memoirs of Harriet Martineau" has found many admirers.

It was announced that the Boston Female Anti-slavery Society would hold a meeting on the 21st of October, 1835, in the Anti-slavery (Stacy) Hall, No. 46 Washington Street. On the morning of that day inflammatory handbills were circulated throughout the city, and threats were freely uttered by the enemies of the cause. The ladies, indeed, became so alarmed at the prospects, that they petitioned the city authorities for protection. No notice was taken of the petition.

To add to the fury of the evil-disposed, a false report was spread abroad, to the effect that George Thompson, one of the most gifted and eloquent men of his age, who had come from England to America, at the request of Mr. Garrison, would be present at the meeting, and would probably deliver an address. The following placard was posted in all parts of the city: —

"THOMPSON THE ABOLITIONIST.

"That infamous foreign scoundrel, Thompson, will hold forth this afternoon at 46 Washington Street. The present is a fair opportunity for the friends of the Union to *snake* Thompson out!

It will be a contest between the Abolitionists and the friends of the Union. A purse of *one hundred dollars* has been raised by a number of patriotic citizens, to reward the individual who shall first lay violent hands on Thompson, so that he may be brought to the Tar Kettle before dark. Friends of the Union, be vigilant!"

One of the morning papers, "The Commercial Gazette," thus alluded to the meeting appointed for the day: —

"It is in vain to hold meetings in Faneuil Hall; in vain that speeches are made and resolutions are adopted, assuring our brethren of the South that we cherish rational and correct notions on the subject of slavery, — if Thompson and Garrison, and their vile associates in this city, are permitted to hold their meetings in the broad face of day, and to continue their denunciations of the planters of the South. They must be put down if we would preserve our consistency. The evil is one of the greatest magnitude; and the opinion prevails very generally, that, if there is no law that will reach it, it must be reached in some other way."

Such language served its purpose. Before the hour appointed for the opening of the meeting, the streets in the vicinity of the hall were filled with men, with their every breath freighted with vengeance. Even a blind man would have detected trouble ahead.

Through this elegantly dressed, culture-boasting crowd, taunted by the insults and vulgarities of these chivalrous friends of their "brethren of the South," the ladies passed into the hall. About thirty responded to the call of the roll.

Then Miss Mary S. Parker read a selection from the Scriptures, and in fervent tones offered up a prayer to Almighty God "for his blessing upon the cause of the bondmen, his forgiveness of his and their enemies, and his succor and protection in the hour of peril."

"It was," says Mr. Garrison, who was present at the meeting by invitation, "an awful, sublime, and soul-thrilling scene, — enough, one would suppose, to melt adamantine hearts, and make even fiends of darkness stagger and retreat. Indeed, the clear, untremulous voice of the Christian heroine in prayer occasionally awed the ruffians into silence, and was heard distinctly, even in the midst of their hisses, yells, and curses."

At the close of the prayer, Mr. Garrison, by the advice of the president, in company with Mr. C. C. Burleigh, went into the anti-slavery office, which adjoined and was separated from the hall by a board partition. His object in thus departing was to preserve the contents of the depository from being destroyed in case the mob should suddenly become furious.

He had just closed the door behind him, and the secretary of the society had just begun to read the annual report, when Mayor Lyman entered the room, and commanded the ladies to disperse. They humbly besought his protection, as they had a right to do: he assured them, that, as they were disturbers of the peace, he was powerless to afford them any protection. Thus baffled by "gentlemen of property and standing," and by their representative the mayor, the ladies quietly adjourned their meeting.

The rioters now rushed into the hall, after having bravely demolished the anti-slavery sign. They appropriated the Testaments and prayer-books, and then turned their attention to Mr. Garrison. By advice of the mayor, in order to escape the mob, he crossed the roof in the rear of the second story of the hall, to a carpenter-shop in the second story of a building in Wilson's Lane. There a friend tried to conceal him, but it was too late. The rioters had discovered his hiding-place, and, amid yells which were heard afar off, dragged him to a window, and were about to throw him out, when the conscience of one of them caused him to interfere. Then they drew him back, and coiled a rope around his body, evidently with the intention of dragging him through the streets of Boston.

Just at that moment a ladder was raised to the window, and Mr. Garrison was permitted to descend. From Wilson's Lane he was dragged, bareheaded, and with his garments torn, into State Street, in the rear of City Hall (now "the Old State House"), over ground stained with the blood of the first martyrs in the cause of liberty and independence in the memorable massacre of 1770.

Arriving at the south door of the hall, an attempt was made by the mayor to protect Mr. Garrison; but only until several respectable citizens lent their assistance, did the attempt prove successful. Finally rescued, Mr. Garrison was taken up to the mayor's room, where he was provided with needful clothing, and was told, that, to preserve his life, he must be committed to jail "as a disturber of the peace." A closed carriage was summoned, and into it the prisoner was put without much difficulty.

"But now," says Mr. Garrison, "a scene occurred that baffles description. As the ocean, lashed into fury by the spirit of the storm, seeks to whelm the adventurous bark beneath the mountain waves, so did the mob, enraged by a series of disappointments, rush like a whirlwind upon the frail vehicle in which I sat, and endeavor to drag me out of it. Escape seemed a physical impossibility. They clung to the wheels, dashed open the doors, seized hold of the horses, and tried to upset the carriage. They were, however, vigorously repulsed by the police; a constable sprung in by my side; the doors were closed; and the driver, lustily using his whip upon the bodies of his horses and the heads of the rioters, happily made an opening through the crowd, and drove at a tremendous speed for Leverett Street. But many of the rioters followed, even with superior swiftness, and repeatedly attempted to arrest the progress of the horses. To reach the jail by a direct course was found impracticable; and after going by a circuitous direction, and encountering many hair-breadth escapes, we drove up to the new and last refuge of liberty and life, when another desperate attempt was made by the mob to seize me, but in vain. In a few moments I was locked up in a cell, safe from my persecutors, accompanied by two delightful associates, — a good conscience and a cheerful mind. In the course of the evening several of my friends came to my grated window, to sympathize and confer with me, with whom I held a strengthening conversation until the hour of retirement, when I threw myself upon my prison-bed, and slept tranquilly."

In the morning the prisoner wrote with a pencil the following inscription upon the walls of his cell: —

"William Lloyd Garrison was put into this cell on Wednesday afternoon, Oct. 21, 1835, to save him from the violence of a 'respectable' and influential mob, who sought to destroy him from preaching the abominable and dangerous doctrine, that 'all men are created equal,' and that all oppression is odious in the sight of God. 'Hail, Columbia!' Cheers for the autocrat of Russia and the sultan of Turkey!

"Reader, let this inscription remain till the last slave in this despotic land be loosed from his fetters."

In the course of the forenoon Mr. Garrison was subjected to the mockery of an examination for form's sake, and then released from custody.

While seated by his study-window in Court Street, the young Boston lawyer, glancing up from the pages of his book, and out into the thoroughfare, caught sight of an assembling crowd of people. Men were hurrying towards the City Hall as fast as their feet could carry them; children were shouting at the top of their voices; and occasionally a woman would turn back, such was her curiosity. What did it signify?

His own curiosity prompted him to forsake his book, and to go out into the street. With hurried strides he wended his way towards the City Hall. There he saw a thousand men, clad in broadcloth and all the other paraphernalia of respectability, dragging a man with a rope around his waist.

"Who is that man?" he inquired.

"William Lloyd Garrison," was the reply of a by-stander.

At once he looked upon the proceeding with indignation, and discerned a violation of the central right of the Saxon's idea of liberty.

He saw the mayor entreating the crowd to maintain order and the peace; but, from the lips of that cowered official, he heard no command of authority. The young lawyer was also a military gentleman, and held a commission in a Suffolk regiment. The colonel of that regiment happened to be standing near him.

"Colonel," said the younger officer, "why not call out the guards? Let us offer our services to the mayor."

In ten words the wiser officer taught his young friend more of the government of the United States than nine years' study had taught him.

"You fool!" replied the latter, pointing to the crowd that surged and pressed before him, "don't you see that the regiment is in front of you?"

Then for the first time it flashed upon the mind of Wendell Phillips — it was he — that our government, with all its merits, in a critical hour when all the passions of men fling themselves against the law, has no reserve force, and that there is no tribunal to which one can appeal, but that at that moment, just so much of law-abiding, self-respecting, intelligent sense as there is in the mob, just so much government have we got, and no more.

Phillips had never thought of this before. He had read Greek and Roman and English history; he had by heart the classic eulogies of brave old men and martyrs: he had even dreamed that he had heard the same tone from the cuckoo lips of Edward Everett, and now he was taught his error.

Into his frenzied brain, thought darted with the speed of an arrow. Intelligence explained, interpreted, the scene before him. True to the old proverb, that "The blood of the martyrs is the seed of the Church," this spectacle of shameless outrage committed against a single, defenceless man, whose only crime was, that he had dared to speak out the unvoiced wrongs of the poorest and most abject beings in the form of man, went home to the heart of Phillips, and stirred his Puritanic blood to the very finger-tips.

Perhaps he could not help it; for, if ever a man was a born fighter, Phillips was that man: and his instincts led him to take up with the weaker side from an innate conviction, that, in such a world as this, ninety-nine times out of a hundred, the right is on the side of the minority. In making up his decision as to what he would do, or where he would stand, the question of power, or wealth, or numbers, never entered into the mind of Phillips.

The young man of twenty-four, with a great, proud family, with a social position higher than that to which most young men attain at twenty-four, with ambition and hope and truth as his safeguards, then and there vowed that he would cast his lot with the anti-slavery people. To this end he had now learned his first lesson: he had become convinced of the righteousness of their cause.

One word more before we close this chapter.

On the twentieth anniversary of the Boston mob, Mr. Phillips delivered a speech in Stacy Hall, Boston, in which he reviewed that terrible event in language profoundly impressive. Whoever fails to read it will ignore one of the finest and most eloquent productions of the modern school of oratory.

CHAPTER V.

THE DÉBUT OF WENDELL PHILLIPS.

The Year 1837. — Slavery the Dominant Power of the Country. — Earnestness of the Abolitionists. — The Lovejoy Tragedy. — Story of the Alton Riots. — The Tidings reach Boston. — Faneuil Hall refused to the Indignant Abolitionists. — Dr. Channing appeals to the Citizens of Boston. — The Hall opened at Last. — A Packed Audience. — Resolutions. — Harangue of Attorney-Gen. Austin. — Its Effect. — Reply of Wendell Phillips. — Great Uproar and Excitement. — The Result.

"Men blame us for the bitterness of our language and the personality of our attacks. It results from our position. The great mass of the people can never be made to stay and argue a long question. They must be made to feel it, through the hides of their idols."

"Give me any thing that walks erect, and can read, and he shall count one in the millions of the Lord's sacramental host, which is yet to come up, and trample all oppression in the dust. The weeds poured forth in nature's lavish luxuriance, give them but time, and their tiny roots shall rend asunder the foundations of palaces, and crumble the Pyramids to the earth." — PHILLIPS.

IT was the year 1837, — a year which marks the dawning of one of the most momentous periods in the history of the American people. Martin Van Buren had been elected to the presidency; and his constituents, the Democratic party, had also secured a decisive majority in the Twenty-fifth Congress. No Congress that preceded was more subservient to the demands of the slave-power. It voted not only to silence the voice of the people, but its own voice as well. It struck down the sacred right of the people to petition for the redress of their grievances, by clamor, menace, and resolution, destroyed the freedom of debate, and hushed the voice of the representatives of the nation.

But although the administration thus begun was unhesitatingly subservient to the demands of the slave-power, and the slave-power itself was far-reaching, the uprising against slavery was not so slight as not to give cause for alarm. Two features of the early stages of this uprising were peculiarly striking and suggestive. There was the manifest failure of those early pioneers "to comprehend the magnitude and inveteracy of the evil to be removed, or the tremendous grasp in which it held the nation in its every department of individual and associated life." There was, too, an enthusiastic but unwarranted confidence in a speedy triumph. Evidences abound. They are seen in the proceedings of anti-slavery conventions and anniversaries, in the anti-slavery reports, speeches, and journals of those days. Even Mr. Garrison, whose abilities and opportunities of judging were certainly not small, shared largely in these illusions of hope, and in this evident under-estimate of the greatness and severity of the contest on which they had entered. Though much be conceded to the charm of novelty, the enthusiasm of youth, and the pardonable confidence of the neophyte, unhackneyed as yet, and without the lessons gained in the stern school of experience, it is difficult to account for these over-sanguine expressions. Especially does this appear in view of the determined opposition they were obliged to encounter almost always and everywhere, in their attempts to reach the popular ear and heart. Not only were they excluded, as they complainingly asserted, from churches and halls, but they were driven by rioters from their own quarters, and hardly permitted to walk the streets without the hootings, and sometimes the more personal and physical violence, of the mob. Nor was this the mere temporary ebullition of the hour. It continued until no inconsiderable number of those early and sanguine men and women felt constrained to come out of both churches and parties, as hopelessly in bondage to this haughty and dominating power of the land. Doubtless it was well that such was the fact. Had they fully comprehended the desperate nature of the struggle, fathomed the depth of their country's degradation and peril, gauged the full measure of its apostasy and the slow progress of truth; had they known the extent of the great and terrible wilderness on which they had entered, and the length of their journeyings to the promised land, — the hearts of many would have sunk within them, and they might have relinquished the attempt before it was well begun.[1]

And now came a tragedy. On the 7th of November,

---

[1] See Wilson, History of the Slave Power; Frothingham, Life of Theodore Parker; Johnson, Garrison and his Times.

1837, Rev. Elijah Lovejoy was murdered by a mob at Alton, Ill.

Mr. Lovejoy was a native of the State of Maine, and a graduate of Waterville College in the class of 1826. At the age of twenty-four he had journeyed to the West, and had become a teacher in one of the schools of St. Louis. Two years later, fortune made him the editor of a political journal of the National Republican party, and an active supporter of Henry Clay. Subsequently he entered the theological seminary at Princeton, N.J., was licensed to preach, and, in the autumn of 1832, returned to Missouri, and established "The St. Louis Observer," a weekly religious journal.

Mr. Lovejoy was not an abolitionist in the full sense of the word, but was a friend of free discussion; and some of his remarks on the subject of slavery gave great offence to the people of St. Louis. "I have sworn eternal hostility to slavery, and by the blessing of God I will never go back:" such were his words.

In the spring of 1836 a negro, who had killed an officer to avoid arrest, was taken out of jail by an excited mob, was carried out of the city, chained to a tree, and burned to death. When, in due time, the matter came before the grand jury, Judge Lawless (an appropriate name surely) expressed in his charge the sentiment, that if a mob be hurried on to its deeds of violence and blood by some "mysterious, metaphysical, and almost electric frenzy," participators in it are absolved from guilt, and are not proper subjects of punishment. "If such be the fact," he said, "act not at all in the matter: the case then transcends your jurisdiction; it is beyond the reach of human law."

Mr. Lovejoy ventured to comment on this infamous charge, and scandalous attempt to blind the eyes of justice. As a result, his office was invaded by a mob, and was ruined. He removed the paper to Alton, Ill.; but his press, on being landed there, was broken into fragments. The citizens reimbursed him for his loss.

Before many weeks had transpired, the pro-slavery party in Alton found cause for complaint in the columns of "The Observer;" and in the month of August, 1837, the office and press were destroyed by a mob. Another press was purchased; but, before it could be set up, it was broken into pieces, and thrown into the Mississippi River.

In the midst of these events, a convention to form a State anti-slavery society, which had been called to meet at Upper Alton, was broken up by a pro-slavery convention. Two days afterwards the convention met, and organized the contemplated society. Among the resolutions adopted was one declaring that "the cause of human rights, the liberty of speech and of the press, imperatively demand that the press of 'The Alton Observer' be re-established at Alton with its present editor," and pledging the society, with the aid of Alton friends, and "by the help of Almighty God," to take measures for its re-establishment.

Naturally, the city was in a state of intense excitement. Violence was anticipated. The arrival of another press was made the occasion of a demonstration which ended only in arson and bloodshed.

The new press arrived on the morning of Nov. 7, and the news of its arrival was spread abroad by the inciters to mob violence by the blowing of horns. The mayor superintended its transfer to the warehouse, and aided in storing it away. During the day, although great excitement prevailed, no wanton act was committed. About nine o'clock in the evening most of the defenders retired, leaving a dozen persons only to face the perils of midnight.

Presently thirty or forty persons, issuing from the grog-shops, approached the door, knocked, and demanded the press. One of the proprietors of the warehouse replied that it would not be given up, and, further, that they had been authorized by the mayor to defend it, and defend it they should, even at the risk of their lives. With a pistol in hand, the leader of the gang announced that they were resolved to have the press at any cost; and, at a signal, stones were hurled against the building, and then shots. The firing was returned; and one of the rioters fell, mortally wounded.

"Burn them out!" shouted the leader. Ladders were obtained, and preparations made to set the building on fire. The mayor came to the defence, also a justice of the peace; and these counselled a surrender of the press, on condition that its defenders should not be injured. But a surrender was not to be thought of by those who believed in a lawful right to protect property. The refusal only added fuel to the popular wrath; and then the cry went up, "Fire the building, and shoot every d—d abolitionist as he leaves!"

The lighted torch was put to the roof. Five of the defenders sallied forth from the building, fired upon the mob, and returned. Mr. Lovejoy and two others then stepped out, and were fired upon by rioters concealed behind a pile of lumber. Mr. Lovejoy received five balls, three of them in his breast. Returning to the counting-room, he exclaimed, "I am shot! I am shot!" and almost instantly expired.

After his death, his friends offered to surrender; but the offer was refused. As they left the burning building, they were fired upon; but no one was killed. The mob then rushed in, seized the press, broke it, and threw the fragments into the river. The next day the body of the martyr was buried by his friends, while his enemies stood near, and exulted over his death.

Thus bravely fell one of the most heroic of that number of noble and earnest men who early consecrated themselves to the purpose of maintaining, at fearful odds, that essential palladium of a republic, — freedom of thought, freedom of speech, and freedom of the press. From that very day Alton "went under a cloud from which she did not emerge for years. Her prosperity was smitten with a moral blight. Her very name became repulsive. Emigrants of intelligence and character could not be attracted to a place whose citizens allowed a man to be ruthlessly murdered for daring to speak against slavery. The grave of the martyr, which was made upon a bluff overlooking the Mississippi, was unmarked for many years; but an appropriate monument now indicates the spot. For centuries to come, that monument will attract more visitors than any other object that Alton will have to show." To the friends of liberty, it will be a shrine, reminding them how much they owe to one noble man, who preferred to die rather than surrender the dearest right of an American citizen.

Nearly a half-century has elapsed since the enactment of that terrible tragedy at Alton, and what changes have taken place! Then the valiant minister of the gospel, hunted like a partridge, and appealing in vain for protection against an infuriated mob, found the officers of the law actuated and awed by the demon of slavery rather than inspired by the genius of freedom. Now that mob is dispersed: many of the leaders came to an ignominious death; the very system of iniquity that urged them onwards and headlong into ruin is dead. When the printing-press of Lovejoy was thrown in fragments into the waters of the Mississippi, it was an act of consecration to freedom of that majestic stream, even as the ashes of the saintly Huss thrown into the Rhine consecrated that storied river to the cause and dominion of Protestantism.

The tidings of the death of Lovejoy were borne like a whirlwind over the broad continent. People who advocated slavery either applauded, or at best excused the bloody act. Those who believed in the freedom of speech and of the press received the news with profound sorrow and regret. Public opinion was thoroughly aroused, — never more so up to this period.

The intelligence reached Boston; and Dr. William Ellery Channing and a hundred of his fellow-citizens applied for permission to call a meeting in Faneuil Hall, for the purpose of giving expression to their horror at the murder of Lovejoy. The application was not immediately granted, on the ground that such a meeting might be interpreted as "the public voice of the city." Undaunted by this decision of the board of aldermen, Dr. Channing at once addressed an appeal to the citizens of Boston.

"Has it come to this? [he asked]. Has Boston fallen so low? May not its citizens be trusted to come together to express the great principles of liberty for which their fathers died? Are our fellow-citizens to be murdered in the act of defending their property, and of assuming the right of free discussion? And is it unsafe in this metropolis to express abhorrence of the deed? If such be our degradation, we ought to know the awful truth; and those among us who retain a portion of the spirit of our ancestors should set themselves to work to recover their degenerate posterity."

Dr. Channing was not an unknown man; and an appeal coming from one who occupied his position, and wielded his influence, could not but make a deep impression. A public meeting was called at the old supreme-court room to "take into consideration the reasons assigned by the mayor and aldermen for withholding Faneuil Hall, and to act in the premises as may be deemed expedient." The meeting was held, a new application was drawn up and presented, — happily with success.

On the 8th of December Faneuil Hall was filled to overflowing. Jonathan Phillips, an eminent citizen, was called to the chair, and opened the proceedings with a few brief remarks. He was followed by Dr. Channing, whose address was most eloquent and impressive. Then a series of resolutions from his pen was read by Mr. Benjamin F. Hallett, and seconded and supported by Mr. George S. Hillard.

Thus far every thing had been decorous, dignified, and in perfect harmony with the occasion. Never did the light of day stream in upon an audience seemingly more in sympathy with the cause of human rights and human freedom.

Suddenly uprose in the gallery James T. Austin, the attorney-general of the Commonwealth, a prominent lawyer, an adroit speaker, and a member of Dr. Channing's congregation. His very manner foreshadowed menace, and his matter was full of insult. With unblushing insolence he declared that Lovejoy had "died as the fool dieth," and compared his murderers with the men who destroyed the tea in Boston Harbor. Alluding to the bondmen, he said, —

"We have a menagerie here, with lions, tigers, a hyena and an elephant, a jackass or two, and monkeys in plenty. Suppose, now, some new cosmopolite, some man of philanthropic feelings, not only toward man, but animals, who believes that all are entitled to freedom as an inalienable right, should engage in the humane task of giving freedom to these wild beasts of the forest, some of whom are nobler than their keepers; or, having discovered some new mode of reaching their understanding, should try to induce them to break their cages, and be free. The people of Missouri had as much reason to be afraid of their slaves as we should have to be afraid of the wild beasts of the menagerie. They had the same dread of Lovejoy that we should have of the supposed instigator, if we really believed the bars would be broken, and the caravan let loose to prowl about our streets."

The speaker probably thought and hoped that his scurrilous utterances would create confusion in the meeting, and defeat its avowed objects. The riotous element of the assemblage, which constituted about one-third, had indeed vociferously applauded, but no more.

Standing among the auditors was a young man, unknown to fame, his brow still wet with the dews of youth, with the best blood of Boston coursing in his veins, the best culture of Harvard in his brain, and

THE DÉBUT OF WENDELL PHILLIPS, 79

with a tongue already set aflame by the righteous indignation that filled his breast. He was a mighty listener, and he had come into that meeting — only to listen.

The attorney-general of the Commonwealth had scarcely retired, when that young man mounted the rostrum. Loud rose the hostile protestations of the partisans of the attorney-general; but with unflinching attitude, calm manner, and serenity of voice, the speaker on the platform held his place. It was a trying, a bitter, ordeal; but it was also an opportunity which comes but once in the lifetime of a man of genius and of mettle.

"Sir, when I heard the gentleman lay down principles which place the murderers of Alton side by side with Otis and Hancock, with Quincy and Adams, I thought those pictured lips [pointing to the portraits in the hall] would have broken into voice, to rebuke the recreant American, — the slanderer of the dead."

A storm of applause and of counter-applause burst from the audience. For a few moments the voice of the speaker was hushed. At length he continued, —

"The gentleman said that he should sink into insignificance if he dared to gainsay the principles of these resolutions. Sir, for the sentiments he has uttered, on soil consecrated by the prayers of Puritans and the blood of patriots, the earth should have yawned, and swallowed him up."

At this point the uproar became furious: the speaker's voice was unheard. "Take that back!" "Take back the 'recreant!'" were the cries on one side! "Go on!"

"Go on!" was the cry on the other. For a moment it seemed as if violence would follow; and two friends of the speaker, George Bond, Esq., and Hon. William Sturgis, came to his side at the front of the platform. They were met with the demands of "Phillips or nobody!" "Make him take back 'recreant:'" "he sha'n't go on till he takes it back!"

Mr. Sturgis raised his hand to the audience, and the din was hushed. "I did not come here to take any part in this discussion," he said, "nor do I intend to: but I do entreat you, fellow-citizens, by every thing you hold sacred; I conjure you by every association connected with this hall, consecrated by our fathers to freedom of discussion, — that you listen to every man who addresses you in a decorous manner."

Unmoved from his position, unabashed by the terrors of the hour, the young man whose voice had enkindled such mighty wrath, resumed his speaking: —

"Fellow-citizens [said he], I cannot take back my words. Surely the attorney-general, so long and well known here, needs not the aid of your hisses against one so young as I am, — my voice never before heard within these walls!"

He closed his speech with the declaration that —

"When liberty was in danger, Faneuil Hall had the right, and it was her duty, to strike the key-note for the Union, that the passage of the resolutions, in spite of the opposition led by the attorney-general, will show more decidedly the deep indignation with which Boston regards this outrage."

By this brave and brilliant utterance, which transcended the most sanguine expectations of the few friends who intimately knew his force of eloquence, and which caused the old "Cradle of Liberty" to echo as never before to exalting and ennobling sentiments, the orator WENDELL PHILLIPS was born.

Such were the events of one short month. The martyrdom of Lovejoy caused Phillips to consecrate culture, learning, and zeal to the advocacy of human rights, and to the denunciation of the wrongs of the oppressed. It placed him also among the foremost and most popular American orators. To his fervid and indignant eloquence, even Attorney-Gen. Austin stands indebted; for it alone will preserve his name to the latest posterity as that of one of the most brutal assailants of the dignity of man.

The meeting in Faneuil Hall was dispersed. The multitude went home impressed, but not, as a majority, convinced. The virus of slavery had taken deep root; and it was hard not to believe, that as Hubbard Winslow, a Boston Congregational clergyman, expressed it a month previous in his Thanksgiving discourse, "the unchristian principles and measures" of the Abolitionists did not tend to fill the land "with violence and blood." A few persons foresaw, however, in the events of the hour, a new revelation of the magnitude and serious character of the contest on which they had entered.

CHAPTER VI.

PHILLIPS AN ABOLITIONIST. — MARRIAGE.

Phillips's Aspirations. — Speech at New Bedford. — The Lyceum-Lecture System. — Phillips delivers his First Lecture. — "The Lost Arts." — Joins the New-England Anti-Slavery Society. — Status of the Colored People. — The Chapmans. — Ann Terry Greene. — Phillips falls in Love. — Marriage. — His Domestic Life. — The Faithful Wife. — Recollections of Mr. Buckingham. — Phillips's First Anti-Slavery Lecture. — Recollections of Edwin Thompson.

"The mightiest intellects of the race, from Plato down to the present time; some of the rarest minds of Germany, France, and England, — have successively yielded their assent to the fact that woman is, not perhaps identically, but equally, endowed with man in all intellectual capabilities. It is generally the second-rate men who doubt, — doubt, perhaps, because they fear a fair field : —

> 'He either fears his fate too much,
> Or his deserts are small,
> That dares not put it to the touch
> To gain or lose it all.'"

"When Infinite Wisdom established the rules of right and honesty, he saw to it that justice should be always the highest expediency." — PHILLIPS.

IN the crowded thoroughfares of Boston, Wendell Phillips found the mission of his manhood. The Garrison mob gave a new bent to his thoughts. At the age of twenty-four he allowed himself to drift into the great struggle which was impending over the republic. From that hour he became interested in the cause of human rights.

Previous to this time he had played the *rôle* of a struggling lawyer, — not, indeed, struggling for bread and butter, but for clients and recognition. Fresh from college, and well knowing of what he was made, and of what he was capable, he had looked forward to a public life, and cherished an ambition to hold a public office. But now he had chosen a different field: he had gone on a different line.

After his graduation Mr. Phillips was invited to speak at New Bedford, Mass. Of this event, Mr. Charles T. Congdon furnishes the following interesting recollections: —

"Massachusetts [he states], in earlier times, was hardly ever in accord with the General Government; but its opposition to the Jackson and Van Buren administrations was particularly bitter, and persistently unbroken. It was intensified by traditions of old quarrels with the Washington powers, which, though long allayed, had still left a root of bitterness. There was a trace of this in the first address which I heard Mr. Wendell Phillips deliver, — a Fourth-of-July oration given in our town (New Bedford) just after he left the university.

"When he stood up in the pulpit, I thought him the handsomest man I had ever seen: when he began to speak, his elocution seemed the most beautiful to which I had ever listened; and I was sure that the orations of Cicero, which I had just begun to thumb, were given to the S.P.Q.R. with much smaller effect. Even then the great orator of the Abolitionists was an admirable speaker; nor did he, though scarcely past his majority, lack the grace and force of language with which the whole country has since become familiar.

"There was, besides, a fresh and youthful enthusiasm, which could not last forever. He had then all the pride of State feeling, which he had probably inherited from his Federal ancestors; and I remember one expression which fell from his lips, which, in the light of his subsequent career, is a little curious. He was speaking of the political history of the State, and of its frequent isolation in politics, and electrified us all by exclaiming, 'The Star of Massachusetts has shone the brighter for shining alone!' I suspect that even then Mr. Phillips's Federal relations were in rather an uncertain condition."[1]

In 1830 the lyceum-lecture system, which has played so important and conspicuous a part in the political and intellectual education of the masses, was started by Horace Mann, Josiah Holbrook, Rev. Dr. Allen, Hon. Amasa Walker, George B. Emerson, and others. Mr. Phillips was among the first to take part in the movement, and as early as 1836 he delivered his first lecture. He selected his subjects from the realm of natural science, of which, perhaps, he was more fond than of the law; and, every winter succeeding, his name appears as one of the lecturers in the stated courses of the day. His lecture on "The Lost Arts," which was probably the most popular and most charming lecture for the people ever delivered in this country, began its career in 1838.

After he had joined the anti-slavery society, in 1837,

---

[1] Reminiscences of a Journalist, by Charles T. Congdon, Boston, 1880.

he gradually abandoned science, and spoke more frequently on the slave-question and on temperance. It was his custom, whenever his auditors would permit him to speak on these themes, to make no charge for so doing. But, if his hearers preferred to listen to a lecture on science instead, he invariably demanded his usual fee. As a rule, they were more in favor of a lecture on science than on slavery or temperance.

During these years the colored people were refused admittance to the lyceum lectures, — a fact which greatly displeased the young aspirant for platform-honors. At first he advocated a special course for the colored people; and, not content with this, he became one of a small group — which included also Ralph Waldo Emerson, George William Curtis, and Charles Sumner — that strenuously refused to lecture before any audience where colored people were not admitted. This had the effect to completely break down the old rule of exclusiveness.

At this period, there lived in what was then Chauncy Place, now Chauncy Street, nearly opposite where the First Church stood, the family of Henry Chapman, a Boston merchant, and a merchant, too, who was one of the first to sacrifice his business interests by espousing the cause of the slave. He was owner of many ships, but none of them with his permission ever carried slaves as freight. Both Mr. Chapman and his wife were greatly interested in the cause of anti-slavery.

Into this family there came, one day, Anne Terry Greene, the daughter of Benjamin Greene, a brother of Sarah (Greene) Chapman. Her father and mother had died while she was yet of tender years. Under the influence of Mr. and Mrs. Chapman, she early became interested in anti-slavery; and, as she had ample property of her own, she became a liberal contributor to the cause.

It was while young Phillips was still a member of the Harvard Law School that he first became acquainted with Miss Greene. It was a sort of chance meeting, the outcome of which is best told in the heroine's own words: —

"It was in old stage-coach days," she once explained. "I, with other girls, was booked for Greenfield, Mass. Wendell Phillips and Charles Sumner agreed to go also. Sumner broke his engagement: Mr. Phillips went. I talked abolition to him all the way up, — all the time there. He listened, came again, and it sealed his fate."

In October, 1837, Mr. Phillips was married to Miss Greene, but not until she had succeeded in fully converting him to the cause of anti-slavery.

It is because that much has been said of the eloquence of Wendell Phillips, and of his remarkable power and grace in public speech, that just here it seems fitting to utter a few words of praise of those other features of his life which so largely depended upon his domestic relations. The home-life of a public man does not belong to the world. Whoever invades its sacredness violates the code of honor. But, to understand what manner of man was Wendell Phillips, one must go a few steps behind the scenes; and to think of the greatest of American orators, and of the part which he enacted during his eventful career, without also thinking of that devoted wife, who was a part of him, and perhaps the greater part, would be doing an injustice to both.

"My wife made me an abolitionist," said Mr. Phillips over and over again to those who had his confidence. For this reason, if for no other, her name should always be spoken with his.

At the time of her marriage she was an invalid, compelled to keep her room, and much of her time her bed, by reason of her weakness and pain. Rarely to be seen by any except a few intimates, she never lost courage, nor wavered in her advocacy of the great truths of humanity. It was her suggestions, the promptings of wifely devotedness and womanly intuition, that inspired Wendell Phillips's loftiest and bravest words in the darkest days of the martyr-age of the great anti-slavery contest. It was his affection for her that gave added tenderness and pathos to his pleas for the suffering slave.

To her he was loving and true indeed; the nurse by day, and the sleepless watcher by night; never flagging in his care, never failing in his delicate and reverent regard to her every want and wish, never going far from home without her approval, always making her quiet chamber the centre of his world.

That centre was full of light and spiritual life; for the wife, though feeble in body, was wise in counsel, strong in soul, and inspired her husband by noble purposes and divine ideals. Faithful and unfailing in his domestic life, his care and thought for her, the chosen among all others, never ceased. She repaid him by lighting his pathway, and keeping his soul up to the fearless courage and uncompromising course which she saw were necessary in

> "The conflict with the crime
> And folly of an evil time."

The world will never forget Wendell Phillips. Even Boston, that spurned and misunderstood him forty years ago, has paid fit reverence to him over his open grave. His work on earth is done, and his true manhood has conquered all hearts. For him, the laurel and the victory. For her, the invalid wife, the very centre of his life, the inspiration of his power, — what? She never doubted his sincerity, she never questioned the nobility of his spirit, she never assailed the sweet purity of his life.

Husband and wife, may their names be always linked in our remembrance! May we never forget how much they owed to each other, how much they helped each other! As often as we recall the burning utterances of the young orator at the Lovejoy meeting, the manly attitude which he assumed towards the fugitive slave, and, above all, that marvellous courage which he put on when he

"Dared to be traitor to Union when Union was traitor to right,"

when the Philistines were howling around him, and were threatening to demolish the roof that sheltered his head, and not only his head, but that also of his wife, may we, in justice to him, think of her who shared his knightly courage, his unselfish consecration to duty, his unspeakable sacrifice and suffering for truth, justice, and freedom!

From the manuscript of Dr. Edgar Buckingham, I cull the following touching passages: —

"I pass from conversations in the privacy of his study and library, to say a word or two of what Mr. Phillips was in his still more private affections. I never saw his wife; though in his conversations and his correspondence with me he often spoke of her, and it was my privilege to exchange many communications with her. He was a lover all his life, — not with the instinctive love of youth alone, but with the secured attachment, the quiet confidence of the heart, the beautiful affectionateness, which, in the later years of the pure and good, is a far superior development of character, and a far richer enjoyment, than the effervescence of youthful days.

"She was, as he wrote me once, his counsel, his guide, his inspiration. Within a year or two, in correspondence with him, I ventured to call her his Egeria; and I think they were both greatly pleased with her being so called. For Egeria was a goddess of ancient Rome, whom no one ever saw, whom Numa, the second king of Rome, after the wars, the tumults, in which that city was long disturbed, were mostly at an end, professed to visit in a secret grotto, to receive instructions from, while he was laboring to establish civil institutions, and to refine the manners of the people, and educate them in the principles and the rights of religion. So the wife of Mr. Phillips was his Egeria, his councillor, his guide, and his inspiration.

"You understand, too, that Mr. Phillips has been for many years laboring for the rights of woman, in relation to government, to social position, to opportunities of education and of employment that should give her a livelihood. And how much loftier a position woman has attained within the last fifty years; how much she has been allowed education, development, usefulness; how much less she is the slave of dress and fashion and pleasure and flattery; how much men are compelled to endure her rivalry and to find themselves under the necessity of greater exertion and nobler aims if they would not decline in honor, and lose the superiority of position which they have long claimed under the title of 'Lords of Creation!' If life was made beautiful to Mr. Phillips by the companionship of an affectionate, cultivated, sympathizing wife, he labored to diffuse through the world the influences he enjoyed; and many thousands of sons will live purer, nobler lives on account of the happiness diffused from these two good, pure, and united hearts. Every maiden who thinks of marriage, and who is to be married, will have a better husband; many a mother will feel that her boys are more secure against intemperance and every other form of corruption; many thousands of husbands will find they have better companions, wives more truly helpmates, guides and means of inspiration."

From the time when Mr. Phillips first began to speak on the slave-question, his services were constantly in demand. The reputation for eloquence which he established for himself at the Lovejoy meeting followed him wherever he went, and undoubtedly carried conviction to many persons disinclined to favor the agitation of the abolition problem.

The first anti-slavery lecture which he ever gave was at Lynn, Mass., in the old Christian meeting-house on Silsbee Street. The house stands nearly opposite where Mr. Williams now preaches. Phillips went there under the auspices of the Young Men's Anti-slavery Society, several of whose members had listened to his famous reply to Attorney-General Austin's harangue in Faneuil Hall.

In 1838 Phillips was again invited to deliver the Fourth-of-July oration in Lynn, at the First Methodist Church. The following reminiscences of this event serve to show something of the earnestness with which Mr. Phillips entered into the cause. They are from the pen of Mr. Edwin Thompson, himself an anti-slavery advocate: —

"We not only engaged Mr. Phillips for the oration [he says], but we also secured the services of Miss Susan Paul, a celebrated teacher of a colored school in Boston. She was the daughter of Thomas Paul, a popular Baptist preacher in Boston, who, though of the colored race, was a man of high standing. His name was a household word in Lynn. At that time children of the colored race could not attend the public schools of Boston, sit with white people in churches, or ride in any public conveyance with them. Miss

Paul came to Lynn with forty of her scholars in carriages which they hired for the occasion. She and her pupils sang such songs as were appropriate in those early anti-slavery days. Of course, it produced a great sensation in Lynn, especially among the young people, who had never seen so many colored children before.

"As Miss Paul and her pupils were obliged to start early from Boston, they had taken but a slight breakfast; and they partook of a lunch at my father's house, which was always open for the friends of every reformatory movement. At the celebration, it so happened that I was called upon to read the Declaration of Independence; which, I suppose, was the reason that Mr. Phillips said he thought I ought to speak publicly in behalf of the slave. I told him I did not think I was qualified to speak as an advocate of the anti-slavery cause. Although I had been engaged in the cause for five years before Mr. Phillips came into the movement, I had never spoken to any great extent on the subject.

"Soon after the conversation with Mr. Phillips, I received an invitation from the Essex County Anti-slavery Society to visit all the towns, and organize societies, get up anti-slavery libraries, and lecture on the subject. I worked under the direction of the martyr, Rev. Charles T. Torrey, who was the corresponding-secretary, who was preaching in Salem as pastor of the Howard-street Church, where the celebrated George B. Cheever, author of the famous 'Deacon Giles' Distillery,' once preached. This appointment, which I suppose came at the instigation of Mr. Phillips, changed my whole course of life, and brought me into a somewhat intimate acquaintance with some of the grandest people I have ever known."

CHAPTER VII.

THE WORLD'S ANTI-SLAVERY CONVENTION.

Begins its Sessions June 12, 1840. — The Rights of Women discussed in the American Anti-Slavery Society. — David Lee Child's Resolutions. — Prominent Delegates. — Freemasons' Hall, London. — Debate on the Admission of Women. — Speech of Mr. Phillips. — The Women rejected. — Adverse Criticism, and Wisdom of Mr. Phillips.

"Theories are but thin and unsubstantial air against the solid fact of woman mingling with honor and profit in the various professions and industrial pursuits of life."

"It is, after all, of little use to argue these social questions. These prejudices never were reasoned up; and, my word for it, they will never be reasoned down. The freedom of the press, the freedom of labor, the freedom of the race in its lowest classes, was never argued to success. The moment you can get woman to go out into the highway of life, and show by active valor what God has created her for, that moment this question is settled forever." — PHILLIPS.

ON the 12th of June, 1840, the World's Anti-slavery Convention began its session in London, England. This fact brings us to a consideration of Mr. Phillips's early advocacy of the rights of women as co-equal with those of men.

When the American Anti-slavery Society was formed, in 1833, some of the women present at the meeting made speeches; and the convention passed a vote of thanks to them for their interest and zeal in the cause.

In 1835 the society wished to delegate Mrs. Lydia Maria Child to visit England in the interests of the anti-slavery cause, and two years later endeavored to secure her services as travelling lecture-agent. In the same year the Misses Grimkè were similarly commissioned.

At the sixth annual meeting of the society, in May, 1839, an attempt was made for the first time to exclude women from active membership. A motion was made by a clergyman (his name is forgotten), that none but men should have their names placed upon the rolls; but this motion was rejected by an overwhelming majority. The same year a woman was put on a committee to "examine and report" on the publication of the annual report. It caused a great commotion among the members; but there was no open revolt until 1840, when for the first time a woman was elected on the business committee of the society. In consequence of this action, a minority of the membership withdrew, and formed another anti-slavery society. This division afterwards extended through many of the State and local anti-slavery organizations.

The World's Anti-slavery Convention was first projected by the English abolitionists. When the American Anti-slavery Society was invited to send delegates, it responded by adopting the following resolutions, offered by David Lee Child, at its annual meeting held in New York, May 12, 1840:—

"*Resolved*, That the American Anti-slavery Society regards with heartfelt interest the design of the World's Convention about to assemble in London, and anticipates from its labors a powerful and blessed influence upon the condition and prospects of the victims of slavery and prejudice wherever they are found.

"*Resolved*, That our beloved friends, William Lloyd Garrison, Nathaniel Peabody Rogers, Charles Lenox Remond, and Lucretia Mott, be, and they hereby are, appointed delegates, to represent this society in the said convention; and we heartily commend them to the confidence and love of the universal abolition fraternity.

"*Resolved*, That the anti-slavery enterprise is the cause of universal humanity, and, as such, legitimately calls together the World's Convention; and that this society trusts that that convention will fully and practically recognize, in its organization and movements, the equal brotherhood of the entire human family, without distinction of color, sex, or clime."

The delegates from other anti-slavery societies in the United States were Wendell Phillips, Anne Greene Phillips, George Bradburn, Henry B. Stanton, Elizabeth Cady Stanton, Professor William Adams, Rev. Henry Colver, Rev. Nathaniel Greene, Rev. Eben Galusha, James Mott, James G. Birney, C. Edwards Lester, Sarah Pugh, Mary Grew, Elizabeth T. Neale (now Mrs. Sidney Howard Gay), Emily Winslow Taylor, Col. J. P. Miller, Isaac Winslow, Abby Kimber, Abby Southwick, Rev. Henry Grew, and perhaps others. Several American clergymen (the clergy always favored reform) who landed in England a few days before the majority of the delegation, busily engaged themselves in fanning the English prejudices into active hostility against the admission of the women to the convention.

The 12th of June was a fair and bright morning, and at an early hour the anti-slavery delegates from the different countries wended their way through the crooked streets of London to Freemasons' Hall. "Entering the vestibule," says a historian of the convention, "little groups might be seen gathered here and there, earnestly discussing the best disposition to make of those women delegates from America. The excitement and vehemence of protest and denunciation could not have been greater if the news had come that the French were about to invade England. In vain these obdurate women had been conjured to withhold their credentials, and not thrust a question that must produce such discord on the convention. Lucretia Mott, in her calm, firm manner, insisted that the delegates had no discretionary power in the proposed action, and the responsibility of accepting or rejecting them must rest on the convention."

The convention was called to order at eleven o'clock, the venerable Thomas Clarkson being in the chair. At the earliest moment Mr. Phillips arose, and made the following motion: —

"That a committee of five be appointed to prepare a correct list of the members of this convention, with instructions to include in such list all persons bearing credentials from any anti-slavery society."

This motion at once opened the debate on the admission of women as delegates.

As soon as an opportunity offered, Mr. Phillips proceeded to argue his motion. He said, —

"When the call reached America, we found that it was an invitation to the friends of the slave of every nation and of every clime. Massachusetts has for several years acted on the principle of admitting women to an equal seat with men in the deliberate bodies of anti-slavery societies. When the Massachusetts Anti-slavery Society received that paper, it interpreted it, as it was its duty, in its broadest and most liberal sense. If there be any other paper, emanating from the committee, limiting to one sex the qualification of membership, there is no proof; and, as an individual, I have no knowledge that such a paper ever reached Massachusetts. We stand here in consequence of your invitation; and knowing our custom, as it must be presumed you did, we had a right to interpret 'friends of the slave' to include women as well as men. In such circumstances we do not think it just or equitable to that State, nor to America in general, that after the trouble, the sacrifice, the self-devotion, of a part of those who leave their families and kindred and occupations in their own land, to come three thousand miles to attend this world's convention, they should be refused a place in its deliberations."

One of the committee who issued the call stated that a second invitation had been issued, in which "the description of those who are to form the convention is set forth as consisting of 'gentlemen.'"

Dr. Bowring said, —

"I look upon this delegation from America as one of the most interesting, the most encouraging, and the most delightful, symptoms of the times. I cannot believe that we shall refuse to welcome gratefully the co-operation which is offered us."

On the other hand, in a most touching appeal to the ladies to withdraw their credentials, the Rev. J. Burnet (another clergyman) said that it would be better that the convention should be dissolved at once than that "this motion should be adopted."

Another clergyman, the Rev. Henry Grew of Philadelphia, said, —

"The reception of women as a part of this convention would in the view of many, be not only a violation of the customs of England, but of the ordinances of Almighty God, who has a right to appoint our services to his sovereign will."

Mr. Phillips was urged on all sides to withdraw his motion. He again arose in support of it. He said, —

"It has been hinted very respectfully by two or three speakers that the delegates from the State of Massachusetts should withdraw their credentials, or the motion before the meeting. The one appears to me to be equivalent to the other. If this motion be withdrawn, we must have another. I would merely ask whether any man can suppose that the delegates from Massachusetts or Pennsylvania can take upon their shoulders the responsibility of withdrawing that list of delegates from your table, which their constituents told them to place there, and whom they sanctioned as their fit representatives, because this convention tells us that it is not ready to meet the ridicule of the morning papers, and stand up against the customs of England. In America we listen to no such arguments. If we had done so, we had never be-here as abolitionists. It is the custom there, not to admit colored men into respectable society; and we have been told again and again, that we are outraging the decencies of humanity when we permit colored men to sit by our side. When we have submitted to brickbats and the tar-tub and feathers in America, rather than yield to the custom prevalent there of not admitting colored brethren into our friendship, shall we yield to parallel custom or prejudice against women in Old England?

"We cannot yield this question if we would, for it is a matter of conscience. But we would not yield it on the ground of expediency. In doing so, we should feel that we were striking off the right arm of our enterprise. We could not go back to America to ask for any aid from the women of Massachusetts if we had deserted them when they chose to send out their own sisters as their representatives here: we could not go back to Massachusetts, and assert the unchangeableness of spirit on the question. We have argued it over and over again, and decided it time after time, in every society in the land, in favor of the women. We have not changed by crossing the water. We stand here the advocates of the same principle that we contend for in America. We think it right for women to sit by our side there, and we think it right for them to do the same here. We ask the convention to admit them: if they do not choose to grant it, the responsibility rests on their shoulders. Massachusetts cannot turn aside, or succumb to any prejudices or customs, even in the land she looks upon with so much reverence as the land of Wilberforce, of Clarkson, and of O'Connell. It is a matter of conscience, and British virtue ought not to ask us to yield."

Mr. Ashurst, in advocating the admission of the women to the convention, put the question very plainly by saying, —

"You are convened to influence society upon a subject connected with the kindliest feelings of our nature; and being the first assembly met to shake hands with other nations, and employ your combined efforts to annihilate slavery throughout the world, are you to commence by saying you will take away the right of one-half of creation? This is the principle which you are putting forward."

He was opposed by another clergyman, the Rev. A. Harvey of Glasgow. He claimed that he had certain views in relation to the teaching of the word of God, and of the "particular" sphere in which woman is to act. "I must say," he remarked, "if I were to give a vote in favor of females sitting and deliberating in such an assembly as this, that I should be acting in opposition to the plain teaching of the word of God." The exquisite refinement of this apostle's conscience almost carried the convention and put a stop to debate.

After a little delay, however, other speakers took the floor, and talked to a late hour. Then the vote was taken, and by an overwhelming majority the women were excluded as delegates to the convention.

"I hope," said Mr. Thompson, — the same George Thompson whom the Boston aristocrats sought to molest, and who, true to the spirit that always governed his acts, was now in favor of the women, — "I hope, as the question is now decided, that Mr. Phillips will give us the assurance that we shall proceed with one heart and one mind."

"I have no doubt of it," replied Mr. Phillips. "There is no unpleasant feeling in our minds. I have no doubt the women will sit with as much interest behind the bar as though the original proposition had been carried in the affirmative. All we asked was an expression of an opinion; and, having obtained it, we shall now act with the utmost cordiality."

Mr. Phillips has been criticised, even by his most ardent admirers, for supposing, that, after being rejected as delegates, these women would "sit with as much interest behind the bar, as in the convention." Why, they ask, did he not himself refuse longer to take part in the deliberations of the convention?

Such criticism is certainly injudicious. To stand in that august assembly, and maintain the unpopular heresy of woman's equality, was a severe ordeal for a young man to pass through; and Wendell Phillips, who accepted the odium of presenting this question to the convention, earned for all time the sincere gratitude of womankind. Every phase of his course at that convention was above criticism. The calm demeanor, mingled with kind regrets, of Mr. Thompson, alone sufficed to disarm resentment. It would have been rash indeed, if, under such circumstances, Mr. Phillips had so far lost sight of the real object of the convention as to have imperilled this object by any action tending to paralyze its results.

CHAPTER VIII.

PROGRESS OF THE ANTI-SLAVERY CAUSE.

Phillips arrives Home from Europe. — Limited Acquaintanceship. — Letter to George Thompson. — The "Remond Case." — A Petition to the Legislature, and its Result. — The Address of O'Connell and his Fellow-Countrymen. — Arrest of George Latimer. — The Action of the Legislature. — A Voice in Congress. — Phillips argues for Disunion. — Discussion. — An Interesting Letter. — Mobs.

"Agitate, and we shall yet see the laws of Massachusetts rule even Boston."

"The community that will not protect its most ignorant and unpopular member in the free utterance of his opinions, no matter how false or hateful, is only a gang of slaves."

"If our agitation has not been wisely planned and conducted, explain for us the history of the last twenty years! Experience is a safe light to walk by, and he is not a rash man who expects success in future from the same means which have secured it in times past." — PHILLIPS.

ON the 12th of July, 1841, Mr. Phillips and his wife arrived home in Boston. During their sojourn on the Continent, they visited many places of interest in France, Italy, and Great Britain, but made few acquaintances. In a letter to his friend Davis of Philadelphia, who applied to him, in 1845, for letters of introduction to notables living on the Continent, he says, —

"As to the second note about foreign parts, let me say I travelled with a sick wife, and made no acquaintances. One or two friends in Paris completed the list, and they have since removed home here. I would add some letters to those you ask for England, but that M. W. C. and W. L. G. are infinitely better names for backers than mine."

While Phillips was abroad, he addressed an open letter to George Thompson in support of the effort then making in England to supersede American cotton by stimulating the production of cotton in India. A single extract from this earnest and eloquent document will bear quotation in this place: —

"How shall we address that large class of men to whom dollars are always a weightier consideration than duties, prices current stronger argument than proofs of holy writ? Our appeal has been entreaty; for the times in America are those 'purs*y* times' when, —

'Virtue itself of Vice must pardon beg,
Yea, curb and woo for leave to do him good.'

"But from India a voice comes, clothed with the omnipotence of self-interest; and the wisdom which might have been slighted from the pulpit, will be to such men oracular from the marketplace. Gladly will we make a pilgrimage, and bow with more than Eastern devotion on the banks of the Ganges, if his holy waters shall be able to wear away the fetters of the slave. God speed the progress of your society! May it soon find in its ranks the whole phalanx of scarred and veteran abolitionists, — no single divided effort, but a united one to grapple with the wealth, influence, and power embattled against you! Is it not Schiller who says, 'Divide the thunder into single tones, and it becomes a lullaby for children; but pour it forth in one quick peal, and the royal sound shall shake the heavens'? So may it be with you! and God grant, that, without waiting for the United States to be consistent, before we are dust the jubilee of emancipated millions may reach us from Mexico to the Potomac, and from the Atlantic to the Rocky Mountains!"

One of the most active and energetic workers in the cause of anti-slavery, at this time, was a well-bred and well-educated colored man named Charles Lenox Remond. His home was in Salem, Mass., where his parents also resided. In 1838 he was appointed an agent of the Massachusetts Anti-slavery Society, in which capacity he rendered abundant and valuable services. He spent the greater part of the year 1841 in Great Britain and Ireland, where he lectured before many large audiences.

Mr. Phillips's interest in Charles L. Remond took him to Salem, on Remond's return from a trip to Europe; and a scene in the old low Salem depot, as related by him and Remond before a committee of the Legislature in that year, shows that the struggle for the rights of the colored people was well prompted.

They took seats side by side in one of the little old cars of that date. A person in authority came in, and ordered Remond to take his seat in a rear second-class car, a mere box with pine seats. Mr. Phillips accompanied Remond to the inferior car, and seated himself beside him. Mr. Phillips was told that he could not remain there, as it was only for colored persons. Mr. Phillips, deprived of the society of his friend, rode in another car to Boston.

The appeal of Remond to the superintendent of the railroad, who stood and conversed with him at the door of the colored people's car, and the cool, unfeeling, though by no means insulting, replies of the superintendent, who was a prominent citizen of Salem and a gentleman of character, were as nigh pathetic as related by Remond before the committee as any words ever heard from human lips. They had no effect on the Legislature; for, a year or two later, a poor black girl, with her little bundle, who had made the same mistake as Remond, was driven out of the car, — the train being stopped for the purpose on one of those precipitous embankments between the islands on the old East-Boston route, — and, screaming and crying for fear she should be left, scrambled along the fearful outside to the negro-car. All the passengers beheld the outrage with absolute indifference. Such was the cowardly indecision in regard to human rights which prevailed at that time.

On the evening of Jan. 28, 1842, a large and overwhelming meeting of the citizens of Boston was held in the old Cradle of Liberty, favorable to the immediate abolition of slavery in the District of Columbia. The resolutions, denouncing Congress for permitting slavery in the District of Columbia, were adopted by an almost unanimous vote, and in the most impressive manner.

The Irish address, signed by Daniel O'Connell,

Father Mathew, and sixty thousand other Irishmen, to the Irish residents in the United States, calling upon them unitedly to espouse the anti-slavery cause, and to identify themselves with the American abolitionists, was then read, and received by the immense assemblage with cheers and loud acclamation of applause. A large number of the Irish inhabitants of Boston and vicinity were present, and responded to the sentiments of the address, and to those which were uttered by the various speakers, in the most enthusiastic manner.

Mr. Phillips offered the following resolutions, which he very eloquently advocated, and which were adopted by acclamation: —

"*Resolved*, That the voice of O'Connell, which now shakes three kingdoms, has poured across the waters a thunder-peal for the cause of liberty in our own land; and Father Mathew, having lifted, with one hand, five millions of his own countrymen into moral life, has stretched forth the other — which may Heaven make equally potent! — to smite off the fetters of the American slave.

"*Resolved*, That we receive, with the deepest gratitude, the names of the sixty thousand Irishmen, who, in the trial-hour of their own struggle for liberty, have not forgotten the slave on this side of the water; that we accept with triumphant exultation the address they have forwarded to us, and pledge ourselves to circulate it through the length and breadth of our land, till the pulse of every man, and especially every man who claims Irish parentage, beats true to the claims of patriotism and humanity."

He then made an address, which, by reason of its importance, is here given in full: —

"I hold in my hand, Mr. Chairman, a resolution expressive of our thanks to the sixty thousand Irishmen who have sent us that token of their sympathy and interest, and especially to those high and gallant spirits who lead the noble list. I must say, that never have I stood in the presence of an audience with higher hopes of the rapid progress and success of our cause than now. I remember with what devoted earnestness, with what unfaltering zeal, Ireland has carried on so many years the struggle for her own freedom. It is from such men — whose hearts lost no jot of their faith in the grave of Emmet, over whose zeal the loss of Curran and Grattan could throw no damp, who are now turning the trophies of one field of victory into weapons for new conquests, whom a hireling press and prejudiced public could never sever a moment from O'Connell's side, — it is from the sympathy of such that we have a right to hope much.

"The image of the generous Isle comes to us, not only 'crowned with the spoil of every science, and decked with the wreath of every muse;' but we cannot forget that she lent to Waterloo the sword which cut the despot's 'shattered sceptre through;' and, to American ears, the crumbled walls of St. Stephen's yet stand to echo the eloquence of her Burke, when, at the foot of the British throne, he took his place side by side with that immortal rebel [pointing to the picture of Washington].

"From a priest of the Catholic Church we might expect superiority to that prejudice against color which freezes the sympathies of our own churches when humanity points to the slave. I remember that African lips may join in the chants of the Church, unrebuked, even under the dome at St. Peter's; and I have seen the colored man in the sacred dress pass with priest and student beneath the frowning portals of the Propaganda College at Rome, with none to sneer at his complexion, or repulse him from society.

"I remember that a long line of popes, from Leo to Gregory,

have denounced the sin of making merchandise of men; that the voice of Rome was the first to be heard against the slave-trade; and that the bull of Gregory XVI., forbidding every true Catholic to touch the accursed thing, is yet hardly a year old.

"Ireland is the land of agitation and agitators. We may well learn a lesson from her in the battle of human rights. Her philosophy is no recluse: she doffs the cowl, and quits the cloister, to grasp in friendly effort the hands of the people. No pulse beats truer to liberty, to humanity, than those which in Dublin quicken at every good from abolition on this side of the ocean. There can be no warmer words of welcome than those which welcome the American abolitionists on their thresholds. Let not any one persuade us, Mr. Chairman, that the question of slavery is no business of ours, but belongs entirely to the South.

"I trust in that love of liberty which every Irishman brings to the country of his adoption, to make him true to her cause at the ballot-box, and throw no vote without asking if the hand to which he is about to trust political power will use it for the slave. When an American was introduced to O'Connell in the lobby of the House of Commons, he asked, without putting out his hand, 'Are you from the South?' — 'Yes, sir.' — 'A slaveholder, I presume?' — 'Yes, sir.' — 'Then,' said the great liberator, 'I have no hand for you!' and stalked away. Shall his countrymen trust that hand with political power which O'Connell deemed it pollution to touch?

"We remember, Mr. Chairman, that, when a jealous disposition tore from the walls of the City Hall of Dublin the picture of Henry Grattan, the act but did endear him the more to Ireland. The slavocracy of our land thinks to expel that 'old man eloquent' with the dignity of seventy winters on his brow (pointing to a picture of J. Q. Adams) from the halls of Congress. They will find him only the more lastingly fixed in the hearts of his countrymen.

"Mr. Chairman, we stand in the presence of at least the name of Father Mathew. We remember the millions who pledged themselves to temperance from his lips. I hope his countrymen will join with me in pledging here, eternal hostility to slavery. Will you ever return to his master the slave who once sets foot on the soil of Massachusetts? [No, no, no!] Will you ever raise to office or power the man who will not pledge his utmost effort against slavery? [No, no, no!]

"Then, may we not hope well for freedom? Thanks to those noble men who battle in her cause the world over. The 'ocean of their philanthropy knows no shore.' Humanity knows no country; and I am proud, here in Faneuil Hall, fit place to receive their message, to learn of O'Connell's fidelity to freedom, and of Father Mathew's love to the real interests of man."

These remarks were received with unbounded applause. With nine cheers, the vast assembly — the influence of which was soon felt throughout the country — adjourned.

It appears in the records of those eventful days, — strange as it may seem now, — that the anti-slavery address of O'Connell and his sixty thousand countrymen was not received well by the Irish residents in the United States. The ebullition of enthusiasm at the meeting held in Faneuil Hall soon cooled down, and a feeling characterized by marked indifference ensued. At a meeting of the Massachusetts Society held in January, 1843, Mr. Garrison offered a resolution bearing upon this indifference and neglect, and declaring the same as "deeply dishonorable to the Irish of this country, and a shame to the land of their birth; proving that Ireland has not sent us her true children, or that the democratic climate of New England is fatal to the liberty-loving spirit."

In the autumn of this year (1842), George Latimer, a native colored man of Virginia, was arrested in Boston without a warrant, and claimed as a slave. The case was brought before the courts, where Chief Justice Shaw ruled that "the statute of the United States authorizes the owner of the fugitive slave to arrest him in any State to which he may have fled."

As soon as tidings of this proceeding were spread abroad, the intensest excitement prevailed. On the 30th of October — a sabbath evening — a large body of citizens met in Faneuil Hall. Speeches were made, and resolutions were presented, protesting, "by all the glorious memories of the Revolutionary struggle, in the names of justice, liberty, and right, in the awful name of God, against the deliverance of George Latimer into the hands of his pursuers."

Letters were also read from John Quincy Adams, George Bancroft, Samuel Hoar, William B. Calhoun, and others. Amid hisses and uproar, Wendell Phillips sought to speak. "When I look," he said, "upon the crowded thousands, and see them trample on their consciences and the rights of their fellow-men at the bidding of a piece of parchment, I say, 'My curse be upon the Constitution of these United States!'"

A few days later a petition, signed by many influential citizens, was presented to the sheriff, demanding the dismissal of the jailer. At the same time another petition was prepared, requesting Gov. Davis to dismiss the sheriff unless he removed the jailer. Then it was that the Rev. Nathaniel Colver agreed to pay the sum of four hundred dollars "on the delivery of free papers, and the surrender of the power of attorney to reclaim his wife." The offer was accepted, and Latimer was released.

The excitement, however, did not end here. A convention was held, and a petition was presented to the Legislature, praying that body to "forbid all persons holding office under the laws of the State from aiding in the arrest or detention of persons claimed as fugitives from slavery; to forbid the use of jails, or other public property, for their detention, and to prepare amendments to the Federal Constitution that should forever separate the people of the State from all connection with slavery."

Subsequently, certain resolves of the Legislature of Massachusetts, proposing to Congress to recommend, according to the provisions of the Fifth Article of the Constitution of the United States, an amendment to the said Constitution, in effect abolishing the representation for slaves, and signed by fifty thousand of the citizens of the State, were laid upon the desk of John Quincy Adams.

The resolutions were presented to the House of Representatives, Dec. 21, 1843. A great sensation was the result. Said Henry A. Wise of Virginia, " I say solemnly before God, as a Southern man, that we are worsted in this fight. From this day forth and forever, I withdraw from the fight. I say to my constituents, that, the way this battle has been fought, there is no hope for your rights. Your interests are doomed to be destroyed."

The New-England Anti-slavery Convention, held in May, 1843, yielded to none of its predecessors in interest to its members and in advantage to the cause. During the day the meetings were held in the Tabernacle in Howard Street: the evening sessions were held in Faneuil Hall. The convention had ordered an address to the slaves of the United States, on the subject of their rights, duties, and hopes; and another to John Tyler, — who was shortly expected in Boston, to assist at the Bunker-hill Monument celebration, — requesting him to emancipate his slaves, to be prepared. Both addresses were submitted to the convention in Faneuil Hall. The address to Mr. Tyler was read by Mr. Phillips, and was enforced with a speech of great power.

This convention was the moving cause of the great movement of the year, best known by the appellation of the Hundred Conventions. In the early part of the year about twenty conventions were held in as many towns, chiefly in Middlesex, Worcester, Norfolk, and Plymouth Counties, in Massachusetts alone. A course of anti-slavery lectures was given during the winter, under the auspices of the Boston Female Anti-slavery Society, by Messrs. Pierpont, Phillips, Quincy, Garrison, Douglass, Bradburn, and Remond, the success of which was highly encouraging. In the summer season Mr. Phillips did excellent work in the neighborhood of Boston, and introduced the subject of abolition into places where it had scarcely been mentioned before. During the year Mr. Phillips was elected general agent of the society. He retained the position until May, 1845, when the pressure of other duties forced him, with regret, to resign.

In 1843 arose in the Garrisonian ranks the discussion whether an abolitionist could rightfully vote or take office under the Constitution of the land, which recognized slavery, gave it a special representation in Congress, and ordered the return of fugitive slaves. Inasmuch as every officeholder swore to support the Constitution, and as every voter did so implicitly, and indeed by his vote asked his candidate to take such an oath, it was urged that no consistent abolitionist could either vote or take office.

Two years before this, Mr. Phillips had taken this ground, and had refused to continue to practise in the courts where an oath to the Constitution was required of each attorney. He started the discussion in the anti-slavery ranks, and in 1844 published an argument, entitled "Can Abolitionists vote or take Office under the United-States Constitution?" in defence of this position, which was unanimously assumed by the American Anti-slavery Society in the same year.

The resolution, written by Mr. Phillips, is in the following words: —

"*Resolved*, That secession from the present United-States Government is the duty of every abolitionist; since no one can take office under the United-States Constitution without violating his anti-slavery principles, and rendering himself an abetter of the slaveholder in his sin."

In 1843 the question whether it was not the duty of the people of the free States to dissolve their political relations with the South, began to be discussed by Mr. Garrison in the colums of "The Liberator." It was, of course, a startling proposition; and many abolitionists, who had all along supposed that their movement had a tendency to preserve the Union, shrank back from it with dread. The discussion, however, was steadily maintained, until at length the American society, and then the whole Garrisonian phalanx, swung solidly round to the same position, and the movement carried aloft the banner, "No union with slaveholders."

Mr. Francis Jackson resigned his office of justice of the peace on the same grounds. From this year until 1861, the cry of disunion was proclaimed in the anti-slavery journals, in pamphlets and tracts, in innumerable conventions, and by the voices of a host of lecturers, with Garrison and Phillips at its head.

In laying down his office, Mr. Jackson wrote a letter containing a calm but clear and able exposition of the reasons which made this course the only one he could honestly pursue. He analyzed the Constitution, and showed what were its compromises, the unworthy services which they demanded of the North, and the political servitude to the slave-power with which it had been visited in consequence of its consenting to them. "That part of the Constitution," said he, "which provides for the surrender of fugitive slaves, I never have supported, and never will. I will join in no slave-hunt. My door shall stand open, as it has long stood, to the panting and trembling victim of the slave-hunter. When I shut it against him, may God shut the door of his mercy against me!"

He thus concluded his letter: —

"The Constitution of the United States, both in theory and practice, is so utterly broken down by the influence and effect of slavery, so imbecile for the highest good of the nation, and so powerful for evil, that I can give no voluntary assistance in holding it up any longer. Henceforth it is dead to me, and I to it. I withdraw all professions of allegiance to it, and all my voluntary efforts to sustain it. The burdens that it lays upon me, while it is held up by others, I shall endeavor to bear patiently, yet acting with reference to a higher law, and distinctly declaring, that, while I retain my own liberty, I will be a party to no compact which helps to rob any other man of his."

This letter, coming as it did from no hot-brained enthusiast, but from a man long known and valued for his practical good sense, and talent for the world's business, attracted a wide attention, and produced a deep impression. It was as well timed as it was well executed, and embodied the views of his fellow-abolitionists in a tangible and intelligible shape.

There can be no doubt, that, in the sixteen years immediately preceding the civil war, this "disunion" movement did much to prepare the Northern people for the crisis which was coming, and through which they were called to pass. Whether it hastened the struggle, is another question. It taught the North to assert that further compromise with the slave-power was impossible: it encouraged the North to do and dare in the cause of liberty. It taught the South that the principle of morality was stronger than the Constitution which was so long a main dependence of the slave-power; and it at least forced from the lips of Mr Wise, and from those who shared his foresight, the confession that Southern interests in the slave-power were doomed to be destroyed.

In an interesting letter addressed to his friend Edward M. Davis, Mr. Phillips thus writes, under date of "May 23, 1844:" —

"Now for questions.

"What is supporting, etc.?

"Why, when an officer takes an oath to support the instrumen

PROGRESS OF THE ANTI-SLAVERY CAUSE.

which prescribes his duties, does it not mean he will perform those duties?

"Why have oaths?

"To secure the carrying out of the provisions of the Constitution, are they not? Did not South Carolina, when the compromise was made in 1789, rely on the oath of Massachusetts, and go home confident that the clauses of that compromise would be fairly carried out, because all officers were to be sworn to do so in all coming time? If the officers of the United States do not in their official capacity do what the Constitution prescribes, then that instrument is a dead letter. Now, in order that it may live, it enjoins that they shall be sworn to support it. Suppose a case: A man claims his slave; the judge refuses to act. Would it not be fair argument for the slaveholder to retort, 'You, sir, assumed a place, and swore to perform its duties: this, you allow, is one (whether morally right, or not, is not the question); it is one set down in the bond. Do you keep your oath, sir, when you refuse this part of your office? I have a claim on you.'

"Suppose the judge to say, 'Now this case has arisen, I will resign.' Would it not be fair to reply to him, 'The country placed you in a certain post: you have no right to determine beforehand, that, on a certain duty arising, you will not perform it.' Suppose a general to assume command, and lead his army to the field, and then, just as the fight began, — resign.

"If the oath is any thing but humbug, it means, that, while the Constitution remains as it is, I will obey and carry it out as it is.

"If it don't mean this, what does it mean?

"2d, Does a man support by taking office when he votes against all pro-slavery measures?

"Try it. Is not his position more than his vote? The senator's duty is to concur in the appointment of judges whose duty it is to return fugitive slaves.

"3d, Can an abolitionist ask and authorize a man to assume such an office as that of judge?

"The representative is to carry out by appropriate laws the pro-slavery clauses of the Constitution. He may be called to elect the President, who is pledged to put down domestic violence, etc.: he is to vote the salaries of the executive officers, whose duties are some of them pro-slavery.

"Now, if, while he does these things, he votes against some pro-slavery measures, is he innocent?

"To vote against every thing which touches slavery would stop the wheels of government. Shall he vote supplies for the Florida war? But I have no time to enlarge on these points. I will only ask, Can the man who has just sworn, as a member of the House of Representatives, to support the Constitution, shelter a fugitive slave in his house, detain, and conceal him from his master? Is this honest dealing, as between man and man?

"4th, Does not this strike a blow against all human governments? Answer first, Don't know: if it's right, don't care. Second, No: we submit, and carry out the will of the majority rightfully in all cases not moral, not of conscience; and government must be so arranged that it shall be understood that no man will take any office under it which requires him to violate his conscience, or fail in his duty. I could go into the House of Commons now, and vote away right and left without violating my conscience.

"5th, Is the position taken for consistency? Then, why pay taxes?

"Taxes are not voluntary. Did Jesus support Nero when he paid a tax? I seek to be in this country like an alien, a traveller. Such can't avoid indirect taxation; but are they responsible for the use government makes of the money? Of course not. We are not responsible for that we can't prevent. Now, I can prevent my money going to government only in two ways, — by voting, which is wrong; by leaving the country, which no one is required to do, because God placing us here is the highest title and message of duty we can have.

"I don't think the position contravenes our section seven Constitution and preamble. Does taking away a political influence weaken us? It does not take away our political influence, only our voting. Who has had more influence on the politics of this country than William Lloyd Garrison, — yet not by voting? 'The Edinburgh Review' has political influence in this country: such we retain, and much more.

"If it did take it away, the question still is, Can we rightfully retain it? Does giving up voting weaken us? Us it may: we may fall into oblivion and neglect. Probably. But the non-voting position, by its disinterestedness, its consistency, its high tone, its absence of suspicion, gives tenfold stronger hold on those about us to make them act.

"Never forget the distinction between weakening us and weakening the cause."

In 1845 Mr. Phillips, in order to aid the discussion, printed an argument entitled, "The Constitution a Pro-slavery Contract; or, Selections from the Madison Papers," the preface to which ends thus: —

"If, then, the Constitution be what these debates show that our fathers intended to make it, and what, too, their descendants, this nation, say they did make it, and agree to uphold, then we affirm that it is a covenant with death, an agreement with hell, and ought to be immediately annulled. No abolitionist can consistently take office under it, or swear to support it.

"But if, on the contrary, our fathers failed in their purpose, and the Constitution is all pure, and untouched by slavery, then Union itself is impossible without guilt. For it is undeniable, that the fifty years passed under this (anti-slavery) Constitution show us the slaves trebling in numbers; slaveholders monopolizing the offices, and dictating the policy, of the government; prostituting the strength and influence of the nation to the support of slavery here and elsewhere; trampling on the rights of the free States, and making the courts of the country their tools. To continue this disastrous alliance longer is madness. The trial of fifty years with the best of men and the best of constitutions, on this supposition, only proves that it is impossible for free and slave States to unite on any terms without all becoming partners in the guilt, and responsible for the sin, of slavery. We dare not prolong the argument; and with double earnestness we repeat our demand upon every honest man to join in the outcry of the American Anti-slavery Society, — No Union with slavery."

During the sessions of the society in the following years, as has already been remarked, this was the prominent topic; and some of Mr. Phillips's best speeches were made to advocate the destruction of the American Church and Union as they then stood.

The discussion touching the question of disunion was, of course, deeply offensive to the public mind; and the speakers were often mobbed. Capt. Rynders, after being defeated one day, turned the American Anti-slavery Society out of its hall. Next year no owner of a hall in New-York City would risk his building for the uses of the society: hence, for several years thereafter, it became necessary to hold the anniversaries in Rochester and Syracuse.

CHAPTER IX.

ERA OF THE FUGITIVE-SLAVE ACT.

James K. Polk becomes President of the United States. — The Annexation of Texas. — Origin of the "Liberty Party." — The Massachusetts Legislature of 1846. — The "Free-Soil Party." — Fleeing from Slavery. — An Outrage in Boston. — Election of Gen. Taylor. — Growth of the Free-Soil Party. — The Fugitive-Slave Bill proposed in Congress. — Debates. — Apostasy of Daniel Webster. — The 7th of March Speech. — Indignation Meetings. — The Act signed by the President. — Faneuil Hall speaks. — Charles Sumner chosen Senator. — The "Shadrach Case." — The "Sims Case." — Public Meetings. — Election of Franklin Pierce. — The Darkest Day in the History of the American Republic.

"Because you have your prejudices, shall there be no history written? Our task is unlike that of some recent meetings, — *history*, not flattery."

"My idea of American civilization is, that it is a second part, a repetition, of that same sublime confidence in the public conscience and the public thought which made the groundwork of Grecian democracy."

"Who can adequately tell the sacredness and the value of free speech? Who can fitly describe the enormity of the crime of its violation? Free speech, at once the instrument, and the guaranty, and the bright, consummate flower, of all liberty." — PHILLIPS.

THE election of James K. Polk to the presidency in 1844, and the annexation of Texas in the following year, largely encouraged and strengthened the pro-slavery party, both in the North and in the South. Many members of the Whig party were depressed in spirits, and had already begun to doubt the expediency of any further contest. The sentiment, if not the action, of Massachusetts was opposed to slavery. Of course this sentiment was not always directly expressed; but then, the opinion prevailed that the anti-slavery cause was at least a righteous one, and that it would eventually receive its vindication. The Democratic party controlled the government: the government was under the control of slavery. The Whig party foresaw two alternatives, — either to go counter to slavery, make a direct issue, and attract to its side the spirit of freedom, of progress, and of the nineteenth century, or to fall back upon the ideas of the dark ages, and to run a race with Democracy for influence and co-operation. In the dilemma arose the "Liberty Party," — a party based on the idea that "any effective opposition to slavery politically must come from the disintegration of the old parties and the combination of their material into the new organization."

At the beginning of the session of the Massachusetts Legislature of 1846, Gov. Briggs laid before it certain resolutions concerning slavery and the action of Massachusetts, which had been adopted by the Legislature of Georgia. Henry Wilson of Natick moved that these resolutions be referred to a special committee, and offered an order that they "be instructed to report a preamble and resolution which should express in fitting terms the hostility of Massachusetts to the institution of slavery." Excitement arose: the motion was vehemently opposed by both Democrats and Whigs; a compromise was tendered, and the committee was left to act without instructions. In defending his motion, Mr. Wilson said that "we must destroy slavery, or slavery will destroy liberty." For himself, Mr. Wilson was ready to act with any man or party — Whig, Democrat, abolitionist, Christian, or infidel — who would lend support to the cause of emancipation.

As the result of the annexation of Texas, the war with Mexico was declared in May, 1846. This aroused at once to action men of all political parties at the North, and changed their minds as to their duties towards slavery. In September a Whig convention assembled in Faneuil Hall, and then and there Charles Sumner and others proclaimed the divorce between conscience and cotton. Mr. Stephen C. Phillips offered some minority resolutions. Daniel Webster was brought in to talk them down, and a scene ensued which will always linger in the memories of those who were present. After this the breach in the Whig party grew wider and wider, and finally led to the formation of the Free-soil party in 1848.

Towards the close of May, 1846, the President of the United States, through the War Department, transmitted a civil request to Gov. Briggs for a regiment of infantry from Massachusetts. His Excellency issued his proclamation on the 26th of that month, calling upon the citizen-soldiers at once to enroll themselves, and to be in readiness when the exigencies of the country should require their services. This course of the governor greatly displeased the abolitionists, inasmuch as the war was a direct consequence of the annexation of Texas; of which act, when in prospect only, he had expressed himself, three years before, in the following emphatic terms: —

"We hold," says the solemn "Appeal to the People of the Free States," signed by him and nineteen other members of Congress, March 3, 1843, — "we hold that the objects of this new acquisition are, *the perpetuation of slavery*, and *the continued ascendency of the slave-power;* . . . that there is *no Constitutional* power delegated *to any department* of government to authorize it; that no Act of Congress or treaty of annexation can impose the least obligation upon the several States of this Union to submit to such an unwarrantable act."

Very naturally, the conduct of the governor, directly opposed to his previous profession of opinion, merited and received a severe rebuke. On the very day the proclamation was issued, the New-England Convention began its annual session in Faneuil Hall. On the following day the meeting was held in the Melodeon, at which time Mr. Phillips arose, and introduced the following resolution: —

"*Resolved*, That at the bar of Liberty and Humanity we impeach George N. Briggs, the author of the proclamation dated yesterday, as perjured on his own principles, as a traitor by his own showing, as one before whose guilt the infamy of Arnold and of the Missouri compromisers becomes respectability and decency; since, under oath to support the Constitution of the United States, he calls on the Commonwealth to rally to a war which is waged to defend and protect an act (the annexation of Texas) which he has himself so often declared 'a violation of the Constitution,' 'equivalent to dissolution,' a triumph of slavery and despotism, one to which it was the basest calumny to suppose that Massachusetts would ever submit; and that we call upon the people to *forget him* as emphatically as they did Mason of Boston, and Shaw of Lanesborough, for their treason in 1820."

This resolution created an intense excitement, not alone in the convention, but also in the community. In the evening the building was crowded to its fullest capacity, and the relations of the Church to slavery was the topic of discussion. On the following day (Thursday) the convention again met in Faneuil Hall. As the morning papers contained Mr. Phillips's resolution, an immense concourse gathered in the hall for the purpose of learning what next was to occur. The Rev. William H. Channing offered a series of resolutions denying the existence of any lawful government of the United States, of any Union, of any obligation of allegiance or countenance to either, and pledging the abolitionists to give no aid or support to the Mexican war, and to exert all efforts to form a new union and a new constitution. These resolutions were sustained, amid mingled cheers and hisses, by Mr. Channing,

Theodore Parker, Mr. Remond, and others, and were enthusiastically adopted.

While the meeting was in progress, a notice was served upon the officers of the convention, that the chairman of the Committee on Public Buildings, Mr. Alderman Jonathan Preston, had directed the superintendent not to allow the hall to be used by the convention for an evening session. Thus the doors were closed against free discussion. A statement of the facts, signed by Jackson, Phillips, Garrison, and Quincy, was published in the morning papers. It concluded as follows: —

"Whether it was the promptings of a base pro-slavery spirit, or a cowardly truckling before the imaginary possibility of a contingent mob, which impelled Mr. Alderman Preston to take this extraordinary and reprehensible course, is a question which it is important only to himself to decide. We would simply ask our fellow-citizens to consider whether he would have dared thus to insult *any* political party, or any *other* philanthropic movement."

It may be a forgotten fact, — and a fact, too, which the prudence of some people might wish to relegate to the shades of oblivion, but which, nevertheless, it is the duty of the historian to record, — that at the dinner of the Ancient and Honorable Artillery Company, held a little later, Gov. Briggs undertook to defend his course on the assumption that he was bound, as a public officer, to do what he did, and that it was for doing a duty "prescribed by the laws," that he had been condemned. The governor evidently lacked intelligence to discern what were " the duties made imperative by his oath of office," and to distinguish between a *command* and a *permission* to do a certain act. President Polk did not pretend, the secretary of war expressly disclaimed, that there was any obligation on the part of the governors of the States, to whom invitations to this work were sent, to come up to it.

The question of caste in the public schools of Boston came prominently before the school committee in 1846 by a petition for the abolition of the colored schools. The committee were guilty of the indiscretion of giving their reasons for their refusing the prayer of the petitioners; and the city solicitor was unwise enough to commit himself, in a written opinion, on the same side. The "arguments" of the first were disposed of in an able minority report, written by Mr. Edmund Jackson, and signed by him and Dr. H. I. Bowditch. The "opinion" of the city solicitor, Mr. P. W. Chandler, was reviewed at length, and with great legal acumen, by Mr. Phillips.

The report of Mr. Jackson and the review of Mr. Phillips were printed and bound together, and extensively circulated. A vote on the question resulted in fifty-nine to sixteen for and against the continuance of the caste-schools.

In 1855 the desired change took place, and was acknowledged by the following resolution, offered by

Mr. Phillips at the ensuing meeting of the Massachusetts Anti-slavery Society: —

"*Resolved*, That this society rejoices in the abolition of the separate colored schools in the city of Boston as the triumph of law and justice over the pride of caste and wealth, and recognizes in it the marked advance of the anti-slavery sentiment of the State."

Meanwhile the annexation of Texas, and the prospective acquisition of Mexican territory, had increased the price of, and the demand for, slaves. The bondmen were filled with dread, and many of the more intelligent among them sought liberty in flight. For a time Eastern Pennsylvania seemed to be the destined place of refuge; and to the judicious counsels and labors of such men as Thomas Shipley, Edward M. Davis, Robert Purvis, William Still, William H. Furness, and to such noble women as Esther Moore, Lucretia Mott, Sarah Pugh, and Mary Grew, all of that State, thousands of these lowly ones were indebted for shelter, food, clothing, and a hearty God-speed.

The frequency of escapes incensed the slave-masters, and made them more vigilant. Numerous instances of kidnapping occurred, in which masters of vessels engaged in the Southern trade bore a prominent part.

In August, 1846, a striking case happened in Boston. The brig "Ottoman," owned by John H. Pierson, and commanded by Capt. James W. Hannum, sailed from New Orleans for Boston. When a few days out at sea, a slave was found secreted in the vessel. In September the vessel arrived in Boston Harbor; and the captain, after transferring the slave on a pilot-boat for safe-keeping, went into the city to arrange with the captain of the bark "Niagara," which was soon to sail for New Orleans, to take him back. The slave managed to escape to South-Boston Point, but was hotly pursued, recaptured, and was "abducted by force from the jurisdiction of the commonwealth, and borne back to slavery."

This proceeding aroused the deepest indignation; and a crowded meeting was held at Faneuil Hall, over which John Quincy Adams presided. Dr. Samuel G. Howe related the facts in the case. John A. Andrew presented a series of resolutions, and these were supported by eloquent speakers. Mr. Sumner characterized the wrong as "an injury and insult to Massachusetts, which should arouse the people to a determination to prevent the repetition of such a crime."

Wendell Phillips attributed the outrage upon the laws to the religious and social institutions of the country. The resolutions, he thought, did not go far enough, and the time had come when the people of Massachusetts should go farther than simply to announce that they would sustain the laws. He would have the people come up to the point, and say, "Law or no law, Constitution or no Constitution, humanity shall be paramount. I would send a voice from Faneuil Hall that shall reach every hovel in South Carolina, and say to the slaves, 'Come here, and find an asylum of freedom here, where no talon of the national eagle shall ever snatch you away.'"

Theodore Parker supported Phillips by asserting, —

"There is a law of God, written on the heart, that cannot be altered or revoked, — that we should do unto others as we would that others should do unto us. When the laws of Massachusetts or the laws of the Union conflict with the laws of God, I would keep God's law in preference, though the heavens should fall. We have officers who tell us that they are sworn to keep the laws of the State and of the United States, and we are born citizens, born to obey the laws; but every bone of my body, and every drop of blood in my system, swears to me that I am amenable to, and must obey, the laws of God."

What was the result? Capt. Hannum boasted that he was justified in his course by the approval of his employer; Mr. Pierson boasted that he had the approval of the merchants of Boston; the merchants of Boston never allowed their opinion in the matter to go upon the records, — a good fortune for their posterity.

In the spring of 1847 Mr. Phillips collected in a pamphlet the papers which he had prepared for "The Anti-slavery Standard" (published in New-York City) in reply to the work of Mr. Lysander Spooner upon the unconstitutionality of slavery. The ingenious sophistry of Mr. Spooner was of no consequence, excepting in so far as it was made the means of blinding the eyes of persons unaccustomed to the construction of laws, and of reconciling them to give their support to the chief political bulwark of slavery, under the delusive idea that it might be made an instrument of its destruction. It is no easy task to prove an axiom, and that which Mr. Phillips had undertaken was little less than this. It was like endeavoring to refute an antagonist who should maintain that there is no regal or aristocratic element in the British Constitution. Mr. Phillips, however, performed his task with great acuteness, learning, and wit. He published the edition of five thousand copies at his own expense, and presented it to the American and the Massachusetts Anti-slavery Societies. The demand for the work in Ohio and New York, the chief fields of the late Liberty party, nearly exhausted the edition.

In 1848 the real anti-slavery fight began. The smouldering embers which the seeming quiet but deep planning of the preceding year had tended to keep alive, now burst into a flame. The Whig party had nominated Zachary Taylor, a slaveholder, for the presidency. Millard Fillmore was their choice for the Vice-Presidency. This action convinced the conscience Whigs that they could no longer trust the policy of the party; and they determined to break up the party, which had shown itself incompetent to deal with the living question of the day. In June a convention of the Free-soil Democrats met at Utica, N.Y., and nominated Martin Van Buren as the presidential candidate of a new party, to represent the doctrine of "undying hostility to the farther extension of slavery." The movement spread, and Free-soil meetings were held in different States. The contest, which followed in a spirited manner, ended in the election of the candidates of the Whig party; and on the 4th of March, 1849, Gen. Taylor was inducted into office.

Gen. Taylor's election seems to have done no great harm, and unconsciously to have been the means of great good; since it led to the formation of the Free-soil party, of which the leading policy was free soil, free speech, free men, and opposition to the extension of slavery and of the slaveholding power. The Liberty party, which was an abolition-political party, was merged into the Free-soil party. This party, which believed in voting as well as talking against slavery (and in this respect unlike the Garrisonians), began in 1839, by casting three hundred and seven votes: it made a gradual increase until it became merged in the Free-soil party and the Republican party. Finally its ideas got control of the country, and effected emancipation in 1863.

At the annual meeting, in January, 1849, of the Massachusetts Anti-slavery Society, Mr. Phillips took occasion to review some of the notable events in the history of the anti-slavery cause in Boston, from the time when Harrison Gray Otis sneeringly said that he heard that the abolitionists, in their madness, put the Bible above the statute-book. He alluded to the time when Peleg Sprague stood in Faneuil Hall, and tried to awaken sympathy with the South by pointing up to the portrait of Washington, and calling him "that slaveholder:" he did not omit to call to mind Richard Fletcher's base attempts to propitiate the South, nor the encouragement given to the murderers of Lovejoy, at Alton, by "that infamous attorney-general, James Trecothick Austin." He proceeded to show what had been the position and attitude of the churches in Boston in the same period. "Where," he asked, "was Hubbard Winslow? Teaching that a minister's rule of duty, as to what he should teach and preach, is 'what the brotherhood will allow and protect.' Where is the pulpit of the Old South? Sustaining slavery as a Bible institution. Where is Park-street Church? Refusing to receive within its walls, for funeral service, the body of the only martyr which the Orthodox Congregationalists of New England have had, Charles T. Torrey, and of whom they were not worthy. Where is Essex-street Church? Teaching that there are occasions when the Golden Rule is to be set aside. And where is Federal-street Church? Teaching that *silence* is the mission of the North with respect to slavery, and closing its doors to the funeral eulogy of FOLLEN, the bosom-friend of the only man who will make Federal-street pulpit to be remembered,

— William Ellery Channing. And I might ask," he said, "where are the New South and Brattle Street, — but they are not."

The annual meeting of the American Anti-slavery Society, held in May, 1849, was one of the most notable in the history of that organization. It was held in the Tabernacle, in New York. Mr. Edmund Quincy proposed a series of resolutions, of which the three following were the concluding ones: —

"*Resolved*, That that which is giving strength, extension, and perpetuity to slavery, — to wit, the Union, — on being overthrown by a peaceful withdrawal from it by the non-slaveholding States, for conscience' sake and for self-preservation, must necessarily weaken limits, and speedily extirpate slavery from the American soil; therefore,

"*Resolved*, That the motto of every Christian and every patriot should be, '*No union with slaveholders, either religiously or politically.*'

"*Resolved*, That this is not a question of expediency on which action may be innocently deferred 'till a more convenient season,' but one of absolute morality, — of obedience to God, and fidelity to mankind, — to be met, and carried out to the letter."

These resolutions, and portions of the impressive speech in support of them, made by Mr. Phillips, were quoted in the halls of Congress, and were copied extensively into the Southern papers. The press of the country generally gave circulation to these "incendiary ideas" by the condemnation they were swift to heap upon them.

ERA OF THE FUGITIVE-SLAVE ACT.

On the 4th of January, 1850, Mr. Mason of Virginia introduced into the Senate of the United States a bill to carry out more effectually the provision of the Constitution in relation to fugitives from service or labor, and asked thereon a speedy report from the Committee on the Judiciary. This was the famous Fugitive-slave Act, which was subsequently adopted, and which excited so much feeling in the free States. In support of this Act, Henry Clay and John C. Calhoun spoke at length; and from their words the friends of liberty received nothing to encourage, but every thing to alarm.

All eyes were then turned toward Mr. Webster, the idolized son, by adoption, of the commonwealth of Massachusetts. The greatest statesman and orator that New England had produced, nurtured in the spirit of the immortal Declaration of '76, and in the avowed purpose of the Constitution to "establish justice," had now an opportunity to crown his venerable head with the laurels of enviable and undying renown. Upon his words the fate of a nation seemed to hang. To redeem this nation from the thraldom of human bondage, by eloquent speech and vote to oppose slavery extension and domination, — all this he promised to do.

The 7th of March came. The Senate Chamber was thronged to overflowing with eager and excited auditors. In words of forceful eloquence, and with a dignity and solemnity of manner which none better than he understood and could command, Mr. Webster began his address. "I speak to-day," he said, "for the preservation of the Union. Hear me, for my cause."

Having thus challenged the attention of his countrymen, Mr. Webster passed rapidly over the events that had transpired from the declaration of war against Mexico to the unanimous adoption by California of its constitution excluding slavery. This he regarded as the main cause of the existing agitation. He then went into an historical review of slavery, of the differences of opinion which had arisen in the North and South on account of its existence, and at length announced that he should support the Fugitive-slave Act "with all its provisions, to its fullest extent."

Mr. Webster's words weighed heavily on the friends of truth, justice, and freedom. Thousands who had loved, honored, and followed him as a trusted leader, now felt themselves paralyzed with grief and disappointment. But this only for a brief season; for, with indignation in their hearts, they soon left him in the hands of his new-found but not steadfast friends, the slaveholding statesmen, who now looked upon Mr. Webster as they did upon their slaves, — as useful but degraded.

The action of Mr. Webster was very strongly condemned by a public meeting in Faneuil Hall on the 25th of March, over which Samuel E. Sewall presided. Theodore Parker introduced a series of resolutions, and supported them with an argument of great thoroughness and force. Mr. Phillips followed with a critical examination of Mr. Webster's unfortunate speech.

The saddest and most astounding evidence of the demoralization of Northern citizens in regard to slavery, and of Mr. Webster's depraving influence upon them, is given in the following letter addressed to him soon after the delivery of his speech on the 7th of March, signed by eight hundred of the prominent citizens of Massachusetts. It was published in "The Boston Daily Advertiser" of April 2, 1850.

"To the Hon. Daniel Webster.

"*Sir,* — Impressed with the magnitude and importance of the service to the Constitution and the Union which you have rendered by your recent speech in the Senate of the United States, on the subject of slavery, we desire to express to you our deep obligation for what this speech has done, and is doing, to enlighten the public mind, and to bring the present crisis in our national affairs to a fortunate and peaceful termination. As citizens of the United States, we wish to thank you for recalling us to our duties under the Constitution, and for the broad, national, and patriotic views which you have sent with the weight of your great authority, and with the power of your unanswerable reasoning, into every corner of the Union.

"It is, permit us to say, sir, no common good which you have thus done for the country. In a time of almost unprecedented excitement, when the minds of men have been bewildered by an apparent conflict of duties, and when multitudes have been unable to find solid ground on which to rest with security and peace, you have pointed out to a whole people the path of duty, have convinced the understanding, and touched the conscience, of a nation. You have met this great exigency as a patriot and a statesman; and, although the debt of gratitude which the people of this country owe to you was large before, you have increased it by a peculiar service, which is felt throughout the land.

"We desire, therefore, to express to you our entire concurrence in the sentiments of your speech, and our heartfelt thanks for the inestimable aid it has afforded towards the preservation and perpetuation of the Union. For this purpose, we respectfully present to you this, our address of thanks and congratulation, in reference to this most interesting and important occasion in your public life.

"We have the honor to be, with the highest respect,

"Your obedient servants,

"T. H. PERKINS, J. W. PAGE,
CHARLES C. PARSONS, THOMAS C. AMORY,
THOMAS B. WALES, BENJ. LORING,
CALEB LORING, GILES LODGE,
WM. APPLETON, WM. P. MASON,
JAMES SAVAGE, WM. STURGIS,
CHARLES P. CURTIS, W. H. PRESCOTT,
CHARLES JACKSON, SAM'L T. ARMSTRONG,
GEORGE TICKNOR, SAMUEL A. ELIOT,
BENJ. R. CURTIS, JAMES JACKSON,
RUFUS CHOATE, MOSES STUART,
JOSIAH BRADLEE, LEONARD WOODS,
EDWARD G. LORING, RALPH EMERSON,
THOMAS B. CURTIS, JARED SPARKS,
FRANCIS J. OLIVER, C. C. FELTON,
J. A. LOWELL,

and over seven hundred others."

On the 9th of July President Taylor died, just in time to defeat his destiny, and to give his successor, Millard Fillmore, an opportunity to sign the Fugitive-slave Act, and thus forever to make his name odious in the annals of his country. The bill was signed on the 18th of September, 1850.

The passage of this Act was the signal for a general commotion throughout the land. On the 14th of October a large and highly important meeting was held in Faneuil Hall "for the denunciation of the law, and the expression of sympathy and co-operation with the fugitive." Charles Francis Adams presided, and made an eloquent address. Other speakers were Frederick Douglass, Theodore Parker, and Wendell Phillips. Instant repeal of the obnoxious statute was demanded, and a vigilance committee of fifty was appointed to take "all needful measures to protect the colored people from the new and imminent dangers to which they were exposed."

The result of Mr. Webster's retreat into the ethics of barbarism was the defeat of the great Whig party at the next election, and, as he had become Mr. Fillmore's secretary of state, the filling of his place in the Senate with Robert Rantoul, jun., for the short term, and for the long term, commencing March 4, 1851, with a sort of twin-brother of Wendell Phillips, named Charles Sumner.

It remains to be seen how the Fugitive-slave Act

worked in the North. In Boston, on the 15th of February, 1851, Shadrach, a colored waiter at the Cornhill Coffee-house, was arrested under a warrant issued by George T. Curtis, United States commissioner, on the complaint of one John de Bree of Norfolk, Va., a purser in the navy. The hearing was postponed until the 18th, and the prisoner was remanded to the custody of the deputy marshal. While his counsel were conferring with him, a number of colored men rushed in, seized Shadrach, carried him away in triumph, and finally sent him in safety to Canada. The excitement was intense. Tidings were sent to Washington, and the President immediately issued a proclamation calling upon all citizens to assist in capturing the fugitive.

On the 3d of April occurred another case. Thomas Sims, a fugitive slave, was arrested in Boston; and, after a hurried and summary examination before Commissioner Curtis, he was given up to his pursuers. The poor slave-youth begged one favor of his counsel. "Give me a knife," said he; "and, when the commissioner declares me a slave, I will stab myself to the heart, and die before his eyes." About midnight the mayor of Boston, attended by his marshal and two or three hundred policemen, all heavily armed, placed Sims on board the "Acorn" (owned by John H. Pierson), and sent him again into bondage. "And this," exclaimed the negro, "is Massachusetts liberty!" He

The Rendition of Anthony Burns

ERA OF THE FUGITIVE-SLAVE ACT.

uttered these significant words on the memorable 19th of April.[1]

On the day following the arrest, a great public meeting was held on Boston Common, which was addressed by Mr. Phillips. On the 8th a rousing convention was held at Tremont Temple of all persons opposed to the Fugitive-slave Act, and the deepest feeling was manifested. On the evening of the same day another and a distinct meeting was held in the same place, which was addressed by Phillips, William Henry Channing, and others. On the 12th, the day of the rendition of Sims, a meeting was held in Washington Hall; and Phillips, Garrison, and Quincy were among the speakers.

After crossing the Rubicon, in 1850, the recreant statesman of Massachusetts found that he could not retrace his steps. With a chagrin which at length carried him into his grave, and yet with a bravado which he must have borrowed from his slaveholding friends, he, in 1852, was led, not only to defend the compromise measures, but even to defame the anti-slavery men and their efforts. He also aspired to the presidency, as a reward for his conduct.

---

[1] Sims was severely whipped after arriving at Savannah, and for two months was kept closely confined in a cell. He was then sent to a slave-pen at Charleston, and thence to a slave-pen at New Orleans. He was purchased by a brick-mason, and taken to Vicksburg, whence, in 1863, he escaped to the besieging-army of Gen. Grant, who gave him transportation to the North. I do not know whether, at the present writing, he is living or dead.

In the election of that year, Franklin Pierce of New Hampshire, the candidate of the Democratic party, was chosen President. It was a victory for the pro-slavery party. All but four States recorded their votes in its favor. It was a victory which implied the indorsement of the compromise measures, and, further, that these measures should be regarded as final. To all this, notwithstanding the anti-slavery agitations which had been going on for nearly half a century, only one hundred and fifty thousand, out of more than three millions, refused to give their sanction. No darker day, not even in the most critical period of the war of the Rebellion, has ever marked the history of the American republic.

CHAPTER X.

A YEAR OF MOBS AND CONVENTIONS.

Friends of Temperance assemble in New York, 1853. — Women excluded from the Convention. — A Busy Autumn. — Comments of "The Tribune." — Rev. Antoinette L. Brown. — Her Experience at the Temperance Convention. — Exclusion of Miss Brown and Mr. Phillips. — The Woman's Rights Convention. — Riotous Disturbances. — Madame Annekè. — Phillips's Bitter Invective. — The Convention forced to adjourn *sine die*.

"My idea of American nationality makes it the last best growth of the thoughtful mind of the century, treading under foot sex and race, caste and condition, and collecting on the broad bosom of what deserves the name of an empire, under the shelter of noble, just, and equal laws, all races, all customs, all religions, all languages, all literature, and all ideas."

"I welcome woman to the platform of the world's teachers; and I look upon the world, in a very important sense, as one great school." — PHILLIPS.

ON the 12th of May, 1853, the friends of temperance assembled in New-York City, to make arrangements for a world's temperance convention. The meeting was held in Dr. Spring's Old Brick Church, on Franklin Square, where "The New-York Times" building now stands. It was organized by nominating the Hon. A. C. Barstow of Rhode Island chairman. The meeting opened with prayer, "asking God's blessing on the proceedings." A motion was then made, that all "gentlemen" present be admitted as delegates. Dr.

Trall of New York moved an amendment, that the word "ladies" be inserted, as there were delegates present from the Woman's State Temperance Society. The motion was carried.

A business committee of one from each State was then appointed. A motion was made, that Susan B. Anthony, secretary of the Woman's State Temperance Society, be added to the business committee; and, after a hot debate, it was ruled out of order. Next Thomas Wentworth Higginson requested that he be excused from serving on the committee, and that his place be filled by Mrs. Lucy Stone. The confusion was increased. A committee of credentials was appointed, to decide who were members of the convention. They reported, that, in their opinion, the call for the meeting was not intended to include female delegates, and that the credentials of the ladies should be rejected. The report was adopted by a vote of thirty-four to thirty-two, ten of those voting being women.

The opening days of the autumn of this year were days of intense excitement in the city of New York. The great World's Fair was in progress; also an anti-slavery, a woman's rights, and two temperance, conventions. On the anti-slavery platform William Henry Channing, Wendell Phillips, William Lloyd Garrison, and other eloquent speakers, were pleading for the black man's freedom; on the woman's rights platform these same men were asserting the equality of their mothers, wives, and daughters; and on the temperance platform they were inculcating noble lessons for both white and black.

The temperance convention, from which, of course, by a previous ruling, women were excluded, was in session in Metropolitan Hall. Truthfully characterized, it was no other than an organized mob, under the complete control of the clergy:—

In "The New-York Tribune," under date of Sept. 7, 1853, Horace Greeley thus summed up the proceedings of the session:—

"This convention has completed three of its four business sessions, and the results may be summed up as follows:—

"First day, crowding a woman off the platform.

"Second day, gagging her.

"Third day, voting that she shall stay gagged. Having thus disposed of the main question, we presume the incidentals will be finished this morning."

It was Antoinette L. Brown (since Rev. Antoinette Brown Blackwell) whom the convention crowded off the platform. How came she there, is a question which must be answered.

On the day of the opening of the World's Temperance Convention, the Woman's Rights Convention was also in session. Miss Brown and Wendell Phillips sat at the latter, reconsidering the matter of the rejection of women. Miss Brown expressed the opinion, that as the Brick-chapel meeting was merely an informal, preliminary meeting, and its decisions of no importance or authority upon the convention proper, perhaps, after all, women would be admitted if proper application were made.

"Go, by all means," said Phillips: "if they receive you, you have only to thank them for rebuking the action of the Brick-chapel meeting. Then we will withdraw, and come back to our own meeting. If, on the other hand, they do not receive you, we will quietly and without protest withdraw, and, in that case, not be gone half an hour."

Miss Brown, Mrs. Caroline M. Severance, and Mr. Phillips then wended their way to Metropolitan Hall.

On arriving at the hall, Miss Brown presented her credentials to the secretary, and went down from the platform. After a little time it was decided that the call admitted all delegates, and, thinking that this decision settled her case, Miss Brown again went upon the platform. In the mean time a permanent organization was effected. Miss Brown arose, and inquired of the president, Neal Dow, if she were rightly a member of the convention. He replied, "Yes, if you have credentials from any abstinence societies." She stated that she had, and then attempted to thank him; but the convention would not receive any expression of thanks. She took her seat, and awaited a better opportunity.

The first day's session came to an end. On going out of the convention, Mr. Phillips stated to persons with whom he came in contact, that a woman delegate had been received by the president, and that she had been insulted, and nobody had risen to sustain her. He said to Miss Brown, "I shall not go to-morrow, but do you go. I can do nothing for you, because I am not a delegate."

That evening a few earnest friends in New York met together, organized a society, and appointed just three delegates to that temperance convention. Those three persons were Wendell Phillips, Mr. Cleveland, — one of the editors of "The Tribune," — and Mr. Gibbon, son-in-law of the late Isaac T. Hopper of New York.

The next morning Miss Brown and the new delegates went to the hall. Mr. Phillips presented his credentials. During the discussion Mr. Phillips took part, and persisted in holding the convention to parliamentary rules. When the preliminary business was over, and various resolutions were being brought forward, Miss Brown arose, and the president gave her the floor. She was invited upon the stand; but, once there, she was not allowed to speak. For the space of three hours she endeavored to be heard. Finally some one insisted that there might be persons voting in the house who were not delegates; and it was decided that the hall should be cleared by the police, and that those who were delegates might come in, one by one, and resume their seats.

There were printed lists of the delegates of the convention; but there were several new delegates, whose names were not on the lists. Mr. Phillips and his colleagues were among the latter. He went to the president, and said, "I rely upon you to be admitted to the hall, for we know that our names are not yet on the list." The president assented.

The delegates were re-admitted by the roll-call: it is needless to add that the two delegates Miss Brown and Wendell Phillips were not called.

We turn now to the proceedings, so far as they fall within our present scope, of the Woman's Rights Convention, which was held in the Broadway Tabernacle on the 6th and 7th of September, 1853. The fact that the Anti-slavery Society held a meeting on Sunday morning, and Antoinette Brown preached to five thousand people the same evening, called out the denunciations of the religious press which intensified the mob spirit, culminating at last in the Woman's Rights Convention.

The Tabernacle, holding three thousand persons, was packed long before the hour of opening. Mr. Channing made an opening prayer; and the president, Mrs. Mott, made a few appropriate remarks. Then the business went on. Among the speakers of the first day were Mr. Garrison, Charles C. Burleigh, Dr. Channing, and Antoinette Brown.

The next morning "The Tribune" stated as follows: —

A YEAR OF MOBS AND CONVENTIONS. 149

"The Woman's Rights Convention was somewhat disturbed last evening by persons whose ideas of the rights of free speech are these: two thousand people assemble to hear a given public question discussed, under distinct announcement that certain persons, whose general views are well known, are to speak throughout the evening. At least nineteen-twentieths come to hear those announced speakers, and will be bitterly disappointed if the opportunity be not afforded them. But one-twentieth have bought tickets, and taken seats on purpose to prevent the hearing of those speakers, by hissing, yelling, and stamping, and all manner of unseemly interruptions."

The second day's proceedings were characterized by blackguardism, defamation, rowdyism, and profanity. The convention seemed entirely under the control of the mob. As it was inconsistent with Mrs. Mott's Quaker principles to call upon the police, she vacated the chair after inviting Ernestine L. Rose to take her place. The president then introduced a German lady, Madame Mathilde Francesca Annekè, editor of a liberal woman's rights newspaper which had been suppressed in Germany.

Madame Annekè attempted to speak, but her voice was drowned by the tumultuous yells of the ruffianly element in the audience. Quick as a flash, Mr. Phillips sprang upon the platform. He said, —

"Allow me to say one word, purely as a matter of the self-respect which you owe to yourselves. We are citizens of a great country, which, from Maine to Georgia, has extended a welcome to Kossuth; and this

New-York audience is now looking upon a noble woman who stood by his side in the battle-fields of Hungary, — one who has faced the cannon of Francis Joseph of Austria, for the rights of the people. Is this the welcome you give her to the shores of republican America? A woman who has proved her gallantry, and attachment to principles, wishes to say five words to you of the feelings with which she is impressed toward this cause. I know, fellow-citizens, that you will hear her."

Madame Annekè then addressed the audience for a few moments, and retired amid a great uproar, which increased when Mr. Phillips presented himself again.

"I am not surprised at the reception I meet," he shouted in a loud voice.

"As presiding officer for this evening," interposed the president, "I call upon the police. The mayor, too, promised to see that our meeting should not be disturbed; and I now call upon him to preserve order. As citizens of New York, we have a right to this protection; for we pay our money for it. My friends, keep order, and then we shall know who the disturbers are."

"You are making a better speech than I can, by your conduct," continued Mr. Phillips. "This is proof positive of the necessity of this convention. The time has been when other conventions have been met, like this, — with hisses. [Renewed hisses.] Go on with your

A YEAR OF MOBS AND CONVENTIONS. 151

hisses: geese have hissed before now. If it be your pleasure to argue the question for us, by proving that the men here, at least, are not fit for exercising political rights" — [Great uproar.]

Again the president called upon the police to maintain order.

"You prove one thing to-night," concluded Mr. Phillips, "that the men of New York do not understand the meaning of civil liberty and free discussion."

Five minutes later the convention was forced to adjourn *sine die*.

"The Tribune" of Sept. 9 commented severely upon these disgraceful proceedings: —

"We do not know whether any of the gentlemen who have succeeded in breaking up the Woman's Rights Convention, or of the other gentlemen who have succeeded in three sessions at Metropolitan Hall in silencing a regularly appointed and admitted delegate, will ever be ashamed of their passion and hostility; but we have little doubt that some of them will live to understand their own folly."

Thirty years have passed over the republic; and later generations, recalling these painful events of the past, would like to ask those gentlemen — what answer?

CHAPTER XI.

PHILLIPS AND THE WOMAN'S RIGHTS MOVEMENT.

A Plan for Action first proposed. — The Call. — Responses. — The Worcester Convention of 1850. — Outline of the Proceedings. — Attitude of the Press. — The Convention of 1851. — Mr. Phillips's Address. — Harriet Martineau. — The Legislature. — The Boston Convention of 1854. — Resolutions. — The Convention of 1855. — Donations. — Assembling of the Seventh National Woman's Rights Convention in New York, 1856. — Mr. Phillips's Speech. — Indifference of Political Parties towards the Movement. — The National Convention of 1858. — The Convention of 1859. — Mr. Phillips makes a Stirring Address. — The Legislatures Memorialized. — The New-England Convention. — Mr. Phillips again. — The "Drawing-Room" Convention. — Mrs. Dall's Lectures. — The Tenth National Convention, 1860. — Marriage and Divorce discussed — Mr. Phillips opposes Discussion. — The Woman Question laid aside. — "After the Slave — then the Woman."

"Throw open the doors of Congress, throw open those court-houses, throw wide open the doors of your colleges, and give to the sisters of the Motts and the Somervilles the same opportunities for culture that men have, and let the result prove what their capacity and intellect really are."

"It is on the ground of natural justice, and on the ground again of the highest expediency, and yet again it is because woman, as an immortal and intellectual being, has a right to all the means of education, — it is on these grounds that we claim for her the civil rights and privileges which man enjoys." — PHILLIPS.

AT an anti-slavery meeting held in Boston, in 1850, an invitation was given from the speaker's desk to all those who felt interested in a plan for a woman's rights convention, to meet in the ante-room. Nine solitary women responded, and went into "the dark and dingy room," to consult together. Of the nine, seven were chosen to call a convention in Massachusetts. We are told, however, that "the work devolved upon one person. Illness hindered one, duty to a brother another, duty to the slave a third, professional engagements a fourth, the fear of bringing the gray hairs of a father to the grave prevented another from serving; but the pledge was made, and could not be withdrawn."

The names of this committee were, Harriot K. Hunt, Eliza J. Kenney, Lucy Stone, Abby Kelley Foster, Dora Taft (Father Taylor's daughter), Eliza J. Taft, and Paulina Wright Davis, — the last named being the one active member.

The call was prepared, and sent forth with earnest letters in all directions. Garrison wrote, —

"I doubt whether a more important movement has ever been launched, touching the destiny of the race, than this in regard to the equality of the sexes. You are at liberty to use my name."

Catherine M. Sedgwick wrote, —

"You do me but justice in supposing me deeply interested in the question of woman's elevation."

Dr. Channing wrote, —

"The new movement has my fullest sympathy, and my name is at its service."

There was also the following: —

"You are at liberty to append my own and my wife's name to your admirable call.

"ANNE GREENE PHILLIPS.
"WENDELL PHILLIPS."

The convention was held in Brinley Hall, Worcester, Mass., Oct. 23 and 24, 1850, and was presided over by Mrs. Paulina W. Davis of Rhode Island. Nine States were represented. There were Garrison, Phillips, Burleigh, Foster, and Pillsbury, leaders in the anti-slavery struggle; Frederick Douglass and Sojourner Truth, representing the enslaved African race; the Channings, Sargents, Parsons, Shaws, from the liberal pulpit and the aristocracy of Boston.

The proceedings, which extended through the greater part of two days, were of a most interesting character. The debates on the resolutions were spicy, pointed, and logical, and were participated in by Phillips, Channing, Garrison, and other able speakers. It is to be regretted, that, in the absence of a phonographic reporter, none of the addresses have been handed down to history.

Before the close of the session, Dr. Channing, from the business committee, proposed a plan for organization, and the principles that should govern the movement. In accordance with his views, a national central committee was appointed, in which every State was represented. Of this committee Wendell Phillips was made treasurer.

It is related that "tidings of this and of the Ohio

convention (same year, in May) travelled across the ocean; and their deliberations were ably discussed by Mrs. John Stuart Mill in 'The Westminster Review,' and great attention was aroused thereby as to the importance of the subject. It is not too much to say, that the whole woman's rights agitation in Old England, as well as in Massachusetts and in New England, may be dated from these conventions of 1850."

Notwithstanding that the "Hen Convention" (so called jocosely) attracted the attention of the English quarterly, only four newspapers in Massachusetts treated the subject with any respect. These were, "The Lynn Pioneer," edited by George Bradburn; "The Liberator," edited by Garrison; "The Carpet Bag" (the "Punch" of those days); and "The Lowell American," a little Free-soil paper edited by William S. Robinson, afterwards known under the *nom de plume* of "Warrington."

Mrs. Harriet H. Robinson remarks that, —

"The central idea of the woman's rights movement was supposed to be a desire on the part of some women to wear men's clothes, and learn to crow; but whether like men, or like barnyard bipeds, was never very clearly defined. When Lucy Stone went to Malden (a suburban town, near Boston), to speak for the first time for woman's rights, a Universalist clergyman announced the proposed meeting from his pulpit, in these words: 'This evening, at the Town Hall, a hen will attempt to crow.' This was thought to be a huge joke."

On the 15th and 16th of October, 1851, the friends

of woman suffrage assembled again in Brinley Hall. The convention was conducted mainly by the same persons who had so successfully managed the proceedings of the previous year. Letters were read from Henry Ward Beecher, Ralph Waldo Emerson, Horace Mann, Angelina Grimkè Weld, Oliver Johnson, and many others. Among the new speakers were several noted suffragists from other States of the Union.

After reading the resolutions, which in great part he had himself prepared, Mr. Phillips delivered his first speech, of which any phonographic report is in existence, in support of the rights of women. It was a remarkable address, as showing not only the manly attitude which Mr. Phillips had taken towards the subject, but also in its severe denunciation of all opposition in the matter. The concluding paragraphs are here given: —

"Woman is ground down, by the competition of her sisters, to the very point of starvation. Heavily taxed, ill paid, in degradation and misery, is it to be wondered at that she yields to the temptation of wealth? It is the same with men; and thus we recruit the ranks of vice by the prejudices of custom and society. We corrupt the whole social fabric, that women may be confined to two or three employments. How much do we suffer through the tyranny of prejudice! When we penitently and gladly give to the energy and the intellect and the enterprise of woman their proper reward, their appropriate employment, this question of wages will settle itself; and it will never be settled at all until then.

"This question is intimately connected with the great social problem, — the vices of cities. You who hang your heads in terror and shame, in view of the advancing demoralization of modern civilized life, and turn away with horror-struck faces, look back now to these social prejudices which have made you close the avenues of profitable employment in the face of woman, and reconsider the conclusions you have made! Look back, I say, and see whether you are surely right here. Come up with us, and argue the question, and say whether this most artificial delicacy, this childish prejudice, on whose Moloch altar you sacrifice the virtue of so many, is worthy the exalted worship you pay it. Consider a moment. From what sources are the ranks of female profligacy recruited? A few, mere giddiness hurries to ruin. Their protection would be in that character and sound common sense which a wider interest in practical life would generally create. In a few, the love of sensual gratification, grown over-strong because all the other powers are dormant for want of exercise, wrecks its unhappy victim. The medicine for these would be occupation, awaking intellect, and stirring their highest energies. Give any one an earnest interest in life, something to do, something that kindles emulation, and soon the gratification of the senses sinks into proper subordination. It is idle heads that are tempted to mischief; and she is emphatically idle, half of whose nature is unemployed. Why does man, so much oftener than woman, surmount a few years or months of sensual gratification, and emerge into a worthier life? It is not solely because the world's judgment is so much harder upon her. Man can immerse himself in business that stirs keenly all his faculties, and thus he smothers passion in honorable cares. An ordinary woman, once fallen, has no busy and stirring life in which to take refuge, where intellect will contend for mastery with passion, and where virtue is braced by high and active thoughts. Passion comes back to the '*empty*,' through 'swept and garnished,' chambers, bringing with him more devils than before. But, undoubtedly, the great temptation to this vice is the love of dress, wealth, and the luxuries it secures. Facts will jostle theories aside. Whether we choose to acknowledge it or not, there are many women, earning two or three dollars a week, who feel that they are as capable as their brothers of earning hundreds, if they could be permitted to exert themselves as freely. Fretting to see the coveted rewards of life forever forbidden them, they are tempted to shut their eyes on the character of the means by which a taste, however short, may be gained of the wealth and luxury they sigh for. Open to man a fair field for his industry, and secure to him its gains, and nine hundred and ninety-nine men out of every thousand will disdain to steal. Open to woman a fair field for her industry, let her do any thing her hands find to do, and enjoy her gains, and nine hundred and ninety-nine women out of every thousand will disdain to debase themselves for dress or ease.

"Of this great social problem, — to cure or lessen the vice of cities, — there is no other solution except what this movement offers you. It is, to leave woman to choose her own employments for herself, responsible, as we are, to the common Creator, and not to her fellow-man. I exhort you, therefore, to look at this question in the spirit in which I have endeavored to present it to you. It is no fanciful, no superficial, movement, based on a few individual tastes, in morbid sympathy with tales of individual suffering. It is a great social protest against the very fabric of society. It is a question which goes down — we admit it, and are willing to meet the issue — goes down beneath the altar at which you worship, goes down beneath this social system in which you live. And it is true, — no denying it, — that, if we are right, the doctrines preached from New-England pulpits are wrong. It is true that all this affected horror at woman's deviation from her sphere is a mistake, — a mistake fraught with momentous consequences. Understand us. We blink no fair issue. We throw down the gauntlet. We have counted the cost: we know the yoke and burden we assume. We know the sneers, the lying frauds of misstatement and misrepresentation, that await us. We have counted all; and it is but the dust in the balance, and the small dust in the measure, compared with the inestimable blessing of doing justice to one-half of the human species, of curing this otherwise immedicable wound, stopping this overflowing fountain of corruption, at the very source of civilized life. Truly, it is the great question of the age. It looks all others out of countenance. It needs little aid from legislation. Specious objections, after all, are not arguments. We know we are right. We only ask an opportunity to argue the question, to set it full before the people, and then leave it to the intellects and hearts of our country, confident that the institutions under which we live, and the education which other reforms have already given to both sexes, have created men and women capable of solving a problem even more difficult, and meeting a change even more radical, than this."

The proceedings of the convention were still further made memorable by the reading of a letter received from Harriet Martineau, which very clearly defined what was her position at that early day.

The interest which Mr. Phillips shared with others in the woman's rights movement continued to grow stronger as the years crept on. Upon no other subject, save anti-slavery, did he bestow so much thought. In April, 1853, an appeal to the citizens of Massachusetts was made, on the question of allowing equal political rights to women. In favor of this appeal, Mr. Phillips made a stirring address before the constitutional convention. He was followed by T. W. Higginson, Theodore Parker, and Lucy Stone. In August of that year, in committee of the whole, the report that "it is inexpedient to act on the petition" of several parties that women may vote, was taken up. This report was, on the next day, adopted by a vote of a hundred and eight to forty-four.

But the ball was kept rolling. On the very day that saw poor Anthony Burns arrested in Boston, and consigned back to hopeless bondage, — June 2, 1854, — the first woman's rights convention ever held in Boston assembled at Horticultural Hall. Though many friends of the women remained in the streets, to witness the sad surrender, still at an early hour the hall was filled with earnest representatives of both sexes.

Among the resolutions reported were the following: —

"*Resolved*, That the common law, which governs the marriage relation, and blots out the legal existence of a wife, denies her right to the product of her own industry, denies her equal property rights, even denies her right to her children, and the custody of her own person, is grossly unjust to woman, dishonorable to man, and destructive to the harmony of life's holiest relation.

"*Resolved*, That the laws which destroy the legal individuality of woman after her marriage, are equally pernicious to man as to woman, and may give to him in marriage a slave, or a tyrant, but never a wife."

Mr. Phillips, Mr. Garrison, and a number of others, took part in the debate.

Sept. 19 and 20, 1855, the convention met again in Boston, with the best attendance that Boston could furnish in intelligence and respectability, and, to a greater degree than usual, clerical. On the first day Mr. Phillips addressed the members, and at other times through the six sessions managed to keep himself busy. It was largely through his efforts that the association obtained the money to enable them to carry on the agitation. Francis Jackson and Charles F. Hovey, always generous towards the reforms of their time, were the first men to make a bequest to the woman's rights movement in Massachusetts. Besides giving liberally from time to time, Francis Jackson left five thousand dollars, in 1858, in the hands of Mr. Phillips; which the latter invested so wisely, and so judiciously managed, that the fund was nearly doubled ere long. Mr. Hovey left fifty thousand dollars to be used in anti-slavery, woman suffrage, and free religion.

In passing, it is well to recall the fact that Lydia Maria Child left a thousand dollars to the movement. With this single exception, no other woman of wealth has ever bequeathed any thing to the enfranchisement of her sex, — a fact singularly strange, when it is remembered that such women never forget colleges, churches, or public charities.

Pursuant to a call issued by the central committee,

the Seventh National Woman's Rights Convention w[as]
held in New-York City, at the Broadway Taberna[cle,]
Nov. 25 and 26, 1856. Mr. Phillips, who was a me[m]-
ber of the business committee, and also treasurer, w[as,]
of course, present. His address in the evening w[as]
thoroughly characteristic, and in interest fairly riv[aled]
that which he made at the Worcester Convention [of]
1851. From the phonographic report, revised by h[im]-
self, the following portion is here given: —

"I would have it constantly kept before the public, that we [do]
not seek to prop up woman: we only ask for her space to let [her]
grow. Governments are not made, they grow. They are [like]
buildings like this, with dome and pillars: they are oaks, w[ith]
roots and branches; and they grow, by God's blessing, in the [air]
he gives to them. Now, man has been allowed to grow; and w[hen]
Pharaoh tied him down with bars of iron, when Europe tied [him]
down with privilege and superstition, he burst the bonds, and g[rew]
strong. We ask the same for woman. Goethe said, that, if [you]
plant an oak in a flower-pot, one of two things was sure to h[ap]-
pen, — either the oak will be dwarfed, or the flower-pot will bre[ak.]
So we have planted woman in a flower-pot, hemmed her in [by]
restrictions; and, when we move to enlarge her sphere, society c[ries]
out, 'Oh, you'll break the flower-pot!' Well, I say, let it bre[ak.]
Man made it; and, the sooner it goes to pieces, the better. Le[t us]
see how broadly the branches will throw themselves, and [how]
beautiful will be the shape, and how glorious against the moo[nlit]
sky, or glowing sunset, the foliage shall appear!

"I say, the very first claim, the middle and last claim, of all [our]
conventions, should be the ballot. Everywhere, in each State, [we]
should claim it, — not for any intrinsic value in the ballot, but

cause it throws upon woman herself the responsibility of her position. Man never grew to his stature until he was provoked to it by the pressure and weight of responsibility; and, I take it, woman will grow up the same way."

This convention was held immediately after the election of James Buchanan to the presidency, and at a time when the anti-slavery problem was the most important and absorbing in the public mind. Gen. Frémont had been the candidate of the Republican party, and the name of Jessie Benton Frémont had been made a rallying-cry of the campaign.

It appears that "the convention, taking advantage of this fact, made an appeal in its resolutions to both the Democratic and Republican parties, to do justice 'to both halves of the human race.'" To the Republican party it said, —

"*Resolved*, That the Republican party, appealing constantly, through its orators, to female sympathy, and using for its most popular rallying-cry a female name, is peculiarly pledged, by consistency, to do justice hereafter in those States where it holds control."

It need hardly be added, that no notice was taken of this appeal by those to whom it was addressed. And yet the Republican party was fast coming into power, made up of men who were old anti-slavery and Free-soil political leaders, whose motto was, Emancipation, free speech, and a free world.

"After Frémont was defeated, it seemed to those who had labored so long for the black man's freedom, and for the rights of woman, as if both causes were lost. The woman movement was silent for a period of three years."

The year 1857 passed without a national convention being held in New York or elsewhere. In the following year, however, the Eighth National Convention was called in New York. The session opened in May. Mr. Phillips, as usual, was one of the speakers.

On the 12th of May, 1859, the Ninth National Convention assembled in the same city. It proved to be a turbulent session; and all the speakers, with one accord, were forced to yield the platform to Mr. Phillips, who, for nearly two hours, "held the mocking crowd in the hollow of his hand." In closing, he said, —

"I will not attempt to detain you longer. ["Go on, go on!"] I have neither the disposition nor the strength to trespass any longer upon your attention. The subject is so large, that it might well fill days instead of hours. It covers the whole surface of American society. It touches religion, purity, political economy, wages, the safety of cities, the growth of ideas, the very success of our experiment. I gave to-night a character of the city of Washington, which some men hissed. You know it is true. If this experiment of self-government is to succeed, it is to succeed by some saving element introduced into the politics of the present day. You know this: your Websters, your Clays, your Calhouns, your Douglases, however intellectually able they may have been, have

THE WOMAN'S RIGHTS MOVEMENT.

never dared or cared to touch that moral element of our national life. Either the shallow and heartless trade of politics had eaten out their own moral being, or they feared to enter the unknown land of lofty right and wrong.

"Neither of these great names has linked its fame with one great moral question of the day. They deal with money questions, with tariffs, with parties, with State law; and if, by chance, they touch the slave-question, it is only like Jewish hucksters trading in the relics of saints. The reformers — the fanatics, as we are called — are the only ones who have launched social and moral questions. I risk nothing when I say, that the anti-slavery discussion of the last twenty years has been the salt of this nation: it has actually kept it alive and wholesome. Without it our politics would have sunk beyond even contempt. So with this question. It stirs the deepest sympathy; it appeals to the highest moral sense; it inwraps within itself the greatest moral issues. Judge it, then, candidly, carefully, as Americans; and let us show ourselves worthy of the high place to which God has called us in human affairs."

A memorial was also prepared and signed by the leaders in the movement, and sent to every Legislature in the nation; but, owing to the excitement caused by the John Brown raid, it commanded but little attention.

On the 27th of May, of this year, the New-England Convention was held in Boston. Rev. James Freeman Clarke made a stirring address, followed by Mrs. Caroline H. Dall, Rev. John T. Sargent, and Mr. Phillips. The speech of Mr. Phillips abounded in felicitous thoughts; and, being still in existence as reported, it will well repay perusal. One paragraph must be quoted here: —

"Many a young girl, in her married life, loses her husband, and thus is left a widow with two or three children. Now, who is to educate them and control them? We see, if left to her own resources, the intellect which she possesses, and which has remained in a comparatively dormant state, displayed in its full power. What a depth of heart lay hidden in that woman! She takes her husband's business, guides it as though it were a trifle; she takes her sons, and leads them; sets her daughters an example; like a master-leader she governs the whole household. That is woman's influence. What made that woman? Responsibility. Call her out from weakness, lay upon her soul the burden of her children's education, and she is no longer a girl, but a woman.

"Horace Greeley once said to Margaret Fuller, 'If you should ask a woman to carry a ship round Cape Horn, how would she go to work to do it? Let her do this, and I will give up the question.' In the fall of 1856 a Boston girl, only twenty years of age, accompanied her husband to California. A brain-fever laid him low. In the presence of mutiny and delirium, she took his vacant post, preserved order, and carried her cargo safe to its destined port. Looking in the face of Mr. Greeley, Miss Fuller said, 'Lo! my dear Horace, it is done. Now, say, what shall woman do next?'" [Cheers.]

On the 1st of June, 1860, a "drawing-room" convention was held at the Meionian, in Boston. It was initiated by Mrs. Caroline H. Dall, with the object of discussing the artistic and æsthetic features of the woman question. Several speakers, including Mr. Phillips, were in attendance, and took part in the discus-ons. On the whole, this convention was probably the most aristocratic meeting of the kind held up to that day. Just previous to this, Mrs. Dall had given a course of twelve lectures in Boston, on the various phases of woman's rights; and these lectures had attracted many ladies of culture and high social position, and induced them to take interest in the cause. It is not too much to affirm, that Mrs. Dall's lectures, and the *résumé* of them which was published in book-form in 1868, and had a wide circulation, exerted an immense influence in forming public opinion, and creating interest on the subjects of which she treated.[1]

The Tenth National Convention, which was held in New York, in May, 1860, was chiefly memorable because of a disagreement which arose during the session. Mrs. Elizabeth Cady Stanton moved a series of resolutions looking towards greater freedom of divorce, and supported them in a lengthy address. Mr. Phillips, to the great surprise of many who were present, objected to the question of marriage and divorce as irrelevant to the platform, and said, —

"The reason why I object so emphatically to the introduction of the question here, is because it is a question which admits of so many theories, physiological and religious, and what is technically called 'free love,' that it is large enough for a movement of

---

[1] The College, the Market, and the Court; or, Woman's Relation to Education, Employment, and Citizenship. By Mrs. C. H. Dall. Boston: Lee & Shepard.

its own. Our question is only unnecessarily burdened with it. I cannot be kept within the convenient limits of this enterprise for this Woman's Rights Convention is not man's convention and I hold that I, as a man, have an exactly equal interest in the essential question of marriage as woman has."

Mr. Phillips moved to lay the resolutions on the table, and even went so far as to object to their being entered on the journal of the convention. Mr. Garrison, while concurring "in opinion with his friend Mr. Phillips," thought that the resolutions ought to be adopted.

The question being put, Mr. Phillips's motion was lost. The resolutions, reported by the business committee, were then adopted without dissent.

In 1861 came the "war of the Rebellion." The women who had so perseveringly worked for their own enfranchisement, now gave all their time and thought to saving the nation, and caring for its brave defenders. Whilst fathers and sons, husbands and lovers, were fighting and bleeding under the stars and stripes, mothers, wives, and sweethearts were busily plying their fingers in the sewing-circles, lending their assistance in the sanitary movement, watching the sick in the hospitals, or closing the eyes of the dying on the battle-field, — as if all this were not enough to have made "justice to woman" the spontaneous cry on the return of the first days of peace.

"It is not the woman's, but the negro's, hour:"

"after the slave, then the woman," said Phillips, in his stirring speeches of the time.

From the beginning of the civil war to 1866, there is no record to be found of any public meeting on the subject of woman's rights, in which any Massachusetts speaker appeared.

CHAPTER XII.

THE PREPARATION FOR WAR.

The Politics of 1853. — Franklin Pierce, President. — The "Kansas and Nebraska Bill." — The Repeal of the Missouri Compromise. — Sumner foresees the "Beginning of the End." — A Convention of the Free-soil Party. — The Republican Party. — Workings of the Fugitive-slave Act. — Arrest of Anthony Burns. — A Famous Meeting. — Indictments found against Phillips, Parker, and Others. — The Result. — A Petition for the Removal of "Slave Commissioner" Loring. — Mr. Phillips's Argument. — "The Crime against Kansas." — Assault on Charles Sumner. — Election of James Buchanan. — The Signs of the Times. — The John Brown Raid. — Mr. Phillips's Eulogy. — His Lecture in Brooklyn. — Mr. Slack's Recollections. — Riotous Feeling in New York and Elsewhere. — Anniversary Meeting in Boston. — A Riot prevented.

"Insurrection of thought always precedes the insurrection of arms."

"God gives us knowledge, keeps for us the weapon: all we need ask for is courage to use it."

"You and I are never to see peace, we are never to see the possibility of putting the army of this nation, whether it be made up of nineteen or thirty-four States, on a peace-footing, until slavery is destroyed."

"A civil war can hardly be any thing but a political war. That is, all civil wars are a struggle between opposite ideas, and armies are but the tools." — PHILLIPS.

FRANKLIN PIERCE took the oath of office on the 4th of March, 1853. Thoroughly incapable of comprehending the past history of his country, it was not strange that his dull or diseased brain should fail

THE PREPARATION FOR WAR. 171

to forecast even the near or immediate future. The most remarkable event in the progress of the anti-slavery conflict happened during his administration. But for this event, which will ever perpetuate his name, President Pierce would long ago have faded out of remembrance.

In December, 1853, Stephen A. Douglas of Illinois proposed a bill in the United-States Senate, to organize the immense region extending from the confines of Missouri, Iowa, and Minnesota to the crest of the Rocky Mountains, and from 36° 30′ north latitude to the British Possessions, into two territories, to be known as Kansas and Nebraska. This bill contained a clause repealing the Missouri Compromise, under the plea that it was "inconsistent with the principle of non-intervention by Congress with slavery in the States and Territories, as recognized by the compromise measures of 1850." The people were taken by surprise; for the question, so destructive to national harmony, and which it was hoped had been settled forever, had assumed a new form. The Missouri Compromise had been deemed a sacred compact between the North and South, and, as such, for the third of a century had received the sanction of all parties.

The debates on the bill extended over many weeks. On the 25th of May, 1854, it passed Congress, and, having been signed on the following day by the President, at once became the law of the land.

"It is at once the worst and the best bill [exclaimed Charles Sumner] on which Congress ever acted! It is the worst bill, inasmuch as it is a present victory of slavery. . . . It is the best bill, for it prepares the way for that 'All hail hereafter' when slavery must disappear. Standing at the very grave of freedom in Kansas and Nebraska, I lift myself to the vision of that happy resurrection by which freedom will be secured hereafter, not only in these Territories, but everywhere under the National Government. More clearly than ever before, I now see 'the beginning of the end' of slavery. Proudly I discern the flag of my country, as it ripples in every breeze, at last become, in reality as in name, the flag of freedom, undoubted, pure, and irresistible. Sorrowfully I bend before the wrong you are about to enact: joyfully I welcome all the promises of the future."

On the 31st of May a State convention of the Free-soil party was held in Boston, in Faneuil Hall, at which a series of resolutions, denunciatory of the Fugitive-slave Bill and the Kansas-Nebraska Act, was passed. "The time has come," it was said, "to forget the past, obliterate the Fugitive-slave Act, and to do what we can to place the country perpetually on the side of freedom."

Shortly afterwards a strong effort was made in the State, to unite the opponents of the repeal of the Missouri prohibition, and to form a political organization that should be untrammelled by slaveholding alliances. On the 20th of July a mass convention of the people at Worcester declared in favor of a new organization, to be called the "Republican" party; and on the 7th

THE PREPARATION FOR WAR. 173

of September the first State convention of the party was held at the same place.

Meanwhile the Fugitive-slave Act was in working order. On the 23d of May Charles F. Suttle of Virginia presented to Edward Greeley Loring of Boston, judge of probate, and commissioner, a complaint praying for the seizure and enslavement of Anthony Burns. The warrant was issued; and on the next day Burns was arrested under the false pretext of burglary, and confined in the Suffolk-county court-house. At first the right of counsel was denied to the prisoner; but, at the remonstrance of Theodore Parker and others, counsel were assigned, and the 27th of May was appointed as the day for the hearing.

On the evening of the 26th a great meeting was held at Faneuil Hall. During the morning and afternoon of that day, certain members of the vigilance committee — including Parker, Phillips, Higginson, Kemp, Stowell, and Dr. Howe — discussed the plan of making a sudden attack on the court-house, and of using the Faneuil-hall crowd to this end. It was voted down, however, three to one. The meeting adjourned about five o'clock, and those gentlemen who were to address the gathering at the hall in the evening were cautioned not to allow the audience to break up for any unprepared attack on the court-house. Between the hour of adjournment and that fixed for the public meeting, certain members of the vigilance committee decided themselves to make the attack.

At the appointed hour Faneuil Hall was filled to overflowing. Samuel G. Howe called the meeting to order; George R. Russell presided; and speeches were made by Parker, Phillips, and others. The suppressed excitement of the audience was intense.

Said Theodore Parker, —

"I am a clergyman and a man of peace. I love peace. But there is a means, and there is an end. Liberty is the end, and sometimes peace is not the means toward it. There are ways of managing this matter [the Burns affair] without shooting anybody. Be sure that these men who have kidnapped a man in Boston are cowards, every mother's son of them; and if we stand up there resolutely, and declare that this man shall not go out of the city of Boston without shooting a gun, then he won't go back. Now, I am going to propose, that, when you adjourn, it be to meet at Court Square to-morrow morning at nine o'clock. As many as are in favor of that motion will raise their hands.

Many hands were raised; and from the audience arose shouts of, "Let's go to-night. Let's pay a visit to the slave-catchers at the Revere House." The question was put, "Do you propose to go to the Revere House to-night? Then, show your hands. It is not a vote. We shall meet at Court Square at nine o'clock to-morrow morning."

At this point in the history, there is a conflict of evidence. It is not possible to determine whether Parker had been informed of the new plan, and waited for the signal agreed upon, but, thinking it was not given, concluded his speech as just quoted; or whether, knowing nothing of the proposed attack, he made it his principal aim, to restrain the audience from rushing away into Court Square. There were indeed cries of alarm around the doors; but those on the platform, supposing them to be feints only, held the audience within the hall.

Before the meeting adjourned, — quietly, of course, — Dr. Howe left the hall, and hurried to Court Square, to see whether the cries which he had heard really meant any thing. Upon arriving at the court-house, he found that a small attack had been made; but the doors were closed: and the crowd, if such it was, had gone. If we suppose the signal to have been given at Faneuil Hall, which is quite improbable, there surely would not have been time for the audience to make its slow way to the square in season to be of any service.

Thus the affair ended. During the remainder of that night, and the whole of the next day, the marines and militia held the streets, and guarded the court-house. The slave was handed over to his master; and on Friday, the 2d of June, he was marched through Court Street and State Street to the wharf, in the centre of a hollow square of armed ruffians, themselves guarded by companies of militia, protected by cannon. The bells of the city tolled a solemn dirge, the streets were draped in black, and the whole scene was as awful as imagination can picture it. Those who witnessed the spectacle will never, never forget it.

After the rendition of Burns, indictments were found against Theodore Parker, Wendell Phillips, Mr. Higginson, Martin Stowell, John Morrison, Samuel T. Proudman, and John C. Cluer. They were defended by John P. Hale, Charles M. Ellis, William L. Burt, John A. Andrew, and Henry F. Durant. The case of Mr. Stowell was first taken up. After proceeding with the arguments for quashing the indictment, Judge Curtis ordered all the writs to be quashed, thus dismissing the cases.

The contemptible action of "Slave Commissioner" Loring excited a deep feeling of disgust and dissatisfaction throughout the State. On account of it, he lost a professorship in Harvard College. Petitions signed by several thousand names were then sent to the Legislature, praying for his removal from his office as judge of probate. The subject was given a thorough hearing and examination. At this hearing, on the 20th of February, 1855, appeared for the petitioners, Wendell Phillips. His argument was lengthy, and covered all the points in issue. It concluded as follows: —

"Gentlemen, the petitioners have no feeling of revenge toward Mr. Edward G. Loring. Let the General Government reward him with thousands if it will. To us he is only an object of pity. There was an hour when one man trembled before him, — when one hapless victim, with more than life at stake, trembled before this man's want of humanity, and ignorance of law. That hour has passed away. To-day he is but a weed on the great ocean of humanity. To us he is nothing: but we, with you, are the Commonwealth of Massachusetts; and for the honor of the State, for the sake of justice, in the name of humanity, we claim his removal. We have a right to a judiciary worthy of the respect of the community. We cannot respect him. Do not give us a man whose judicial character is made up of party bias, personal predilection, bad law, and a reckless disregard of human rights, and whose heart was too hard to melt before the mute eloquence of a hapless and terrified man! Do not commit to such a one the widows and orphans of the commonwealth! Do not place such a man on a bench which only able and humane and Christian men have occupied before! Do not let him escape the deserved indignation of the community, by the technical construction of a statute! The Constitution has left you, as the representatives of the original sovereignty of the people, the power to remove a judge when you think he has lost the confidence and respect of his constituents. Exercise it! Say to the United States, 'The Constitution allows the return of fugitive slaves. Find your agents where you will: you shall not find them on the supreme or any inferior bench of Massachusetts. You shall never gather round that infamous procedure any respectability derived from the magistracy of the commonwealth. If it is to be done, let it be done by men whom it does not harm the honor or the interest of Massachusetts to have dishonored and made infamous!'

"Mr. Chairman, give free channel to the natural instincts of the commonwealth; and let us — let us be at liberty to despise the slave-hunter, without feeling that our children's hopes and lives are prejudiced thereby! When you have done it, — when you have pronounced on this hasty, reckless, inhuman court its proper judgment, the verdict of official reprobation, — you will secure another thing. The next slave commissioner who opens his court will remember that he opens it in Massachusetts, where a man is not to be robbed of his rights as a human being, merely because he is black. You will throw around the unfortunate victim of a cruel law, which you say you cannot annul, all the protection that Massachusetts incidentally can. And, doing this, you will do something to prevent seeing another such sad week as that of last May or June, in the capital of the commonwealth. Although you cannot blot out this wicked clause in the Constitution, you will render it impossible that any but reckless, unprincipled, and shameless men shall aid in its enforcement. Such men cannot long uphold a law in this commonwealth.

"The petitioners ask both these things; claiming especially to have proved that you can do this work, and that, if you love justice or mercy, you ought to do it."

The committee reported an address to the governor in favor of the prayer of the petitioners, which both the House and the Senate adopted. The governor's council also approved it, but Gov. Gardner refused to grant the prayer. After the inauguration of Gov. Banks, in 1858, a similar petition was presented, which resulted in the removal of Loring.

By the passage, in 1854, of the Kansas and Nebraska Act, a vast extent of territory was laid open, both to free and servile labor; and immigration at once began to set in from the North and South, thus bringing freedom and slavery hand to hand, and face to face. In the autumn of 1855 confusion reigned in the territory. Outrages of almost every kind were committed; and property, belonging in the most part to the free-State settlers, was destroyed. In the spring of 1856 a bill

THE PREPARATION FOR WAR.

was presented in Congress "for the admission of Kansas into the Union." In the course of the heated discussion which followed, Mr. Sumner made his celebrated speech entitled "The Crime against Kansas."

It created an intense madness in the hearts of the Southern and slaveholding leaders. "Such words are damaging." "He has the audacity of a Danton." "He must be silenced." Such were some of the remarks of the Southern chivalry.

On the 22d of May, two days after his speech, Mr. Sumner, while seated at his desk in the Senate Chamber, engaged in writing, and after the Senate had adjourned, was assaulted and beaten to the floor by Preston S. Brooks of South Carolina. The senator fell forward, bleeding and insensible. "Do you want the pieces of your cane?" asked a page of the Senate of the cowardly ruffian. "Only the gold head," was the response. "The next time kill him, Brooks," said his companion, who stood in the doorway with a pistol in his hand. "Come let us go and take a drink." They did so.

As soon as the news reached Boston, a meeting was called in Faneuil Hall. "We must stand by him," said Gov. Gardner, "who is the representative of Massachusetts, under all circumstances."

In the presidential election of 1856 John C. Frémont, the candidate of the Republican party, was defeated. James Buchanan, the choice of the Democratic party, was elected. If the Democratic victory was appalling, the Republican defeat was by no means insignificant. The signs of the times pointed to the one fact, that Republican thought and feeling were increasing. Many influences helped to swell this increase, notably the labors of the American Anti-slavery Society and its affiliated associations. The members of this society were not voters; they refrained from all political action; and still, they were workers, and their work told. They were the bitterest opponents of the slave-power; and their weapons — the printing-press, orators, public meetings, and conventions — were such as not even the slave-power could much longer resist. The band of heroes who fought and fell at Thermopylæ are not more worthy of renown than the band of noble men and women, who, by thought and words and deeds, exposed their lives to the perils and encroachments of the slave autocracy of the South.

But the crowning event of the decade was yet to happen. The raid on Harper's Ferry and its failure, the capture, trial, conviction, and execution of John Brown and his followers, are matters which have passed into history, and will not soon be erased. The circumstances of this affair are full of interest, and must now be related.

It was in March, 1858, that Brown, at the suggestion of Theodore Parker, visited Boston, and first made known the plan of his proposed invasion of Virginia. He found ardent sympathizers, who lost no time in raising the requisite funds. At a meeting of the secret committee, held at the Revere House in May, it was agreed that the assault should be deferred till the spring of 1859. After leaving Boston, Brown went to the Kennedy farm on the Maryland side of the Potomac, — five miles from Harper's Ferry, — which he had rented, and which he now made his rendezvous. During the summer and autumn, recruits came to him, and due preparations were made. Just before the assault Frederick Douglass visited him, and, for the first time, learned of Brown's purpose to attack Harper's Ferry. Vainly urging him to join the enterprise, Brown said, "Go with me, Douglass. I don't want you to fight. I will protect you with my life; but I want you to be there when the bees swarm, and help put them into the hive." Brown undoubtedly believed that the slaves were ready to rise on their masters, would fight for liberty, and only needed a leader and a plan.

On the 16th of October, 1859, in the evening, Brown assembled his little forces, consisting of fourteen white and five colored men, armed and equipped for war. A little after ten o'clock they entered the town, took possession of the United-States armory buildings, stopped the trains of the railroad, cut the telegraph-wires, captured a number of the citizens, liberated several slaves, and held the town about thirty hours. After some fighting, in which several persons were killed and wounded, Brown retired to the engine-house, where he was finally overpowered and captured by a detachment of United-States marines, under the command of Col. Robert E. Lee, afterwards commander-in-chief of the Confederate forces. Brown was wounded in several places. Eight of his band, including two of his sons, were killed or mortally wounded; six were captured; and five made their escape.

During his confinement at the guard-house, Brown was visited by Gov. Wise, to whom he frankly stated the motives and purposes of his action. To others he remarked, "You people at the South had better prepare yourselves for a settlement of this question, which will come up sooner than you are prepared for it."

Brown was indicted "for murder, and other crimes," brought to trial, convicted, and, on the 2d of November, was sentenced to be hung. He was defended by George H. Hoyt, — a young lawyer of Boston, — Samuel Chilton of Washington, and Henry Griswold of Ohio. On the 2d of December the last act in this drama of blood was performed.

Immediately after the execution, the body was delivered to the custody of friends, and was carried to the North. At New York, Mr. Phillips joined the little *cortége;* and they proceeded rapidly towards North Elba. They buried him on the 8th with services as "simple and unostentatious as were the character and life of the martyr himself, as was, too, the community in which he had lived, and for which he had labored."

THE PREPARATION FOR WAR.

Over the grave of the dead, Mr. Phillips could not but speak eloquently, and with such pathetic and pointed utterances as the event would suggest to one in sympathy with the objects of the deceased.

"What lesson shall those lips teach us? [spoke the orator, closing his eulogy]. Before that still, calm brow let us take a new baptism. How can we stand here without a fresh and utter consecration? These tears! how shall we dare even to offer consolation? Only lips fresh from such a vow have the right to mingle their words with your tears. We envy you your nearer place to these martyred children of God. I do not believe slavery will go down in blood. Ours is the age of thought. Hearts are stronger than swords That last fortnight! How sublime its lesson, — the Christian one of conscience, of truth! Virginia is weak, because each man's heart said amen to John Brown. His words, — they are stronger, even, than his rifles. These crushed a State. Those have changed the thoughts of millions, and will yet crush slavery Men said, 'Would he had died in arms!' God ordered better, and granted to him and the slave those noble prison-hours, — that single hour of death; granted him a higher than the soldier's place, — that of teacher: the echoes of his rifles have died away in the hills; a million hearts guard his words. God bless this roof! make it bless us. We dare not say bless you, children of this home! you stand nearer to one whose lips God touched, and we rather bend for your blessing. God make us all worthier of him whose dust we lay among these hills he loved! Here he girded himself, and went forth to battle. Fuller success than his heart ever dreamed God granted him. He sleeps in the blessings of the crushed and the poor; and men believe more firmly in virtue, now that such a man has lived Standing here, let us thank God for a firmer faith and fuller hope."

Like most, if not all, of the opponents of slavery at that time, Mr. Phillips seemed to have no conception of the nature of the conflict itself, or of the forces that would be needful to root up and destroy American slavery. Even John Brown, whose methods were conceived in folly, was a better prophet. "I do not believe," said Mr. Phillips, "slavery will go down in blood." One year later than the utterance of this assertion, South Carolina passed her ordinances of secession, and fired the train which ushered in the civil war.

Truthfully has it been written, that "whatever diversities in judgment, or errors of estimate, there may have been, Mr. Phillips did not err when, standing by the open grave of John Brown, he said that his words were stronger than his arms, and that, while the echoes of his rifles had died away among the hills of Virginia, his words were guarded by a million hearts. When, a few months later, the uprising nation sent forth its loyal sons to battle, his brave, humane, and generous utterances were kept in fresh remembrance. The 'John Brown Song,' extemporized in Boston Harbor, and sung by the Massachusetts Twelfth, marching up State Street, down Broadway, and in its encampment in Pleasant Valley, on the banks of the Potomac, struck responsive chords that vibrated through the land. Regiment after regiment, army after army, caught up the air; and in the camp, on the march, and on the battle-field, brave men associated the body 'mouldering in the ground,' and the 'soul still marching on,' of the heroic old man, with the sacred idea for which he died, and for which they were fighting." [1]

The execution gave rise to signal discussions both at home and abroad. "Slaughtered," wrote Victor Hugo, "by the American Republic, the crime assumes the proportions of the nation which commits it." In America, John Brown was the hero of the hour. The press, the pulpit, and the platform resounded with conflicting discussions. In every city and town public meetings were held. The majority of people, while not doubting the honesty and good intention of the man, condemned his act: these same people also regarded slavery as "wise, just, and benevolent," and stigmatized the abolitionists as "drunken mutineers." A very few, including the anti-slavery people, repudiated John Brown's methods, saying with the poet Whittier, —

> "Perish with him the folly
>   That seeks through evil, good;
> Long live the generous purpose,
>   Unstained with human blood!
> Not the raid of midnight terror,
>   But the thought that underlies;
> Not the outlaw's pride of daring,
>   But the Christian sacrifice."

In November, on the day before Brown received his

---

[1] Henry Wilson, Rise and Fall of the Slave-power, ii. p. 600.

sentence, Mr. Phillips lectured at Henry Ward Beecher's church in Brooklyn, N.Y., on "The Lesson of the Hour." He said,—

"I think the lesson of the hour is insurrection. [Sensation.] Insurrection of thought always precedes the insurrection of arms. The last twenty years have been an insurrection of thought. We seem to be entering on a new phase of this great American struggle."

Farther on he said,—

"I said the lesson of the hour was insurrection. I ought not to apply that word to John Brown of Ossawattomie, for there was no insurrection in his case. It is a great mistake to call him an insurgent. . . . But John Brown violated the law. Yes. On yonder desk lie the inspired words of men who died violent deaths for breaking the laws of Rome. Why do you listen to them so reverently? Huss and Wickliffe violated laws: why honor them? George Washington, had he been caught before 1783, would have died on the gibbet for breaking the laws of his sovereign. Yet I have heard that man praised within six months. Yes, you say, but these men broke bad laws. Just so. It is honorable, then, to break bad laws, and such law-breaking history loves, and God blesses. Who says, then, that slave-laws are not ten thousand times worse than any those men resisted? Whatever argument excuses them, makes John Brown a saint."

The following interesting reminiscence is furnished by Mr. Charles W. Slack:—

"When John Brown lay in the Charlestown (Va.) prison, awaiting execution, it fell to my lot to organize the meeting in Tremont Temple for the relief of his impoverished family. The gathering had been suggested at the weekly meeting of the Parker Fraternity. Mr. Parker was then sick in Europe. John A. Andrew, not then governor, said he would preside. Mr. Emerson accepted my invitation to speak for the literature of New England, Rev. J. M. Manning for the Congregational theology held by John Brown, Rev. G. H. Hepworth for Unitarian good works, and Mr. Phillips for the anti-slavery cause, in whose behalf Brown was condemned. The meeting was held on a Saturday evening. Mr. Manning, in accepting a participation, apologized in advance for a possible tardiness in being present; as he should try to finish his next day's sermon before he came. Mr. Hepworth was the most confident and ready adapter of himself to the occasion, despite the conservative quality of many of his congregation, — and the only one to prevaricate himself out of the meeting. Every thing went well, except Hepworth's self-condemnatory letter, saying he did not understand both sides of the question could be considered in the discussion; which drew the retort from Andrew, that he was not aware that there were two sides to the question whether or not John Brown's family should starve. Emerson made a fine address; and so did Andrew and Phillips, of course: but little Manning, with heroic pluck unusual in the ministry of that day, put the crowning sheaf on the occasion by claiming to represent the church of Sam Adams and Wendell Phillips. 'I thought I might not get here,' he said; 'but I made an effort, and here I am: and I want all the world to know that I am not afraid to ride in the coach when Wendell Phillips sits on the box.'"

That meeting passed off without disturbance from outside influences. But when, about a month later, Mr. Phillips and other friends tried to raise funds for the family of John Brown by a public meeting in New York, they were confronted by perhaps the fiercest mob that Phillips ever saw.

The following reminiscence of Mr. Hamilton Willcox, of Staten Island, illustrates the intense bitterness with which the advocates of the abolition of slavery were in those days regarded : —

"In the fall of 1859 [says Mr. Willcox] the North-Shore lecture committee, which for some time maintained a yearly course of lectures in the Park Baptist Church, Port Richmond, resolved to change their plan from having the discourses given by residents of the Island, to the 'lyceum' method of inviting distinguished lecturers from abroad. They announced a course including Horace Greeley, Henry Ward Beecher, Rev. Dr. Chapin, and Wendell Phillips. The topics were not political, but literary."

"The Richmond County Gazette" at once made a vehement attack upon Mr. Phillips, and upon the lecture committee, of which George William Curtis was the chairman, for inviting a fanatical agitator to address an audience, although upon a topic remote from the political dissensions of the day. The mob element echoed the sentiment expressed by "The Gazette," and its mutterings were openly heard. A letter written by George A. Ward of New Brighton was published in "The Gazette," protesting against the attitude of that newspaper upon the subject. "The Gazette" printed the letter, and editorially admitted the truth of part of it, but repeated its objections to Phillips's lecturing on Staten Island, because, among other grounds, of the dreadful fact that "woman's rights conventions and like assemblages have frqeuently been enlightened by

THE PREPARATION FOR WAR. 189

him." Before the time set for the lecture of Mr. Phillips, which was to be upon the subject, "The Lost Arts," the remarkable Harper's Ferry episode occurred, and the name of John Brown became the synonyme of all that is to be detested. When, therefore, the strong pro-slavery element of Staten Island heard that Wendell Phillips had spoken, at meetings held in Cooper Union, New York, and Plymouth Church, Brooklyn, to raise funds for Brown's family, words on Brown's saintly qualities, the furious wrath of the baser part of the pro-slavery men was roused. Placards appeared along the North Shore, calling on the people to prevent Phillips being heard on Staten Island. A crowd on a North-Shore boat proposed to throw overboard, and drown, George William Curtis, chairman of the offending lecture committee; and it was stated afterwards, that, had he not landed at New Brighton instead of at Snug Harbor as usual, he would have been in great danger.

Although a riot was imminent, no steps were taken by the sheriff and his deputies to avert it. Accordingly, about twenty of the friends of Phillips and the cause he advocated formed themselves into a guard for the purpose of defending the speaker from a possible attack, and maintaining the peace.

"Before the lecture, in the early evening [says Mr. Willcox], Mr. Corbett and his friends posted themselves at the church-gate. There were no gas-lamps in the streets then, and the light was dim. Nearly every man who entered expected a bloody riot, and was well armed. By eight o'clock a large and excited assemblage occupied the road and sidewalk, loudly objecting to Phillips's speaking; though his subject was not politics. Prominent near the gate was a Virginian named J. M. C. Loud. This worthy was forward in denouncing Phillips as 'an enemy to the Union.' When a lady drove up, Victor LeGal of West Brighton, followed by several roughs, rushed to her carriage-door, and said, 'I advise you, madam, not to go in: there is going to be trouble.'

"'What trouble, sir?' said she calmly.

"'Two hundred of us,' said LeGal, 'have sworn to tear this man from the desk, and plant him in the Jersey marshes.'

"The lady looked him steadily in the face, and replied, —

"'I don't think that will be allowed, sir.'

"'Well,' said LeGal, 'if you know you have force enough to prevent it, go ahead!'

"'I do not say any such thing,' answered the lady; 'but this is not a political meeting. I have come to hear a literary lecture, and I think there will be decent men enough here to check any disturbance.'

"The intrepidity of this heroic woman abashed the crowd, and, without doubt, discouraged them from attempting to storm the church in which the lecture was delivered. It was afterward learned that LeGal spoke the real purpose of the leaders of the gang, who meant to row Mr. Phillips to a salt marsh whence he could not escape, and leave him there, to be drowned by the rising tide ere daybreak.

"Mr. Phillips left his carriage at some distance from the church-door, and, wrapped in his cloak, went forward on foot. In the dim light he passed unnoticed through the multitude; but, just as he reached the gate, a rough, who had doubtless helped to disturb anti-slavery meetings in New York, recognized him. Grasping his shoulder, the fellow shouted to the populace, —

"'Let me introduce you to Wendell Phillips!'

"The ruffian was instantly dragged off, and Mr. Phillips entered unharmed.

"Mr. Curtis, who evidently apprehended trouble [the narrator continues], took the platform, and introduced Mr. Phillips, who proceeded to deliver his address.

"Voices from the street cried, 'Fetch him out! Fetch him out!' The janitor and his aid closed and fastened the outer door, and Mr. Phillips proceeded with his lecture. Some member of the mob outside took a ladder to a window on the south side of the church, and, climbing up, pulled the blind open. Some one inside at once jerked it back, and fastened it shut. This made a loud noise for several minutes. The assembly all looked round, but sat still. Mr. Phillips stopped, and stood watching the matter, till the noise ceased, and then went on with perfect self-possession.

"When the lecture ended, — which it did earlier than the rowdies expected, — the speaker, instead of waiting to be spoken to by his hearers as usual, stepped at once to the pew where Mrs. Shaw and Mrs. Curtis sat, and, giving an arm to each, joined the stream of people moving out, being about midway of the line. In the midst of the outgoing congregation he passed unnoticed through the mob, and walked away. When all the audience had passed out, Mr. Shaw in a hurried manner rushed forth, and sprang into his carriage, which was driven quickly off. A rabble pursued it, yelling, cursing, and throwing stones; but, when they had gone some distance, a friend of the speaker shouted, 'You're too late! He's not in there!' Mortified and discouraged, the mob stopped the chase, and dispersed."

The first anniversary of Brown's execution was remembered in Boston by a public meeting proposed to be held at Tremont Temple. The times were fraught with danger. The South was on the eve of an outbreak. Abraham Lincoln had been elected President. The conservative papers were bitterly opposed to the idea of holding a public meeting. But the anti-slavery people had a fixed purpose; and Joseph Story Fay, J. Murray Howe, and other rioters, by taking possession of the hall, made that purpose successful.

Finding that the use of Tremont Temple was denied to them, Mr. Phillips and his associates were forced to look elsewhere. The Joy-street church was opened to them.

"There [says Mr. Slack, who was present at the meeting] Phillips spoke with regal magnificence and dauntless courage; while the court-way beside the church, and the street in front, were filled with angry and yelling Union-savers. They thought Phillips could not emerge without passing through their ranks, and they were prepared for violence towards them. But there was a rear passage-way, very narrow, from the meeting-house through to South Russell Street; and out by that avenue, single file, walked Phillips and his friends, and thence up the hill to Myrtle, and so to Joy, Street, and across the Common to Mr. Phillips's Essex-street residence. When the mob heard that Mr. Phillips had escaped, they rushed up the hill, and overtook his escort just as it had descended the stone steps leading to the Beacon-street mall. They found a cordon of young men, forty or more in number, who, with locked arms and closely compacted bodies, had Phillips in the centre of their circle, and were safely bearing him home. Timidity, or a conviction that an assault would be fruitless, prompted them to take satisfaction at the discovery only in yells and execration."

CHAPTER XIII.

PHILLIPS DURING WAR-TIME.

The Outbreak of Rebellion. — Winter of 1860-61. — The Fight for Free Speech in Boston. — The Personal-Liberty Act. — Status of the Press. — The Virginia Peace Commission. — President Lincoln inaugurated. — The First Gun. — The Country aroused. — Phillips at New Bedford. — The Call for Troops. — The Patriotism of the Press. — The Memorable April Twenty-first. — A Morning Meeting in State Street. — Wendell Phillips in Music Hall. — "Under the Flag." — State Conventions. — The Question of Slavery ignored. — The Year 1862. — The Emancipation Proclamation. — Ratification Meeting. — Phillips favors arming the Colored Men. — The "July Riot." — Progress of the War. — The Thirteenth Amendment. — Peace. — Return of Troops. — Woman Suffrage. — Conventions of 1866-69.

"Civil war needs momentous and solemn justification. I think that the history of the nation and of the government, both, is an ample justification to our own times and to history for this appeal to arms."

"I believe in the possibility of justice, in the certainty of union. Years hence, when the smoke of this conflict clears away, the world will see under our banner all tongues, all creeds, all races, — one brotherhood, — and on the banks of the Potomac, the genius of Liberty, robed in light, four and thirty stars for her diadem, broken chains under her feet, and an olive-branch in her right hand."

IN his valedictory address, delivered on the 3d of January, 1861, Gov. Banks alluded to one topic which had a direct bearing on the war which was so soon to open. The Legislature of 1858 had passed an Act for the protection of personal liberty, which was intended to mitigate the harsh provisions of the Fugitive-slave Law. Judge Story had ruled that the Constitution contemplated the existence of a "positive, unqualified right on the part of the owner of a slave, which no State law or regulation can in any way qualify, regulate, control, or restrain."

This opinion of the Supreme Court was approved by the State Legislature, and confirmed by the Supreme Judicial Court. Said Gov. Banks, —

"It is not my purpose to defend the constitutionality of the Fugitive-slave Act. The omission of a provision for jury trial, however harsh and cruel, cannot in any event be supplied by State legislation. While I am constrained to doubt the right of this State to enact such laws, I do not admit, that, in any just sense, it is a violation of the national compact. It is only when unconstitutional legislation is enforced by executive authority that it assumes that character, and no such result has occurred in this State. . . . I cannot but regard the maintenance of the statute — although it may be within the extremest limits of constitutional power, which is so unnecessary to the public service, and so detrimental to the public peace — as an inexcusable public wrong. I hope by common consent it may be removed from the statute-book, and such guaranties as individual freedom demands be sought in new legislation." [1]

In the election of 1860, there were four gubernatorial candidates in the Massachusetts field. John A

---

[1] These and other words embraced in Gov. Banks's address were made prominent pretexts by the Disunion party to justify a dissolution of the Union.

Andrew of Boston was the candidate of the Republican party, Erasmus D. Beach of Springfield of the Douglas wing of the Democrats, Amos A. Lawrence of Boston of the Conservatives, and Benjamin F. Butler of Lowell of the Breckinridge wing of the Democrats. Mr. Andrew received a majority over all the opposing candidates of upward of thirty-nine thousand votes. The eight councillors elected, and all the members of Congress, were Republicans. The presidential electors in favor of the election of Mr. Lincoln of Illinois, and of Mr. Hamlin of Maine, for President and Vice-President of the United States, received about the same majority as did Mr. Andrew for governor.

The winter of 1860-61 was one never to be forgotten. Party feeling ran high, and ideas clashed sometimes with a fury which seemed to know no bounds. At the most critical moments Mr. Phillips was always in the van. His courage never failed him: indeed, he appeared to be the happiest when facing extreme danger.

Driven out of Tremont Temple, the standing-committee of the Twenty-eighth Congregational Society (Rev. Theodore Parker) invited Mr. Phillips to speak on Sunday, Dec. 16, 1860, from their pulpit in Music Hall.

"The society [says Mr. Slack] was in possession of the hall Sunday forenoons by a written lease from the directors of the Music-hall Association. When it became known that Mr. Phillips was invited to that pulpit, the directors became alarmed; and a special meeting was convened, to consider their duty in the premises. It was a long and exciting session, lasting till midnight. A majority of the directors were disposed to revoke the lease, and shut up the hall. The standing-committee of the society, who were in attendance at the hall, threatened a suit for damages if they did. The directors wanted to know who would be responsible if injury were done to the hall through Mr. Phillips's presence. The standing-committee referred them to the mayor. The directors shivered like a mainsail subjected to a tack of the craft. The standing-committee, conscious they had law, as well as right, on their side, were firm as a rock. They would not yield a jot of their possession. John P. Putnam, afterwards judge, of the directors, was their friend in counsel as well as sympathy; and he informed his colleagues, that the position of the standing-committee was impregnable, and must be acknowledged, whatever came to the building. It was something after midnight before word came out from their council, that the directors would interpose no objection to the use of the hall the next forenoon as purposed. With the late John R. Manley, the clerk of the society, I carried the decision to Mr. Phillips, who was up, and awaiting the result. He said, 'It is well! I will be ready!' We left, and the next morning Music Hall saw a crowd within its walls never exceeded since. Mr. Phillips was on hand in due course, calm as nature on a spring morning. Whoever heard that discourse never will forget it. It was, from beginning to end, one terrible arraignment of the mob-spirit in America. He used no rose-water flavor in describing the rioters of the Tremont Temple gathering, but in the most scathing language made personal issue with the well-known social and political leaders on that occasion. As he poured out his blistering anathemas, I sat trembling lest I should hear the snap of a pistol that should send a ball into his glowing and pulsating form. But there was no violence attempted. His sympathizers fully equalled the malecontents; and the mayor, on the appeal of the directors of the hall, had the audience interspersed with policemen in plain clothes. When the services were over, and Mr. Phillips withdrew from the hall by the Winter-street entrance, court and street were found to be filled by the baffled rioters ready for assault. Just then two sections of young men, double file, took Mr. Phillips, with a friend on each side of him, between them, and escorted him up Washington Street to his residence in entire safety. This escort was fully armed, and it would have been a sad day for the mob had Mr. Phillips been assaulted. For nearly a week after, a portion of these young men remained on duty at Mr. Phillips's house for his protection.

Gov. Andrew was inaugurated on the 5th of January, 1861; and in his address he reviewed the gloomy condition of the country, and alluded to the position which Massachusetts and her great statesmen had always held in regard to it.

The annual meeting of the New-England Anti-slavery Society followed the next month. Again was the Tremont Temple invaded, but under different circumstances. A large number of the German-Turners were present, armed, every man of them, with the purpose of putting an end to whoever dared usurp the control of the meeting. The body of the house was filled with ladies and gentlemen. An especial effort was made to have the ladies — in contrast to the John Brown meeting, which was composed almost exclusively of men. Indeed, the anti-slavery ladies always had the finest courage; and, where danger lurked, they were sure to be present. No overt act of violence or usurpation was attempted, but the result of breaking up the meeting was achieved in a different way. Wherever the mob could penetrate on the sides of the hall, in the aisles, etc., both below and in the gallery, they did so; and by groans, shuffling of the feet, stamping, outcries, etc., — a perfect roar of bedlamite noise, — they prevented any thing being heard from the platform. Mayor Wightman had the hall studded with policemen, but with orders to make no arrests unless overt acts were committed. The mob knew of these orders, and hence their course of proceeding. Finally the mayor ordered the closing of the hall for the public safety. Phillips, Garrison, and the abolitionists, protested in vain. Finally Gov. Andrew, just inaugurated, was appealed to, to lend the militia or a police force; Mr. Phillips being the impassioned orator. Gov. Andrew, while sympathizing with the anti-slavery men, could not accede to their wish, — first, because the militia could not be ordered out without a request from the mayor, which he was not disposed to make; and, second, because he had no police-force amenable to his order. This lack led to the subsequent establishment of the State constabulary, and the occasion gave great momentum to the cause of free speech on the part of many hitherto conservative about abolitionism. The war was nearly on, and sagacious men saw that the

North had gone far enough. The Joy-street church once more held the baffled abolitionists; and Wightman began to lose favor, and was retired the next year. Two additional discourses from Music Hall, by Mr. Phillips, one on Jan. 20, and the other on Feb. 17, added still further to the excitement of the hour.

The following letter, written by Lydia Maria Child, and addressed to her friend, Mrs. Shaw, vividly recalls some of these scenes: —

MEDFORD, January, 1861.

"Tired in mind and body, I sit down to write you, and tell you all about it. On Wednesday evening I went to Mrs. Chapman's reception. The hall inside was beautiful with light and banners; and, outside, the street was beautiful with moonlight and prismatic icicles. All went on quietly: people walked about, and talked, occasionally enlivened by music of the Germania Band. They seemed to enjoy themselves, and I (being released from the care of unruly boys, demolishing cake, and spilling slops, as they did last year) did my best to help them have a good time. But what with being introduced to strangers, and chatting with old acquaintances half forgotten, I went home to Derne Street very weary, yet found it impossible for me to sleep. I knew there were very formidable preparations to mob the anti-slavery meeting the next day, and that the mayor was avowedly on the side of the mob. I would rather have given fifty dollars than attend the meeting, but conscience told me it was a duty. I was excited and anxious, not for myself, but for Wendell Phillips. Hour after hour of the night I heard the clock strike, while visions were passing through my mind of that noble head assailed by murderous hands, and I obliged to stand by without the power to save him.

"I went very early in the morning, and entered the Tremont Temple by a private labyrinthine passage. There I found a company of young men, a portion of the self-constituted body-guard of Mr. Phillips. They looked calm, but resolute and stern. I knew they were all armed, as well as hundreds of others; but their weapons were not visible. The women friends came in gradually by the same private passage. It was a solemn gathering, I assure you; for though there was a pledge not to use weapons unless Mr. Phillips or some other anti-slavery speaker was personally in danger, still nobody could foresee what might happen. The meeting opened well. The anti-slavery sentiment was there in strong force, but soon the mob began to yell from the galleries. They came tumbling in by hundreds. The papers will tell you of their goings on. Such yelling, screeching, stamping, and bellowing I never heard. It was a full realization of the old phrase, 'All hell broke loose.'

"Mr. Phillips stood on the front of the platform for a full hour, trying to be heard whenever the storm lulled a little. They cried, 'Throw him out!' 'Throw a brick-bat at him!' 'Your house is a-fire: don't you know your house is a-fire? Go put out your house.' Then they'd sing, with various bellowing and shrieking accompaniments, 'Tell John Andrew, tell John Andrew, John Brown's dead!' I should think there were four or five hundred of them. At one time they all rose up, many of them clattered down-stairs, and there was a surging forward toward the platform. My heart beat so fast I could hear it; for I did not then know how Mr. Phillips's armed friends were stationed at every door, and in the middle of every aisle. They formed a firm wall, which the mob could not pass. At last it was announced that the police were coming. I saw and heard nothing of them, but there was a lull. Mr. Phillips tried to speak, but his voice was again drowned. Then, by a clever stroke of management, he stooped forward, and addressed his speech to the reporters stationed directly below him. This tantalized the mob; and they began to call out, 'Speak louder! we want to hear what you're saying;' whereupon he raised his voice, and for half an hour he seemed to hold them in the hollow of his hand. But, as soon as he sat down, they began to yell and sing again, to prevent any more speaking. But Higginson made himself heard through the storm, and spoke in very manly and effective style; the purport of which was, that to-day he would set aside the subject of slavery, and take his stand upon the right of free speech, which the members of this society were determined to maintain at every hazard. I forgot to mention that Wendell Phillips was preceded by James Freeman Clarke, whom the mob treated with such boisterous insults that he was often obliged to pause in his remarks. After Mr. Phillips, R. W. Emerson tried to address the people; but his voice was completely drowned. After the meeting adjourned, a large mob outside waited for Mr. Phillips; but he went out by the private entrance, and arrived home safely.

"In the afternoon meeting the uproar was greater than it had been in the forenoon. The mob cheered and hurrahed for the Union, and for Edward Everett, for Mayor Wightman, and for Charles Francis Adams. The mayor came at last, and, mounting the platform, informed his 'fellow-citizens' in the galleries, that the trustees of the building had requested him to disperse the meeting, and close the hall. Turning the meeting out-of-doors was precisely what they wanted him to do."

The purport of the remainder of this letter was, that, on the mayor's complying with the demand that he should read the letter aloud to the meeting, it appeared that the trustees had desired him to disperse the *mob*, and not the meeting. Mr. Edmund Quincy, the presiding officer, thereupon called upon the mayor to fulfil his duty, and eject the mob from the hall, which was done within ten minutes, to the intense chagrin of the rioters, and the discomfiture of the mayor; and the meeting proceeded without further interruption. Mayor Wightman, on leaving the hall, promised that an adequate force of police should be sent to protect the evening meeting; and he then returned to the City Hall, to issue an order that the hall should be closed, and no meeting permitted there that evening. These events took place at the annual meeting of the Massachusetts Anti-slavery Society, on the 24th of January, 1861.[1]

In January the Personal-liberty Bill came before a committee of the Legislature. This committee met in a small room in the State House, to discuss the bill and an attempt was made to report against it, for it had been the policy of some of the frightened "Union savers" in other States to repeal this bill. Mr. Phillips and other anti-slavery people, on being informed of this intention on the part of the committee, crowded into the committee-room, and nearly filled it. Mr. Phillips and others made stirring speeches, and demanded a public hearing, which was granted. On the 1st of February the first number of "The Tocsin," a campaign newspaper, appeared. Elizur Wright, F. W.

---

[1] See Letters of Lydia Maria Child, p. 147.

Bird, F. B. Sanborn, and William S. Robinson contributed articles for its columns. Its prospectus declared it to be "published by an association of Republicans who are in earnest, and who will be heard." Its motto was, "No compromise with slavery." The six numbers which appeared contained articles against the repeal of the Personal-liberty Bill, in favor of radical anti-slavery measures, and denouncing the Virginia peace commission.

Virginia had called upon all States who wanted to adjust the slavery question, to send four commissioners to that State, to confer on the subject. A meeting was held in February, on State Street, Boston, at which many bankers and brokers were present. A committee of four representative persons was chosen, to instruct the Legislature to respond to this call. Very properly, the Legislature took no notice of this interference; but finally an order passed its branches, and seven commissioners were appointed. Many of the Republicans were opposed to this commission, and so was Gov. Andrew at first; but he "afterwards caved in, as he did on the Personal-liberty Bill."

At this time, the only anti-slavery paper of political value published in Boston was "The Bee;" but such short-lived campaign sheets as "The Straight Republican," "The Tocsin," and afterwards "The Reveille," did a good work of their kind. All of the other papers advocated a timid policy, and did not heartily support the new abolition governor and President. The Hunker and Doughface element was in the ascendant.

On the 4th of March, 1861, the people of the United States witnessed the departure of the old, and the advent of the new, administration, in the midst of pending serious national calamities. On that day Abraham Lincoln was inaugurated as President of the national government. Although rumors of revolt, of assassination, and of a destruction of the Capitol, were rife, the solemn and impressive ceremonies were completed without disaster or crime. In his inaugural address, President Lincoln said, —

"In your hands, my dissatisfied fellow-countrymen, and not in mine, is the momentous issue of civil war. The government will not assail you: you can have no conflict without yourselves being the aggressors. You have no oath registered in heaven to destroy the government; while I shall have the most solemn one to 'preserve, protect, and defend it.'"

Mr. Lincoln had been obliged to go secretly to Washington in February: five States had seceded, and the Southern Confederacy had chosen Jefferson Davis for its president.

Events crowded upon one another with rapid succession. On the 13th of April came the tidings that Fort Sumter had fallen. The news went like a thunderbolt through the land. The martial spirit of the nation was aroused. Law, order, peace, the foundations of the republic, had been outraged; and never did British blood or Celtic ire leap quicker at an insult offered to their nation's honor than did the American spring to redeem his flag from this deep disgrace. In view of the myrmidons of rebellion belching their fires upon the cherished institutions of the Union, the President of the United States had nothing to do but to strike in return. There was no cause, no time, for deliberation. From the south to the north, from the east to the west, went the cry, To arms! Then followed a proclamation, calling forth seventy-five thousand of the militia of the several States; Congress was ordered to assemble on the Fourth of July; the ports of South Carolina, Georgia, Alabama, Florida, Mississippi, Louisiana, Texas, Virginia, and North Carolina, — the seceded States, — were declared to be in a state of blockade.

At last the war had begun. No party throughout the country was more astonished than was the abolition party, whose hatred of slavery was chronic, whose martyr spirit was felt and acknowledged, whose policy was aggressive, — a party which made no compromises, which sought no offices, which asked no favors, and which gave no quarter. As we have seen, this party had interpreted the Constitution as a pro-slavery instrument, the Union as "a covenant with hell." Up to the very day when the secessionists fired upon Sumter, the party had thus spoken, and had shown consistency in all their acts.

But earnest men are not always reliable prophets.

On the evening of the 9th of April, 1861, Mr. Phillips delivered a speech at New Bedford, Mass., from which we select the following curious and remarkable passages: —

"The telegraph [said Mr. Phillips] is said to report to-night, that the guns are firing, either out of Fort Sumter, or into it; that to-morrow's breeze, when it sweeps from the North, will bring to us the echo of the first Lexington battle of the new Revolution. Well, what shall we say of such an hour? My own feeling is a double one. It is like the triumph of sadness, — rejoicing and sorrow. I cannot, indeed, congratulate you enough on the sublime spectacle of twenty millions of people educated in a twelvemonth up to being willing that their idolized Union should risk a battle, should risk dissolution, in order, at any risk, to put down this rebellion of slave States.

"But I am sorry that a gun should be fired at Fort Sumter, or that a gun should be fired from it, for this reason: The Administration at Washington does not know its time. Here are a series of States girding the Gulf, who think that their peculiar institutions require that they should have a separate government. They have a right to decide that question, without appealing to you or me. A large body of people, sufficient to make a nation, have come to the conclusion, that they will have a government of a certain form. Who denies them the right? Standing with the principles of '76 behind us, who can deny them the right? What is a matter of a few millions of dollars, or a few forts? It is a mere drop in the bucket of the great national question. It is theirs, just as much as ours. I maintain, on the principles of '76, that Abraham Lincoln has no right to a soldier in Fort Sumter.

"But the question comes, secondly, 'Suppose we had a right to interfere, what is the good of it?' You may punish South Carolina for going out of the Union: that does not bring her in. You may subdue her by hundreds of thousands of armies, but that does not make her a State. There is no longer a Union: it is nothing but boy's play. Mr. Jefferson Davis is angry, and Mr. Abraham Lincoln is mad; and they agree to fight. One, two, or three years hence, if the news of the afternoon is correct, we shall have gone through a war, spent millions, required the death of a hundred thousand men, and be exactly then where we are now, — two nations, a little more angry, a little poorer, and a great deal wiser; and that will be the only difference: we may just as well settle it now as then.

"You cannot go through Massachusetts, and recruit men to bombard Charleston or New Orleans. The Northern mind will not bear it: you can never make such a war popular. The first onset may be borne; the telegraph may bring us news, that Anderson has bombarded Charleston, and you may rejoice; but the sober second thought of Massachusetts will be, 'wasteful, unchristian, guilty.' The North never will indorse such a war. Instead of conquering Charleston, you create a Charleston in New England, you stir up sympathy for the South. Therefore it seems to me, that the inauguration of war is not a violation of principle, but it is a violation of expediency.

"To be for disunion, in Boston, is to be an abolitionist: to be against disunion is to be an abolitionist to-day in the streets of Charleston. Now, that very state of things shows that the civilization of the two cities is utterly antagonistic. What is the use of trying to join them? Is Abraham Lincoln capable of making fire and powder lie down together in peace? If he can, let him send his army to Fort Sumter, and occupy it.

"But understand me: I believe in the Union, exactly as you do, in the future. This is my proposition: 'Go out, gentlemen: you are welcome to your empire; take it.' Let them try the experiment of cheating with one hand, and idleness with the other. I know that God has written bankruptcy over such an experiment. If you cannonade South Carolina, you cannonade her into the sympathy of the world. I do not know *now* but what a majority there is on my side; but I know this, if the telegraph speaks true to-night, that the guns are echoing around Fort Sumter, that a majority is against us; for it will convert every man into a secessionist. Besides, there is another fearful element in the problem; there is another terrible consideration: we can then no longer extend to the black race, at the South, our best sympathy and our best aid.

"We stand to-night at the beginning of an epoch, which may have the peace or the ruin of a generation in its bosom. Inaugurate war, we know not where it will end: we are in no condition to fight. The South is poor, and we are rich. The poor man can do twice the injury to the rich man, that the rich man can do to the poor. Your wealth rides safely on the bosom of the ocean, and New England has its millions afloat. The North whitens every sea with its wealth. The South has no commerce, but she can buy the privateers of every race to prey on yours. It is a dangerous strife when wealth quarrels with poverty.

"Driven to despair, the Southern States may be poor and bankrupt; but the poorest man can be a pirate: and, as long as New England's tonnage is a third of that of the civilized world, the South can punish New England more than New England can punish her. We provoke a strife in which we are defenceless. If, on the contrary, we hold ourselves to the strife of ideas, if we manifest that strength which despises insult, and bides its hour, we are sure to conquer in the end.

"I distrust these guns at Fort Sumter. I do not believe that Abraham Lincoln means war. I do not believe in the madness of the Cabinet. Nothing but madness can provoke war with the

Gulf States. My suspicion is this: that the Administration dares not compromise. It trembles before the five hundred thousand readers of 'The New-York Tribune.'

"But there is a safe way to compromise. It is this: seem to provoke war. Cannonade the forts. What will be the first result? New-York commerce is pale with bankruptcy. The affrighted seaboard sees grass growing in its streets. It will start up every man whose livelihood hangs upon trade, intensifying him into a compromiser. Those guns fired at Fort Sumter are only to frighten the North into a compromise.

"If the Administration provokes bloodshed, it is a trick, — nothing else. It is the masterly cunning of the devil of compromise, the Secretary of State. He is not mad enough to let these States run into battle. He knows that the age of bullets is over. If a gun is fired in Southern waters, it is fired at the wharves of New York, at the bank-vaults of Boston, at the money of the North. It is meant to alarm. It is policy, not sincerity. It means concession; and, in twelve months, you will see this Union reconstructed, with a constitution like that of Montgomery.

"New England may, indeed, never be coerced into a slave confederacy. But when the battles of Abraham Lincoln are ended, and compromises worse than Crittenden's are adopted, New England may claim the right to secede. And, as sure as a gun is fired to-night at Fort Sumter, within three years from to-day you will be thirty States gathered under a Constitution twice as damnable as that of 1787. The only hope of liberty is fidelity to principle, fidelity to peace, fidelity to the slave. Out of that, God gives us nothing but hope and brightness. In blood, there is sure to be ruin."

The lecture "was interrupted by frequent hisses."
On the 15th of April Gov. Andrew received a telegram from Washington, urging him to send forward at

once fifteen hundred men. The drum-beat of the long roll had been struck. On the morning of the 16th, volunteers began to arrive in Boston. The first to reach the capital were the three companies of the Eighth Regiment, belonging to Marblehead, commanded by Capts. Martin, Phillips, and Boardman. On the same day the Fifth Regiment was ordered to report, and on the 17th Brig.-Gen. Benjamin F. Butler was detailed to command the troops at six o'clock on the afternoon of the 16th. The Third, Fourth, and Sixth Regiments were ready to start. Meanwhile new companies were being raised in all parts of the State.

As if by magic, the entire character of the State was changed; from a peaceful, industrious community, it became a camp of armed men; and the hum of labor gave place to the notes of fife and drum. And, amid the excitement that everywhere prevailed, men and women were anxious to do something, and in some way to be useful. Hundreds of the wealthier citizens of Massachusetts pledged pecuniary aid to soldiers' families. The Boston banks offered to loan the State three million six hundred thousand dollars, without security, while other banks in the State manifested similar liberality. Gentlemen of the learned professions tendered their services, while ladies of every rank in life showed their willingness to minister to the sick and wounded men in the hospitals.

The people of Massachusetts were deeply moved by

the departure of the three-months' men, and the attack made upon the Sixth Regiment in the streets of Baltimore. Meetings were held in city and town. Speeches were made by the most distinguished orators of the day. In some of the towns the people were called together by the ringing of church-bells, and in others by the public crier.

The newspapers of the Commonwealth spoke with one voice. Party spirit was allayed: political differences were forgotten. The past was buried with the past. "The Boston Post," the leading Democratic newspaper of New England, published, on the morning of April 16, the following patriotic appeal to the people: —

"Patriotic citizens! choose you which you will serve, — the world's best hope, — our noble Republican Government, — or that bottomless pit, — social anarchy. Adjourn other issues until this self-preserving issue is settled. Hitherto a good Providence has smiled upon the American Union. This was the morning star that led on the men of the Revolution. It is precisely the truth to say, that, when those sages and heroes labored, they made UNION the vital condition of their labor. It was faith in Union that destroyed the tea, and thus nerved the resistance to British aggression. Without it, patriots felt they were nothing; and with it they felt equal to all things. The Union flag they transmitted to their posterity. To-day it waves over those who are rallying under the standard of the LAW; and God grant, that in the end, as it was with the old Mother Country, after wars between White and Red Roses and Roundheads and Cavaliers, so it may be with the daughter; that she may see PEACE in her borders, and all her children loving each other better than ever!"

"The Liberator" spoke with equal spirit in support of the government; and the religious press, without exception, invoked the blessing of Heaven upon our soldiers, and the holy cause they had gone forth to uphold.

On Sunday morning, April 21, an immense meeting was held in State Street, in front of the Merchants' Exchange. It had been announced in the newspapers of the preceding day, that Fletcher Webster — the sole surviving child of Daniel Webster — and other gentlemen would speak. Mr. Webster began his address from the steps of the Merchants' Exchange. The position was unfavorable: the crowd could not hear, and calls were made to adjourn to the rear of the old State House. The adjournment was carried. The crowd remained in the street; and Mr. Webster spoke from the rear balcony, facing State Street.

In the afternoon Wendell Phillips delivered an address in the great Music Hall, which was crowded in every part. Thousands were unable to gain admission. Many persons were afraid that he would not be permitted to speak, and that if he attempted to sustain the position which he assumed in his speech at New Bedford, ten days before, a riot would be the result. The first sentence uttered by Mr. Phillips, however, gave

"Many times this winter, here and elsewhere, I have counselled peace, — urged, as well as I knew how, the expediency of acknowledging a Southern Confederacy, and the peaceful separation of these thirty-four States. One of the journals announces to you that I come here this morning to retract those opinions. No, not one of them! [Applause.] I need them all, — every word I have spoken this winter, — every act of twenty-five years of my life, to make the welcome I give this war hearty and hot. Civil war is a momentous evil. It needs the soundest, most solemn, justification. I rejoice before God to-day for every word that I have spoken counselling peace; but I rejoice also, with an especially profound gratitude, that now, the first time in my anti-slavery life, I speak under the stars and stripes, and welcome the tread of Massachusetts men marshalled for war. [Enthusiastic cheering.] No matter what the past has been or said, to-day the slave asks God for a sight of this banner, and counts it the pledge of his redemption. [Applause.] Hitherto it may have meant what you thought, or what I did: to-day it represents sovereignty and justice. [Renewed applause.] The only mistake that I have made, was in supposing Massachusetts wholly choked with cotton-dust, and cankered with gold. [Loud cheering.] The South thought her patience, and generous willingness for peace, were cowardice: to-day shows the mistake. She has been sleeping on her arms since '83, and the first cannon-shot brings her to her feet with the war-cry of the Revolution on her lips. [Loud cheers.] Any man who loves either liberty or manhood must rejoice at such an hour. [Applause.]

"Let me tell you the path by which I, at least, have trod my way up to this conclusion. I do not acknowledge the motto, in its full significance, 'Our country, right or wrong.' If you let it trespass on the domain of morals, it is knavish. But there is a full, broad sphere for loyalty; and no war-cry ever stirred a generous people that had not in it much of truth and right. It is sublime, this rally of a great people to the defence of what they think their national honor! A 'noble and puissant nation rousing herself like a strong man from sleep, and shaking her invincible locks.' Just now we saw her 'reposing, peaceful and motionless; but, at the call of patriotism, she ruffles, as it were, her swelling plumage, collects her scattered elements of strength, and awakens her dormant thunders.'

"But how do we justify this last appeal to the God of battles? Let me tell you how I do. I have always believed in the sincerity of Abraham Lincoln. You have heard me express my confidence in it every time I have spoken from this desk. I only doubted sometimes whether he were really the head of the government. To-day he is at any rate commander-in-chief.

"The delay in the action of government has doubtless been necessity, but policy also. Traitors within and without made it hesitate to move till it had tried the machine of government just given it. But delay was wise; as it matured a public opinion definite, decisive, and ready to keep step to the music of the government march. The very postponement of another session of Congress till July 4 plainly invites discussion, — evidently contemplates the ripening of public opinion in the interval. Fairly to examine public affairs, and prepare a community wise to co-operate with the government, is the duty of every pulpit and every press.

"Plain words, therefore, now, before the nation goes mad with excitement, is every man's duty. Every public meeting in Athens was opened with a curse on any one who should not speak what he really thought. 'I have never defiled my conscience from fear or favor to my superiors,' was part of the oath every Egyptian soul was supposed to utter in the Judgment-Hall of Osiris, before admission to heaven. Let us show to-day a Christian spirit as sincere and fearless. No mobs in this hour of victory, to silence those whom events have not converted. We are strong enough to tolerate dissent. That flag which floats over press or mansion at the bidding of a mob, disgraces both victor and victim.

"All winter long I have acted with that party which cried for peace. The anti-slavery enterprise to which I belong started with peace written on its banner. We imagined that the age of bullets was over; that the age of ideas had come; that thirty millions of people were able to take a great question, and decide it by the conflict of opinions; that, without letting the ship of state founder, we could lift four millions of men into Liberty and Justice. We thought, that if your statesmen would throw away personal ambition and party watchwords, and devote themselves to the great issue, this might be accomplished. To a certain extent it has been. The North has answered to the call. Year after year, event by event, has indicated the rising education of the people, — the readiness for a higher moral life, the calm, self-poised confidence in our own convictions that patiently waits — like master for a pupil — for a neighbor's conversion. The North has responded to the call of that peaceful, moral, intellectual agitation which the anti-slavery idea has initiated. Our mistake, if any, has been, that we counted too much on the intelligence of the masses, on the honesty and wisdom of statesmen as a class. Perhaps we did not give weight enough to the fact we saw, that this nation is made up of different ages, — not homogeneous, but a mixed mass of different centuries. The North *thinks*, — can appreciate argument, — is the nineteenth century, — hardly any struggle left in it but that between the working-class and the money-kings. The South *dreams*, — it is the thirteenth and fourteenth century, — baron and serf, — noble and slave. Jack Cade and Wat Tyler loom over its horizon; and the serf, rising, calls for another Thierry to record his struggle. There the fagot still burns which the doctors of the Sorbonne called, ages ago, 'the best light to guide the erring.' There men are tortured for opinions, the only punishment the Jesuits were willing their pupils should look on. This is, perhaps, too flattering a picture of the South. Better call her, as Sumner does, 'the Barbarous States.' Our struggle, therefore, is between barbarism and civilization. Such can only be settled by arms. [Prolonged cheering.] The government has waited until its best friends almost suspected its courage or its integrity, but the cannon-shot against Fort Sumter has opened the only door out of this hour. There were but two. One was compromise: the other was battle. The integrity of the North closed the first: the generous forbearance of nineteen States closed the other. The South opened this with cannon-shot, and Lincoln shows himself at the door. [Prolonged and enthusiastic cheering.] The war, then, is not aggressive, but in self-defence; and Washington has become the Thermopylæ of Liberty and Justice. [Applause.] Rather than surrender that capital, cover every square foot of it with a living body [loud cheers]: crowd it with a million of men, and empty every bank-vault at the North to pay the cost. [Renewed cheering.] Teach the world once for all, that North America belongs to the stars and stripes, and under them no man shall wear a chain. [Enthusiastic cheering.] In the whole of this conflict, I have looked only at Liberty, — only at the slave. Perry entered the battle of the Lakes with 'DON'T GIVE UP THE SHIP!' floating from the mast-head of the 'Lawrence.' When with his fighting-flag he left her crippled, heading north, and, mounting the deck of the 'Niagara,' turned her bows due west, he did all for one and the same purpose, — to rake the decks of the foe. Steer north or west, acknowledge secession or cannonade it, I care not which; but, 'Proclaim liberty throughout all the land unto all the inhabitants thereof.' [Loud cheers.]

The speech was remarkable, not only for its force and vigor, its patriotic and elevated sentiments, but for its strong contrast with the speech which we have previously quoted.

Mr. Slack's recollections of this eventful afternoon are interesting. He said, —

"The outbreak of the rebellion was soon to come. Less than three months after the breaking-up of the January meeting, Sumter was fired upon. This was Friday, April 12, 1861. On Sunday week following, Mr. Phillips was again invited to the Music-hall pulpit, but under what differing circumstances! The Union flag had been fired upon; our national sovereignty was at stake; the President had called for volunteers to put down the rebellion. The divorce between slavery and the government was at hand! The standing-committee had the spirit of all the free North. They dressed their pulpit in the national colors. Over the occupant's head was an arch of bunting, decked with laurel and evergreen. Thousands crowded into the hall. Mr. Phillips was promptly on hand, with — for the first time in his public career — an audience wholly in sympathy with his expected speech. The atmosphere was charged with patriotism. Men's faces, especially those of the old abolitionists, were aglow with a confident hope. Again was Mr. Phillips equal to the occasion! He welcomed the national outbreak as the sure precursor of the death of human slavery in republican America. He built up his magnificent expectancy of the results of the war, sentence by sentence, thrilling the audience with grand and noble aspiration. He yielded, in the furnace of his patriotic and humane warmth, all his old-time predilections, and stood, disinthralled, for the Union and the flag, the Constitution of the fathers, and its future interpretation in the interest of liberty on this continent. How the audience applauded! How they cheered! The men who were there to mob him three months before, now were his strongest indorsers. They crowded the platform to congratulate him when he closed, and joy and satisfaction beamed on every countenance. It had been a Pentecostal season; and the divine outflow of humanity, justice, and the rights of man, had baptized every one of that immense throng! It required no phalanx of armed men to escort Mr. Phillips home that day; for he was almost, figuratively, borne in the arms of a grateful citizenship to his modest abode!"

Mr. Phillips's address (now published in the collected edition of his works) was thoroughly reported by Mr. Yerrington for the "Boston Journal," and the other papers also had it in type. Before the papers went to press, a committee of prudential friends of the government caused the speech to be suppressed, for fear of losing the support of the War Democrats: but, on the fact becoming known, the friends of Mr. Phillips had the speech issued as an extra to the "Anglo-African" paper, and circulated on the street-corners; and over a hundred thousand copies were disposed of.

The people in the State were a unit in support of the war. The officers and men of the regiments were composed of all parties; and, in the selection of men to be commissioned, politics were never regarded. It was the desire of a large portion of the Republican party, that, in the nomination of State officers, representative men of both the Republican and Democratic parties should be placed upon the ticket.

The Republican convention met at Worcester on the 1st of October, and renominated Mr. Andrew for the governorship. The marked feature of the convention was a speech of Charles Sumner, which as it openly advocated proclaiming freedom to the slaves, and using colored men as soldiers in the armies of the Union, gave great offence to the convention, and to the Republican party in the State. The criticisms on this speech which appeared in the press at the time, show very plainly that the Republican party of Massachusetts did not favor the abolition of, or any interference with, slavery. Three days after the convention was held, "The Boston Daily Advertiser," in a leading editorial, remarked, —

"The convention certainly disavowed any intention of indorsing the fatal doctrines announced by Mr. Sumner, with a distinctness that can hardly be flattering to that gentleman's conception of his own influence in Massachusetts. The resolutions offered by Rev. James Freeman Clarke, as a crucial test of the readiness of the convention to adopt open abolitionism as its creed, went to the table, and were buried, never to rise."

Farther on it said, —

"It may not appear so to Mr. Sumner and his supporters, and it

> may be forgotten by some who oppose him, but we hold it for an incontestable truth, that neither men nor money will be forthcoming for this war if once the people are impressed with the belief, that the abolition of slavery, and not the defence of the Union, is its object, or that its original purpose is converted into a cloak for some new design of seizing this opportunity for the destruction of the social system of the South. The people are heart and soul with the government in support of any Constitutional undertaking. We do not believe that they will follow it if they are made to suspect that they are being decoyed into the support of any unconstitutional and revolutionary designs."

The Democratic convention, which met at Worcester, on the 18th of September, nominated a ticket composed of "War Democrats." All of the speakers condemned the rebellion, and favored "conquering a peace." At the election in November, the entire Republican ticket was chosen.

Meanwhile the war was progressing. During the year 1862, events thickened fast; but as yet there were no decisive results. The Union armies had met the enemy on many battle-fields: alternate victory and defeat had marked the contest. Notwithstanding that the days were dark and gloomy, the loyal people of the North were learning many lessons. The administration, as well as the people, had been educated to an anti-slavery point.

On the 22d of September, 1862, the President issued his proclamation of freedom to the enslaved, to take effect on the first day of the new year. "Africa was carried into the war." The black man was made a soldier, with a musket in his hand, and on his body the uniform of a loyal volunteer.

On Sunday, Jan. 4, 1863, Mr. Phillips spoke to a crowded audience in the Boston Music Hall, upon the President's Proclamation. He took the occasion to note the great progress which the cause of freedom had made during the two years preceding, and the encouraging indications of the triumph of justice, to which, in spite of all obstacles, the nation was rapidly marching on. Mr. Phillips accepted the Proclamation as a step in the progress of the work; although he did not admit that it gave all that was desired, or which even the exigency of the war demanded. From his summing up of the situation, and his eloquent closing paragraph, the following is quoted: —

"I know what men say about our President's omitting Tennessee from his list of rebel States, and sparing certain Louisiana districts. No matter: he is only stopping on the edge of Niagara, to pick up and save a few chips. He and they will go over together. I know also the threats of the Democratic party, — the party of re-action. But they will not save any more chips than he. The mighty current is too strong for any reluctance of individuals, or mad ambition of desperate parties. Saints and sinners, we are all borne onward; and, even if some eddy or close nook of a few years may delay our progress, the result is certain. God's hand has launched the nation on a voyage whose only port is Liberty. Neither the reluctance of the captain, nor the mutiny of the cabin-boys, will matter much. And this is why I, once a Disunionist, cling to the Union. Once it had neither the right nor the wish to interfere with slavery. Then we sought to break it. That Sumter cannon gave it the *right*, — the *right of war*. Every day since has ripened the *wish*. A blundering and corrupt cabinet has made it at last an *inevitable necessity*, — Liberty or Death! The cowardice of Webster's followers in the cabinet has turned his empty rhetoric into solemn truth; and now honest men are not only at liberty, but bound, to live and die under his motto, — 'Liberty and Union, now and forever, one and inseparable.'

. . . .

"But, after all, what is the President's Proclamation to us? Nothing but a step in the progress of a people, rich, prosperous, independent, in spite of the world. But let me open for you the huts of three million of slaves, and what is that Proclamation there? It is the sunlight, scattering the despair of centuries. It is a voice like that of God, that gives the slave the right to work and to walk, the right to child and to wife. It is a word that makes the prayers of the poor and the victim the corner-stones of the Republic. Other nations since Greece have built their nationality on a Thermopylæ, or a great name, — a victory, or a knightly family. Our corner-stone, thank God! is the blessings of the poor. Our flag floats in the prayers of four millions, who recognize it as the pledge of their freedom. The hut of the Carolinas! They may curse that paper in ceiled houses, but the blessings of the poor bear it up to the throne of God. Our flag floats in the thanksgiving of the slave. I know it will succeed. Such a breeze never wafted a banner to defeat. The old slave, who sought the 'Kingfisher' in the Gulf of Mexico, thirty miles from the shore, in a wretched skiff of boards, rudely nailed together, when the commander asked him, 'Why! didn't you know that a breath would have sent you to the bottom?' said, 'Lor', massa, God Almighty never brought me down here to send me to the bottom.'

So, God never brought the Union of 1787 to the height of that act, to sunder it in pieces!" [Enthusiastic applause.]

> "'Thou, too, sail on, O Ship of State!
> Sail on, O UNION, strong and great!
>
> . . . .
>
> Sail on, nor fear to breast the sea!
> Our hearts, our hopes, are all with thee,
> Our hearts, our hopes, our prayers, our tears,
> Our faith triumphant o'er our fears,
> Are all with thee, — are all with thee!'"

[Loud and prolonged applause.]

There is no part of the military history of Massachusetts of greater interest than the part which relates to the recruiting and organization of the colored regiments, which went forth to battle for the freedom of the race. Wendell Phillips was one of the first to favor such a movement, and on every possible occasion he urged its practicability. Authority was received from the secretary of war, by an order dated Jan. 26, 1863, to raise a colored regiment in Massachusetts. The first authority given by the governor to any person, to recruit colored men in the State, was dated Feb. 7; and the regiment was filled to the maximum by May 14. Before its organization was completed, so many colored men were anxious to enlist, that it was decided to raise another regiment. These two regiments were called the Fifty-fourth and the Fifty-fifth. Capt. Robert G. Shaw, of the Second Regiment Massachusetts

Infantry, was designated as colonel, and Capt. Edward N. Hallowell, of the Twentieth Regiment, as lieutenant-colonel of the Fifty-fourth.

It was a pathetic sight to see this regiment march through the streets of Boston. Three hundred of them, it was said, were fugitive slaves. They had a cowed look, as if used to beseeching: they did not gaze among the throngs which filled the sidewalks, with the eager, hungry gaze of the white soldier, as if in search of a friendly face. Poor fellows! many of them had never known a friend. But here and there a colored woman, with proud and joyful look, walked by the side of her soldier. History has kept the record of how well they fought, and how nobly they died, for their country.

It seemed to many that "God was ready for the Union armies to be victorious," since the "iron-skin" brigade had hardly begun to fight when victory was achieved. Grant advanced; Meade forced Lee back into Virginia; and the cry, "On to Richmond!" began to sound in earnest. Vicksburg and Port Hudson surrendered, and all was no longer "quiet on the Potomac." Says one who lived through these never-to-be-forgotten scenes, —

"The South grew poorer as the North became richer and more prosperous. Confederate scrip was given by the peck for a gold dollar; while money was plenty at the North, with gold at 2.25. Fortunes were made every day, and "shoddy" began to be a sigficant word. The soldier sent home his pay; and families that before the war had only the bare necessities of life, now revelled in luxury. While at the South, almost every man and boy was a conscript, our quota was filled without a second draft; and —

"We are coming, Father Abraham, three hundred thousand more,"

was sung in every town and city at the North. Many a young man, trained from his cradle in anti-slavery principles, enlisted for the sole purpose of "getting one good lick at slavery." The people were right at last, and led the dominant party along the line of freedom. Even the conservative portion, who had so long objected to the needed medicine, were now willing, as it was coarsely expressed, to "swallow the negro."

The happiest man in Boston was Wendell Phillips; for at last he saw the day breaking upon the colored race, and heard the shackles falling from their oppressed souls. Slavery had, indeed, become a sin of the past.[1]

On the 11th and 12th of March of this year, Mr. Phillips delivered his noble panegyric on Toussaint L'Ouverture in New York and Brooklyn. Although prepared some years before, and adjudged "only a sketch" by its author, a more remarkable condensation

---

[1] "You remember Charles Sprague's description of scenes he witnessed from a window near State Street? First, Garrison dragged through the streets by a mob; second, Burns carried back to slavery by United-States troops, through the same street; third, a black regiment, marching down the same street, to the tune of 'John Brown,' to join the United-States army for the emancipation of their race. What a thrilling historical poem might be made of that!"— See *Letters of L. M. Child*, p. 235.

of a remarkable man's life does not stand on record It proved to be, to many people, a conclusive answer t the absurd talk of those who affirmed that the negroe would not fight. The address may be found in th first volume of Mr. Phillips's "Speeches and Lectures.

After seven months of war, on the 8th day of Jar uary, 1861, a meeting of gentlemen, who saw tha slavery was the "origin, or mainspring, of the Rebe lion," appointed a committee to consider the propriet of organizing an Emancipation League. This con mittee, after most careful consideration at several mee ings, finally reported the constitution to a meeting hel on the 19th of the same month. The organization the League was completed by the choice of officers, o the 29th of January, 1862.

The meeting of the League on the 25th of May, 186: was one of the most animated of all. Robert Collye of Chicago made a telling speech, but the great even was the debate between Mr. Phillips and Senator Wi son. Mr. Phillips began his speech by referring to th inauguration of the League, and then alluded to the d feats and mistakes of the administration and of the R publican party, which had not even learned wisdom i the way mentioned by the proverb, "He that will n be ruled by the rudder, shall be ruled by the rock. He praised Gen. Butler, and hoped he might yet con to believe in a God. Finally he demanded, in th name of the four millions of negroes now called upo to arm in defence of the country, that they should not only be protected from the "barbarity" of the Southern leaders, but from the hatred of their own officers, some of whom might be base enough to betray them in battle.

Senator Wilson rose, and thought Mr. Phillips severe in his remarks, but admitted that there had been many errors on the part of the government. This led to a prolonged discussion, interspersed with some bitterness, which it would serve no useful purpose to recall.

On the Fourth of July, there was a grand celebration at Framingham, Mass. The regular annual mass-meeting of the Friends of Freedom was held there, under the auspices of the Massachusetts Anti-slavery Society. Besides Mr. Phillips, other speakers were Mr. Garrison, Mr. Remond, and Mr. Evans, on English workmen. The prevailing feeling was one of confidence in the success of the Union cause, and the destruction of slavery by war, not by peace. The address made by Mr. Phillips was, perhaps, the most remarkable delivered by him during the war.

Not everybody who lived in Boston sympathized with the cause for the Union. "Copperheads," as they were called, were numerous, and at times noisy in their hostile demonstrations. On the evening of the 14th of July a body of these "oppositionists" assembled in Boston, in the neighborhood of the armory of the Eleventh Battery, in Cooper Street. The rioters attacked the armory with stones and other missiles, and towards midnight the mob increased in violence and numbers. The soldiers in their comparatively small room, with guns loaded, awaited the assault without trepidation. At length the mob wearied of throwing stones, and made a concerted movement to force open the doors, and to gain possession of the few pieces of cannon inside. The word was given to fire. Several of the rioters were killed, and many more were wounded. That one volley ended the demonstration.

On the 3d of September the Democratic party held a State convention at Worcester, and nominated Henry W. Paine of Cambridge for governor. The feeling of the convention was opposed to the policy of the national administration, and the resolutions passed were a general indictment against the same. George B. Loring of Salem, whose remarkably false prophecy did not prevent him from subsequently taking shelter under the Republican wing, where he remains to-day, an office-holder, addressed to his fellow Democrats the following assertion: —

"This administration will pass away as the idle wind. Its name will live in history only as an administration which subverted the rights of the people, until they rose in their might, and overthrew it."

At the election in November, Mr. Andrew received a majority of the votes cast, and was, therefore, continued in office.

In the autumn of this year appeared the first volume of the collected edition of Mr. Phillips's lectures and speeches. The collection was prepared by James Redpath, under the advice and direction of the orator. The appearance of the volume created something of a stir. Horace Greeley, reviewing it in "The Independent," said,—

"Mr. Phillips's speeches and lectures were well worth collecting; they form a chapter of the history of our age; they seem to have been well edited. . . . I doubt that any other living lawyer's collected speeches would sell so extensively as these."

"The Hartford Evening Press" said,—

"We regard this volume as fit, and sure, to become classic, the production of one of the true New-World orators."

The editor of "The New-York Evangelist" wrote,—

"We know nothing better calculated to send a thrill of patriotic fire, like lightning, through the heart, than some of these eloquent speeches; and, in behalf of our readers, we tender to the publisher our hearty thanks that he has brought them before the public in so elegant a form."

A correspondent of "The Portland Press" thus wrote,—

"We understand that Edward Everett is soon to visit the West. We should be glad to hear him in this region: next to Wendell Phillips, he is the most eloquent man in the country.

"A gentleman in Washington told me a short time since, that he was about to furnish his son, as an aid to his education, the writings of Wendell Phillips, with directions to write off and study; these presenting the finest specimens of eloquence, especially of American eloquence."

On the 31st of December Mr. Phillips repeated his famous Cooper Institute speech on "The Amnesty," before the Mercantile Library Association in Boston. Many persons at the time regarded this speech as an attack on the President and Secretary Chase. Nevertheless, everybody was anxious to read it; and, while many abused Phillips, but few came forward to answer his arguments.

On the evening of Dec. 22, 1863, a very large audience assembled at Cooper Institute, New York, to hear Mr. Phillips's criticism on the President's "Amnesty Proclamation." No more momentous questions were ever presented to a people than those contained and involved in this proclamation; and it was held by Mr. Phillips, that the freest discussion of these questions was among the highest duties of patriotism. While many people at the time doubted the practicability of the proclamation, others believed that it was feasible, and that such strictures as Mr. Phillips had to offer were merely an attack upon the President, and his secretary, Mr. Chase. The speech itself was read by everybody, however, and was one of the most logical and memorable ever delivered by the great orator. At the present time it may well be counted as one of the most important commentaries upon that momentous period of our national history. On the 26th of January, 1864, Mr. Phillips spoke again on the subject, at a meeting (annual) of the Massachusetts Anti-slavery Society. In concluding, he said, —

"Massachusetts is a democratic State, because every man owns his farm, and works on it. New York is like Massachusetts; Illinois the same; and we stretch away to the West, democrats, because every man has something to do, and does it. He may shut off his covetous neighbor, a hundred acres, right and left, and say, 'Here at last I am sovereign.' Good! such a mood against capitalists and armies: only preserve it. Make over the South in the same likeness; plant the same seeds: then let the States come back when you please."

An official call summoning a people's convention to meet at Cleveland, O., on the 21st of May, "for consultation, and concert of action, in respect to the approaching presidential election," was looked upon by outsiders as one of the signs of the times. It meant strong dissatisfaction no less with those at the head of affairs than with those who had convened at the Baltimore convention, and who were suspected of a design to manipulate that convention to suit a foregone conclusion relative to the presidential election. Above all, the call to the people to send delegates to Cleveland indicated the growing demand for a more radical policy to bring the war to a successful and early conclusion, and to establish a lasting peace on the basis of universal freedom and justice to all, irrespective of race or color.

The call was signed by Hon. B. Gratz Brown of Missouri, and forty-one others, citizens of influence in their respective States. The following letter from Mr. Phillips forms a part of the history of the convention: —

JUDGE STALLO.

Dear Sir, — Since you asked my judgment as to the course to be taken in nominating a candidate for the presidency, I have been requested to sign a call for a convention for that purpose, to meet at Cleveland in May next.

Let me tell you the national policy I advocate.

Subdue the South as rapidly as possible. The moment territory comes under our flag, reconstruct States thus: Confiscate and divide the lands of rebels, extend the right of suffrage as broadly as possible to whites and blacks, let the Federal Constitution prohibit slavery throughout the Union, and forbid the States to make any distinction among their citizens on account of color or race.

I shall make every effort to have this policy pursued. Believing that the present administration repudiates it, and is carrying us to a point where we shall be obliged either to acknowledge the Southern Confederacy, or to reconstruct the Union on terms grossly unjust, intolerable to the masses, and sure soon to result in another war, I earnestly advise an unpledged and independent convention, like that proposed, to consider public affairs, and nominate for the presidency a statesman and a patriot.

Yours faithfully,
WENDELL PHILLIPS.

BOSTON, April 21, 1864.

On the 23d of May the members and friends of the Emancipation League met in Tremont Temple, Boston, to transact the usual business of such occasions. Mr.

Phillips was one of the speakers. He made a brilliant address, which was listened to with rapt attention. At the close, a gentleman in the audience arose, and inquired of Mr. Phillips if he considered himself a citizen of the United States, and in duty bound to support the Constitution. Mr. Phillips replied that every man and woman born on the soil of the United States was a citizen; but, so far as regarded the support of the Constitution by voting, he could not do it until its pro-slavery clauses were stricken out. The fault he found with the administration, he said, was, that, having had the means in their hands of amending the Constitution so that any abolitionist could vote under it, they had not done so.

The interrogator said he did not see how any one in Mr. Phillips's position could appreciate that of Mr. Lincoln, and it seemed to him that Mr. Phillips had misrepresented the position of the President. Mr. Phillips replied, that he, in common with all other abolitionists, agreed with Mr. Lincoln in his view of the Constitution. He found no fault with Mr. Lincoln for saying, that, as President of the United States, he had no right to abolish because he thought it a sin. All he (Phillips) said in that point of view, was, that no negro was bound to entertain any gratitude to Mr. Lincoln; because he had distinctly declared that he had never done any thing for the negro out of regard for him, only out of regard for the white man.

During the fall and winter of 1864 Mr. Phillips's voice was heard often in public. In the last week of October, he spoke at Tremont Temple on "The Presidential Election," and stated that he had dared, for twenty years, for the sake of the negro, to risk a division of the Union, and that he now dared, for his sake, to risk a division of the Republican party. "I dread Mr. Lincoln's re-election," he said, "because the pressure against him is diminishing; and only under such pressure has he ever done an anti-slavery act."

Though it was evident that the audience was strongly Republican in politics, the force and justice of many of his statements drew frequent and vigorous applause from the listeners.

On the 6th of December Mr. Phillips gratified another large audience in Boston by his philanthropic discussion of "The Situation." So general was the approbation of the effort, that the orator wittily remarked in private that he needed only to have an income of thirty thousand dollars to become "highly respectable."

The annual meeting of the Anti-slavery Society opened on the 25th of January (1865); and Music Hall, Boston, was filled with a choice company of the old and tried friends of freedom, together with a multitude of more recent converts. The session lasted three days, and the leading theme of discussion was "Reconstruction." Mr. A. Bronson Alcott, in a brief address, paid a beautiful tribute to Mr. Garrison, and predicted that his work was to be taken up, and carried on to completion, by younger hands, and that the leadership would pass naturally into the hands of his "son and disciple, Wendell Phillips."

Mr. Garrison followed, disclaiming any leadership. Mr. Phillips then remarked that nothing could be more painful to him than any thing said on that platform which placed him, seemingly, in an attitude of antagonism to Mr. Garrison. Whatever the value of his anti-slavery labors, he owed it all to his teacher and leader. As to the leadership of Garrison, no denial of it had ever come from any but his own modest lips.

Mr. Phillips then reverted to the topic of the hour, reconstruction, — the admission of Louisiana with her system of negro apprenticeship, which he thought was merely a modified form of slavery. Among other things, he affirmed, "I will attend to the amendment of the Constitution when I have leisure; but one thing at a time. The question now is, Shall Louisiana be admitted? The White House has set its foot down that she shall: I have set my foot down that she sha'n't."

The speaker, it was remarked at the time, was never more sublimely inspired than in this defiant declaration. The vote was taken on the resolutions, and Mr. Phillips's series was carried without a dissenting voice.

He was, therefore, master of the situation in the old-school anti-slavery organization.

At the risk of interrupting our narrative, we must revert to some of the leading events in the progress of the war. A hasty recapitulation alone will suffice.

In May, 1864, Grant had made the declaration, which will go far to save his name from oblivion, that he would "fight it out on this line if it takes all summer," and was in hot pursuit of Gen. Lee. In September Atlanta was taken by Sherman, and Sheridan was achieving his victories in the valley of the Shenandoah. In December Savannah surrendered, and the "back of the Rebellion was broken." Gen. McClellan had been nominated for the presidency by the Democrats, in opposition to President Lincoln. Intense excitement prevailed, which only those who witnessed it can now understand. Mr. Lincoln was re-elected by an unexpectedly large majority.

On the 6th of January, 1865, Charleston was evacuated; and the old flag again waved its stars and stripes over the ramparts of Fort Sumter. Wilmington had been captured, and Sherman was marching northward. On the 20th of March the Confederate Congress adjourned *sine die;* and, in May, Jefferson Davis, the president of the Confederacy, was taken prisoner. The Confederates were on the point of arming their slaves, but it was too late. On the 2d of April Richmond fell: on the 9th Gen. Lee surrendered, and

President Lincoln (who, on the 4th of February preceding, had consummated the crowning act of his life, by signing the amendment to the Constitution prohibiting slavery forever) went to the front.

The people of the North were rejoiced. But the oil of joy was suddenly changed for mourning. On the 14th of April the President was assassinated; and he was gone, — again and forever to the front. It was a sad, sad day for the nation; and South as well as North shared in the universal sorrow.

The war was over. On both sides the soldiers had done their part well. Each believed itself in the right: each had acted as God had given it to see the right. Far be it from our purpose to now recall old animosities, or open anew wounds that time has healed. We live for the future, guided by our recollections of the past.

> "Under the sod and the dew,
> Waiting the judgment day,
> Love and tears for the 'blue,'
> Tears and love for the 'gray.'"

The regiments had come home. As though they had lain them down but yesterday, they took up the hammer, the trowel, the hoe, or the pen. It was a grand spectacle, worthy of the Republic. Said Wendell Phillips, "There never was such a thing known before in the history of the world as so large an army of soldiers disbanding, and returning peacefully to the environments of civil life."

On the afternoon of the 25th of July of this year (1865) occurred the annual school festival in Boston. The following recollections of Mr. Slack, relative thereto, are interesting. He says, —

"It was very nearly twenty years ago, that, chancing to be on the school committee of Boston, I suggested to the sub-committee in charge, that Wendell Phillips be invited to speak at the annual school festival in Music Hall. I knew he had never received an invitation carrying civic honor, since he took his stand with the abolitionists in 1835. Social and political, if not religious, influences were all against his recognition. I nevertheless ventured the suggestion, and warmly advocated it. The committee was a kindly and sympathetic one, but feared popular opposition. They thought he might say some ultra or exasperating thing. I said, Let us have the courage to try him. I will answer that the city will be honored, and the company delighted.' After much talk and deliberation I brought my colleagues to say, that if I would take the invitation in charge, and be personally responsible if any thing disagreeable occurred, they would assent to the selection. I only too gladly accepted the trust, and at once conferred with Mr. Phillips. The invitation touched him. He said to me, that though a Boston school-boy, and always a dweller in the city which he loved as his very being, this was the first intimation he had ever received that he was deemed worthy to represent her. Mr. Phillips attended the festival, and, after the mayor's welcome, was called up. He spoke, only as he could speak, of his schooldays, and gave a vivid portraiture of his part with his associates in the reception of Gen. Lafayette in 1824. The description and whole speech were simply charming, — not a word misplaced or ill-timed, not a sentence that was not charged with graceful cadence, and most attractive courtesy. Everybody was delighted,

Mr. Phillips's address was not long, but abounding in reminiscences. It is here given in full, for the benefit of the young people of to-day.

"FELLOW-CITIZENS,— I was invited by the mayor to address the scholars of the schools of Boston; but like my friend Mr. Dana, who preceded me, I hardly know in what direction to look in the course of this address for the scholars. I can hardly turn my back on them, nor can I turn my back on you. I shall have to make a compromise, — that everlasting refuge of Americans. I recollect, that when I was in college, when any classmate came upon the stage, we could recognize in the audience where the family, the mother, or sister, or the father, were, by noticing him when he made his first bow. He would look toward them, and they would invariably bow in return. By this inevitable sign I have distinguished many a mother, sister, and father among the audience to-day.

"This is the first time for many years that I have participated in a school festival. I have received no invitation since 1824, when I was a little boy in a class in the Latin School, when we were turned out on yonder Common in a grand procession at nine o'clock in the morning. And for what? Not to hear eloquent music, — no: but for the sight of something better than art or music, that thrilled more than eloquence, — a sight which should live in the memory forever, the best sight which Boston ever saw, — the welcome of Lafayette on his return to this country, after an absence of a score of years. I can boast, boys and girls, more than you. I can boast that these eyes have beheld the hero of three revolutions, this hand has touched the right hand that held up Hancock and Washington. Not all this glorious celebration can equal that glad reception of the nation's benefactor by all that Boston could offer him, — a sight of its children. It was a long procession; and, unlike other processions, we started punctually at the hour published. They would not let us wander about, and did not wish us to sit down. I there received my first lesson in hero-worship. I was so tired after four-hours' waiting, I could scarcely stand; but when I saw him — that glorious old Frenchman! — I could have stood until to-day.

"Well, now, boys, those were very small times compared with this. Our public examinations were held up in Boylston Hall. I do not believe we ever were afforded banners: I know we never had any music. Now they take the classes out to walk on the Common at eleven o'clock. We were let out into a small place, eight feet by eleven, solid walls on one side, and a paling on the other, which looked like a hencoop. There the public Latin scholars recreated themselves. They were very small times compared with these. As Mr. Dana referred to the facilities and opportunities that the Boston boys enjoy, I could not but think what it is that makes the efficient man. Not by going with the current: you must swim against it to develop strength and power. The danger is, that a boy with all these facilities, books, and libraries, may never make that sturdy scholar, that energetic man, we would wish him to become. When I look on such a scene as this, I go back to that precedent alluded to by you, sir, — to him who travelled eighteen miles, and worked all day, to earn a book, and sat up all night to read it. By the side of me, in this same city of Boston, sat a boy in the Latin School who bought his dictionary with money earned by picking chestnuts. Do you remember Cobbett? and Frederick Douglass, whose eloquent notes still echo through these arches, who learned to read from the posters and bits of writing on the highway? and Theodore Parker, who laid the foundation of his great library with the dictionary for which he spent three weeks in picking berries?

"Boys, you will not be moved to action by starvation and want. Where will you get the motive-power? You will have the spur of ambition to be worthy of the fathers that have given you these opportunities. Remember, boys, what fame it is you bear up, — this old name of Boston. A certain well-known poet says it is the hub of the universe. Well, this is a gentle and generous satire. In Revolutionary days they talked of the *Boston* revolution. When Samuel Johnson wrote his work against the American colonies, it was *Boston* he ridiculed. When the king could not sleep over night, he got up, and muttered, "*Boston.*" When the proclamation pardon was issued, the only two excepted were the two *Boston* fanatics, John Hancock and Sam Adams. But what did Boston do? They sent Hancock to Philadelphia, to write his name first on the Declaration of Independence in letters large enough, almost, for the king to read on the other side of the ocean. Boston then meant *liberty*. Come down forty or fifty years. What did Boston mean when the South went mad, and got up a new flag, and said they would put it in Boston on Faneuil Hall? It was Boston that meant liberty, as Boston had meant independence. And, when our troops went out in the recent war, what was it that gave them their superiority? It was the brains they carried from these schools. When Gen. Butler was stopped near the Relay House with a broken locomotive, he turned to the Eighth Regiment, and asked if any man could mend it; and a private walked out of the ranks, and patted it on the back, and said, "I ought to know it: I made it." When we went down to Charleston, and were kept seven miles off from the city, the Yankees sent down a Parrott gun that would send a two-hundred-pound shot into their midst. The great ability of New England has been proved.

"Now, boys, 'the glory of a father is his children.' That father has done his work well who has left a child better than himself. The German phrase is, 'Lord, grant I may be as well off to-morrow as yesterday!' No Yankee ever uttered that prayer. He always means that his son shall have a better starting-point in life than himself. 'The glory of a father is his children.' Our fathers made themselves independent seventy or eighty years ago. It remains for us to devote ourselves to liberty, and the welfare of others, with the generous willingness to be and to do towards others as we would have others do to us. Now, boys, this is my lesson to you to-day, stated as an Irishism: You are not as good as your fathers, unless you are better. You have your father's example,— the opportunities and advantages they have accumulated, — and to be only as good is not enough. You must be better. You must copy only the spirit of your fathers, and not their imperfections. There was an old Boston merchant, years ago, who wanted a set of china made in Peking. You know that Boston men, sixty years ago, looked at both sides of a cent before they spent it; and, if they earned twelve cents, they would save eight. He could not spare a whole plate, so he sent a cracked one; and, when he received the set, there was a crack in every piece. The Chinese had imitated the pattern exactly. Now, boys, do not imitate us, or there will be a great many cracks. Be better than we. We have invented a telegraph, but what of that? I expect, if I live forty years, to see a telegraph that will send messages without wire, both ways, at the same time. If you do not invent it, you are not as good as we are. You are bound to go ahead of us. The old London physician said the way to be well was to live on a sixpence, and earn it. That is education under the laws of necessity. We cannot give you that. Underneath you is the ever watchful hand of city culture and wealth. All the motive we can give you is the name you bear. Bear it nobly! I was in the

West, where they partly love, and partly hate, the Yankee. A man undertook to explain the difference between the time by a watch in Boston and in Chicago. It was but a bungling explanation at best. He asked me what I thought of it? I answered him as a Boston man should: 'We always do what we undertake to do — thoroughly.' That is Boston. What Boston claims you should know, know it. Boston has set the example of doing: do better. Sir Robert Peel said, in the last hours of his life, 'I have left the Queen's service; I have held the highest offices in the gift of the crown; and now, going out of public life (he had just removed the tax from bread), the happiest thought I have is, that, when the poor man breaks his bread in his cottage, he thanks God that I ever lived.' Fellow-citizens, the warmest compliment I ever heard was breathed into my ears from the lips of a fugitive from South Carolina. In his hovel at home he had said, 'I thank God for Boston, and hope, before I die, I may tread upon its pavements.' Boston has meant liberty and protection. See to it in all coming time, young men and women, you make it stand for good learning, upright character, sturdy love of liberty, willingness to be and do unto others as you would have others be and do unto you. But make it, young men and women, make it a dread to every man who seeks to do evil! Make it a home and a refuge for the oppressed of all lands!"

The closing paragraphs of this whole-hearted and beautiful address, so eloquently inculcating the lesson " to be and do unto others as we would have others be and do unto us," recalls the following incident: —

One day during the war Mr. Phillips spoke before the lyceum at Gloucester, Mass., and, returning home by the cars the next morning, fell in with a lady who got upon the train at a way-station. She was a Southern refugee, who had been suddenly reduced from affluence to poverty, and was supporting herself and her fatherless children by giving an occasional lecture before a country audience. It was a struggle; for the field was full, and she was almost unknown and friendless: but with a brave heart she worked on, never asking a dollar of aid from any society or individual. Mr. Phillips saw her get upon the car, and asked her to take a seat beside him. It was a winter day; and she was thinly clad, shivering from the exposure of a long ride in the open air of the cold morning. Observing this, Mr. Phillips asked, —

"Where did you speak last night?"

She told him it was at a town about ten miles distant from the railway.

"And — I wouldn't be impertinent — how much did they pay you?"

"Five dollars, and the fare to and from Boston."

"Five dollars!" he exclaimed; "why, I always get fifty or a hundred: and your lecture must be worth more than mine, — you can give them facts, I only opinions."

"Small as it is, I am very glad to get it, Mr. Phillips," answered the lady. "I would talk at that rate every night during the winter."

He sat for a moment in silence: then he put his hand into his pocket, drew out a roll of bank-notes, and said, in a hesitating way, —

"I don't want to give offence, but you know I preach that a woman is entitled to the same as a man if she does the same work. Now, my price is fifty or a hundred dollars; and, if you will let me divide it with you, I shall not have had any more than you, and the thing will be even."

The lady at first refused; but, after a little gentle urging, she put the bank-notes into her purse. At the end of her journey, she counted the roll, and found it contained fifty dollars, — every dollar that he had received for his lecture at Gloucester. It may add a point to this simple incident to say (what is the truth) that the lady was a niece of Jefferson Davis.

The American Anti-slavery Society held a meeting in Boston, on the 24th of January, 1866, with a very slim attendance. On the next day the Massachusetts Society assembled, bent, on the part of its officers, on dissolving. Mr. Garrison, Edmund Quincy, Mr. Buffum, and others, favored this course earnestly; but Mr. Phillips, Mr. S. S. Foster, and others, resisted the movement, and carried their side handsomely. The address which Mr. Phillips made on the occasion, was remarkable for the closeness of its logic, its earnestness of purpose, its familiarity with current events, its pertinency of illustration, and its downright good sense.

The resistance of Mr. Phillips to the dissolution of the Anti-slavery Society greatly nettled Mr. Garrison, and caused him to send a letter to "The Independent," wherein he defined his position on the questions of the day, and expressed his indignation at the misrepresentations and aspersions of certain gentlemen with whom he had long "been associated in the anti-slavery struggle," — meaning mainly Mr. Phillips. Mr. Garrison showed plainly that he considered the breach between himself and Mr. Phillips one which could never be bridged. He quoted largely from Mr. Phillips's speech at the late meeting, exclaimed "*Et tu, Brute!*" and went on to accuse Mr. Phillips of an undue fondness for speech-making, of "swollen self-complacency," and of "egotistical assumption," and the like. Everybody regretted the breach; but it must be said, that, in all their personal intercourse, Mr. Phillips treated his old associate with the utmost respect, even with deference. Mr. Phillips, in public, was bound to defend his own views; and it may be added, that his audiences invariably coincided with him. Possibly it was Mr. Phillips's success which nettled Mr. Garrison. It was, at least, singular, that a reformer like Mr. Garrison, who had ever held that individual conscience and conviction should be the guide of conduct, should now be unwilling to follow this opinion when it conflicted with his desire to have the anti-slavery agitation terminate with his own retirement from the field.

On the 13th of April Edward W. Green, convicted on a charge of murder, was hung in the Cambridge jail.

Many persons believed him innocent; and Mr. Phillips went so far as to publish a letter to Gov. Bullock, criticising in scathing terms the action of that official in the hanging. Again Mr. Phillips's clear vision anticipated the verdict of the future. "The New-York Tribune" printed the letter, and remarked editorially, —

"The execution of that man was one of the most culpable that any State has ever been guilty of, and the day is not distant when governor and council and court will be equally glad to escape — if they can — the responsibility for it. We believe Mr. Phillips's letter rests on a basis of facts that cannot be impeached."

"The Boston Daily Advertiser," which, throughout its whole history, has appeared to have a very indifferent opinion of the value of its own columns, allowed one George Sennott to pour out a column or more of ribaldry in response to Mr. Phillips.

On the 29th of April Mr. Phillips addressed the members of the Twenty-eighth Congregational Society, on the subject of "Capital Punishment." It was an able *exposé* of the whole field, and creditable to the heart and brain of its author.

At the annual anti-slavery gathering at Framingham, on July 4, Mr. Phillips spoke on "The Meaning of the War." It gave rise to much dissension; and many people went home railing against the speaker for his assault on the Republican party and its leaders, who, he thought, were playing the old game of politicians, holding their principles in abeyance, while they sought to save a party. Others there were, however, who had memories, and who recalled how many times Mr. Phillips's judgment of men had been confirmed, his prophecies of evil sadly fulfilled.

In its issue of Aug. 18, "The Boston Commonwealth" published the following letter, addressed to the editor: —

"EDITOR COMMONWEALTH, — The forthcoming Congressional election offers to the Republicans of the third district of Massachusetts an opportunity of service to the country such as is seldom presented to any people.

"The representative man of the republican idea in America may now be placed in Congress, where he belongs by right of his matchless eloquence, his profound and sagacious statesmanship, his patriotism without a flaw, his heroic courage, and his chivalric devotion of a life to the best interests of his country and of mankind, — WENDELL PHILLIPS.

"The Republic needs Wendell Phillips in Congress: the Republican party needs him there. For that post of duty he is fitted by more varied capabilities than fall to the lot of most men, even among the justly eminent. Had the policy which Mr. Phillips marked out as the proper method for the conduct of the war, been adopted, the nation might have been saved the years of struggle, the sacrifice of life, the waste of treasure, all uselessly expended before the government approached that method, to which it was finally obliged to come. Had the plan of reconstruction, laid down by Mr. Phillips, been adopted, we should have preserved, and not have lost, the results of victory: we should have had already settled the questions which may now produce another war before they are adjudicated. His was the conception of the statesman, his the policy of security. As he has been followed, we have won:

as he has been rejected, we have lost. The intelligence of the country recognizes these facts; its fairness admits them; its instinctive appreciation 'of the right man in the right place' will hail the advent of Wendell Phillips in Congress with enthusiasm and confidence.

"The Republicans of the third district have the opportunity and the power to place him there. The honor can be theirs: the benefit will be their country's. L. B."

About the same time the Boston "Voice" remarked editorially, "What John Bright is to Parliament, the workingmen of the third Massachusetts district can make Wendell Phillips to Congress." It is very doubtful if Mr. Phillips would have accepted the nomination.

It must be plain to every reader of this chapter, that Mr. Phillips, though unmindful of office, kept close watch of all office-holders. Nothing seemed to escape him. A close student of events and transactions, he was also a severe critic of the men connected with them. In the autumn of this year his voice was heard on "The Perils of the Hour," and it had no uncertain ring. "Five years ago," he exclaimed, "we had a traitor in the White House! He has been five years explaining why his administration was a failure. We have a traitor now in the White House. Do your duty; and, in 1869, he will be explaining why he did not succeed."

In November Mr. Phillips paid his respects, in a public lecture in Boston, to "the swindling Congress;"

that is, the Thirty-ninth. It is needless to say that it created something of a sensation, even at the seat of government, as any one now reading it over will readily surmise.

The year 1867 found Mr. Phillips as active as ever. That the war was over, that negro slavery was forever blotted out throughout this broad land, were not sufficient excuses for him to still his voice. On the 24th of January he spoke at the State House, Boston, on the new "Constitutional Amendment," which had been nine months before the country, and which he thought, "practically speaking," would "never be of any importance." Still later, he took up the life of Daniel O'Connell, and considered it a "great example," and declared, that, if the green flag should ever wave over Castle Green, it would be accomplished only by men who had O'Connell as their example. His remarks on O'Connell were particularly pleasing to "The Pilot," whose pro-slavery editor wrote, —

"Fortunate will Mr. Phillips be when his acts are history, and he has passed away from the scenes of busy life, if there shall some large-hearted man arise in this his own, or in any other, country, who with equal fidelity, with the same spirit of justice, and with powers as rare as his own, shall attest the work of his life, and crown the altar of his fame, as fully and impartially as he has done those of Daniel O'Connell."

During this year Mr. Phillips was a frequent contributor to the columns of "The Anti-slavery Standard." Most of his articles were on the current issues of the day; and, in the fall of the year, his pen appeared to be dipped in gall, so bitter were the sentences which it wrote. While Sumner, Wilson, and Butler, and all the rest, were discussing the great events of the time, Mr. Phillips's clarion notes were echoed from sea to sea, and found as many interested listeners. "If 1861," he wrote, in one of his articles, "will stand in our history as the year of treason, 1867 will surely be marked, on the same page, as the year of dunces, — at Washington." Occasionally he wrote on temperance and prohibition, — subjects which he also discussed, in strong words, from the platform.

On the 18th of November Mr. Phillips lectured in one of the suburban towns on Grant. He was rather sharp on the general's reticence, but insisted that the people must, before 1869, be so educated that Grant, if his election were inevitable, should be compelled to be a Republican and a radical. Mr. Phillips stated that he would not trust Sumner or Stevens because they talk well, but because their lives are guaranties that they would do well. But no one believed that any such man as Sumner or Stevens would ever be made president.

The only public address which he made in the year 1868, was in the month of May, at the Ladies' Fair held in Boston. The object of this fair was, to raise funds in aid of the Cretan struggle; and Mr. Phillips spoke eloquently in behalf of this object.

On the 29th of January of the following year Mr. Phillips spoke on "The Political Situation" in Horticultural Hall, Boston. It was throughout a most severe arraignment of the Republican party and its leaders.

"Be it known to all men and women, that hereafter, on every platform, when Henry Wilson and others fling in my face the merits and successes of the Republican party, I arraign them, first, for three months of admitted murder at the South in keeping Andrew Johnson in the presidential chair without the sham of an excuse for not impeaching him. I arraign them for not giving us a Constitutional amendment. I arraign them for not giving us a political bill."

On the 27th and 28th of the same month the New-England Labor-Reform Convention assembled in Boston. Mr. Phillips was one of the speakers, and favored the eight-hour movement in an eloquent address. He proposed the following resolution, which was adopted unanimously: —

"*Resolved*, That from motives of public policy, and in justice to the only opportunities enjoyed by the laboring-classes, we ask the opening of the Public Library at the usual hours on Sunday."

In April, before a special committee of the Legislature, Mr. Phillips spoke of trades' unions, not defending them, but claiming that they were the only means of self-protection the laboring-classes have. The whole system, he thought, was to be defended on that ground. He was in favor of a commission, but feared that a satisfactory one could not be obtained. He did not expect the rights of the laboring-people would be secure until the Republican party took hold of them, which would be when the power of the workingmen was felt at the ballot-box. Failing in having a proper commission, he would have an officer appointed as an inspector or commissioner of labor, with a good salary, who should have the power to require exhibits from corporations that all laws in regard to labor have been observed, and with power to compel their observance. He wanted the same officer to collect information in regard to the annual average hours of actual labor each day, deducting absence for sickness, etc., rates of wages, rents, prices of provisions, some estimate of the social and comfortable condition of the laboring-classes, and, in fact, all matters relating to the laboring-classes. Such a step he also considered merely a temporary one, the great remedy to come when the power to protect themselves at the ballot-box is in the hands of the laboring-classes.

Since the death of Mr. Phillips, a controversy has arisen in the columns of the Boston daily press relative to the "mobbing" of William Lloyd Garrison in the memorable year 1835. As if knowing that the voice best able to speak on this subject was forever hushed, a score of "witnesses" have recently come to the front, bearing their "testimony" in regard to the disgraceful event. At the time of the mob, Miss Harriet Martineau was passing, for the first time, through the streets of Boston, and, very naturally, inquired as to its significance. Blushing with shame, but not hesitating to deceive, Boston society told her that it was "post-time, and people are hurrying for the mail." If at that early day Boston society shuddered at its lawlessness, what wonder is it, that, ever since that day, it has sought to cover up its disgrace? Mr. Phillips, though dead, yet speaketh; and in the issue of "The Boston Commonwealth" of Nov. 13, 1869, a printed correspondence which passed between him and Theodore Lyman will enable interested persons to decide for themselves which one of the two contestants had the stronger arguments and data to bring forward.[1]

---

[1] In this matter Mr. Theodore Lyman denied the statement made by Mr. Phillips in one of his lectures, — "The Question of To-morrow," — that Mayor Lyman "besought, instead of commanding, that day, and was, metaphorically speaking, on his knees to the mob." I quote now from Mr. Phillips's first reply: —

"His son disbelieves this, because such conduct would be very unlike his father. *He* was in his cradle that day. *I* was in Washington Street. I *saw* his father beg and sue: I *heard* him beseech and entreat that mob to disperse, and preserve order. He never once commanded, or sought to *control*, it. He never vindicated his office by even attempting to rally a force, and *maintain* order. Had he issued one command, even one that was disobeyed, he would have done all that in him lay to redeem Boston; and I should have honored him. I saw him consent, if not assist, at tearing down the anti-slavery sign, and throwing it to the mob to propitiate its rage. The city was mine as well as his; and I hung my head, ashamed of it and him. He was lamentably wanting on that occasion in all that befits a magistrate. He broke his pledge, made a week before, to the Female Anti-slavery Society. The only

Everybody, not excepting Mr. Phillips and Mr. Garrison, could not help respecting the filial feeling that prompted Col. Lyman to defend the memory of his father. Unfortunately, however, the facts could bear no other construction than that put upon them by the orator. Mayor Lyman was probably the first, but certainly the best, of the many Boston mayors who yielded to the mob-spirit that has been as frequently, if not as violently, displayed in Boston, as in any other American city. The burning of the Charlestown convent, the Garrison mob, the Broad-street riot, the Shadrack and Burns rescue riots, the mobs of December, 1860, and January and February, 1861, and the draft riot of 1863, are cases in point; and only one of these mobs

---

order he issued that day was one ordering its members, legally met in their own hall, to disperse. He never commanded the mob to disperse. . . . The mayor did well in giving Mr. Garrison the only refuge which Boston, under such a mayor, could furnish, — its jail. . . . Twenty years ago I said, 'The time will come when sons will deem it unkind and unchristian to remind the world of acts their fathers take pride in.' That hour has come. I refer to old shames, not to insult the dead, but to control the living. I have no ill-will toward Mayor Lyman. His services to the cause of education are an honor to his memory; and, if report can be trusted, he bitterly repented his weakness on that shameful day. But evil-doers have one motive more to restrain them, if they can be made to feel that their children will blush for the names they inherit. I bring these things up, to show the world that reformers have terrible memories; and that, even if base acts win office and plaudits to-day, the ears of the actors' children will tingle at the report of them half a century hence." — *Vide* the Boston Advertiser, Nov. 2 *seq.*, 1869; also Phillips's Speeches, first series.

was dealt with on the Napoleon plan of putting it down first, and hearing its excuses afterward. Boston had tampered with mobs for twenty years, when Gov. Andrew, in the Cooper-street riot of 1863, applied the short and sharp remedy that never fails. But he might have tried it in 1861 with credit to himself and the State.

It is a notable fact, that almost all the Boston mobs have been "broadcloth" riots, and could have been quelled by a few policemen acting under decisive orders. When, in 1861, Mr. Phillips was subjected to the riotous element, Mr. Wightman, the mayor, was, as usual, on the side of the mobs. If Gen. Lyman, or his son, had then been mayor, they would, undoubtedly, have put a stop to the demonstrations; but Mayor Wightman rather took pride in them.

Nobody has ever had a better right than Wendell Phillips to talk about Boston mobs. He saw every one of them that disgraced the city since the days of his father, John Phillips, the first mayor. He knew who originated them, who figured in them, who praised them in the newspapers, and who subsequently made confession of their shame at them. The topic, however, was never a very agreeable one for discussion in Boston; and this was, perhaps, the reason why Mr. Phillips returned to it so often.

CHAPTER XIV.

NEARING THE END.

The Fifteenth Amendment. — Phillips nominated for Governor. — Arraigns the Republican Party. — Meeting of the Reform League. — Convention. — A Labor Platform. — The Butler Campaign of 1871. — Phillips at Steinway Hall. — "Courts and Jails." — Phillips supports Grant. — Letter to the Colored Citizens of Boston. — The Days of the White Leaguers. — Opposition Meetings. — Phillips on Finance in 1875. — Phillips on Daniel O'Connell. — Sir Harry Vane. — The Grant-Sumner Controversy. — Phillips on License. — Letter to "the Liberal Clergy." — Phillips vs. Crosby. — The Irish Crisis. — Phillips at Cambridge. — Reminiscences of Dr. Clarke. — Letter of Parker Pillsbury. — Declining Years. — Phillips's Last Speech. — Illness. — Death and Burial.

"From Boston to New Orleans, from Mobile to Rochester, from Baltimore to St. Louis, we have now but one purpose; and that is, having driven all other political questions out of the arena, having abolished slavery, the only question left is labor — the relations of capital and labor."

"I hail the labor-movement for two reasons; and one is, that it is my only hope for democracy."

"I believe in the temperance movement. I am a temperance man of nearly forty years' standing; and I think it one of the grandest things in the world, because it holds the basis of self-control. Intemperance is the cause of poverty, I know; but there is another side to that; poverty is the cause of intemperance." — PHILLIPS.

ON the 9th of April, 1870, there was a large gathering of the members and friends of the American Anti-slavery Society, at Apollo Hall, New-York City, to commemorate the passage of the Fifteenth Amendment to the Constitution of the United States, by which "Liberty is proclaimed to all the land, and to the inhabitants thereof," and to formally withdraw the Society from the reformatory field as a no longer needed agency. It was an historical occasion, and all hearts were blended by the combined emotions of joy and gratitude.

The meeting was called to order by Mr. Phillips, since the resignation of Garrison the president of the Society, who made an eloquent address. He was followed by other speakers, and numerous letters from members unable to be present were read. The occasion was simple, without a single boast, hearty, no parade, but a natural mixture of sadness and triumph. The members afterwards met and disbanded. The army was mustered out because the enemy had surrendered; and, as Mr. Phillips said, the last orders were "Close the ranks, and go forward!" to new reforms.

At the Labor Reform Convention, held at Worcester on the 8th of September, Mr. Phillips was nominated for governor. Previous to this he was made the nominee of the Prohibitory party. In acknowledgment of his nomination he submitted the following letter: —

BOSTON, Sept. 12, 1870.

CHARLES COWLEY, *Esq.*

Dear Sir, — You send me notice that the Labor Reform party of Massachusetts, which met at Worcester on the 8th inst., has done me the honor to nominate me for the office of governor.

I have no wish to be governor of Massachusetts: and, flattering as is this confidence, I thoroughly dislike to have my name drawn into party politics; for I belong to no political party. But I see nothing in your platform from whicn I dissent, and the struggle which underlies your movement has my fullest and heartiest sympathy.

You are kind enough to say that my life has been given to the cause of workingmen. The adoption of the fifteenth amendment sweeps in all races, and gives the cause a wider range. Capital and labor — partners, not enemies — stand face to face, in order to bring about a fair division of the common profits. I am fully convinced, that hitherto legislation has leaned too much — leaned most unfairly — to the side of capital. Hereafter it should be impartial. Law should do all it can to give the masses more leisure, a more complete education, better opportunities, and a fair share of profits. It is a shame to our Christianity and civilization, for our social system to provide and expect that one man at seventy years of age shall be lord of many thousands of dollars, while hundreds of other men, who have made as good use of their talents and opportunities, lean upon charity for their daily bread. Of course, there must be inequalities. But the best minds and hearts of the land should give themselves to the work of changing this gross injustice, this appalling inequality. I feel sure that the readiest way to turn public thought and effort into this channel, is for the workingmen to organize a political party. No social question ever gets fearlessly treated here till we make politics turn on it. The real American college is the ballot-box. On questions like these, a political party is the surest and readiest, if not the only, way to stir discussion, and secure improvement.

If my name will strengthen your movement, you are welcome to it.

Allow me to add, that, though we work for a large vote, we

should not be discouraged by a small one. Last year's experience shows your strength, and the anti-slavery movement proves how quickly a correct principle wins assent if earnest men will work for it Yours truly,

WENDELL PHILLIPS.

BOSTON, Sept. 13, 1870.

Dear Sir, — When your Convention nominated me for governor of the State, it was agreed, for reasons satisfactory to it and to me, that no official notice of the nomination should be sent me, and no formal acceptance asked.

A maturer consideration of the whole subject convinces me that it is best I should express my profound sense of the honor you do me, my entire agreement with you in the necessity of a distinct, special political party, and my willingness, that, in rallying such a party, you should make such use of my name as seems best.

As temperance men, you were bound to quit the Republican party, since it has deceived you more than once. Any prohibitionist who adheres to it proclaims beforehand his willingness to be cheated, and, so far as political action is concerned, betrays his principles. The Republican party deserves our gratitude. It has achieved great results. It will deserve our support whenever it grapples with our present living difficulties. A party must live on present service, not on laurels, however well earned.

I have no wish to be governor of Massachusetts. But, to rally a political party, disinterested men must give years to the work of enlightening the public mind, and organizing their ranks. In that work, I am willing to be used. My inclinations would induce me to decline the nomination; but I dare not do so in view of the vast interests involved in your movement, which call on each one of us to make every sacrifice to insure its success.

No one supposes that law can make men temperate. Occasionally some sot betrays the average level of liquor intelligence, by fancying that to be our belief and plan. Temperance men, on the contrary, have always known and argued that we must trust to argument, example, social influence, and religious principle, to make men temperate. But law can shut up those bars and dramshops which facilitate and feed intemperance, which double our taxes, make our streets unsafe for men of feeble resolution, treble the peril to property and life, and make the masses tools in the hands of designing men to undermine and cripple law.

The *use* of intoxicating liquors rests with each man's discretion. But the *trade* in them comes clearly within the control of law. Many considerations — and among them the safety and success of republican institutions — bid us put forth the full power of the law to shut up dram-shops. We have never yet ruled a great city on the principle of self-government. Republican institutions, undermined by intemperance, are obliged to confess that they have never governed a great city here, on the basis of universal suffrage, in such way as to preserve order, protect life, and secure free speech.

New York, ruled by drunkards, is proof of the despotism of the dram-shop. Men whom murderers serve that they may escape, and because they have escaped the gallows, rule that city. The ribald crew which holds them up could neither stifle its own conscience, nor rally its retinue, but for the help of the grog-shop. A like testimony comes from the history of our other great cities. State laws are defied in their streets; and by means of the dram-shop, and the gilded saloons of fashionable hotels, their ballot-box is in the hands of the criminal classes, — of men who avowedly and systematically defy the laws. Indeed, this is the case in Boston.

Since your nomination was made, I have been honored with another by the workingmen of Massachusetts. Their cause is a powerful ally of yours. Whatever lifts the masses to better education and more self-control, and secures them their full rights, helps the temperance cause. Indeed, theirs is a radical movement, broad as the human race, and properly includes every thing that elevates man, and subjects passion and temptation to reason and principle.

But the only bulwark against the dangers of intemperance is prohibition. More than thirty years of experience have convinced me, and as wide an experience has taught you, that this can only be secured by means of a distinct political organization. Thoroughly as I dislike to have my name used in a political canvass, I do not feel that I have the right to refuse its use if you think it will strengthen your party.

I am, very respectfully yours,

WENDELL PHILLIPS.

On the 18th of October Mr. Phillips enunciated his views on the questions of the hour in an eloquent address at Music Hall. For some weeks previous he had been the object of much severe criticism by persons who doubted his fitness as a "political leader." An opportunity to respond was now furnished to him. In the first place he arraigned the Republican organization as "a party with but one idea, — that of territorial limitation." Next he made an attack on "Warrington" for certain alleged statements, and was not particularly complimentary to Gov. Claflin. Lastly, he was cruelly unjust to Francis W. Bird and his associates of the "Bird Club," whom he accused of being "a vast controlling and black-mailing institution in the politics of Massachusetts." Altogether, the address was unfortunate: it gave rise to a controversy which continued through many weeks, and which ended with no satisfactory results. It is unpleasant to recall it; and, the sooner it is forgotten, the better will it be. But such vexations are part of the fate of all who get prominently into the whirl of politics.

On the 9th of May, 1871, the Reform League convened in New-York City. A letter was read from Senator Sumner, regretting that he could not attend the meeting, and recommending the Americans to give up the war-dance around San Domingo. The annual report dealt with the South, and with the Indian and Chinese questions. Mr. Phillips spoke nearly an hour, dealing chiefly with the Southern difficulty and the labor-reform question. He approved Senator Sumner's San Domingo policy, and regretted the insult offered him. Certain remarks, not complimentary to "The Tribune," drew out a long reply by Mr. Greeley.

The labor and prohibitory conventions respectively met on Sept. 4, 1871, at South Framingham, Mass., and in Boston. In the former Mr. Phillips presided: there were present some four hundred and twenty-five delegates, of whom eight or ten were women. Mr. Phillips said, on taking the chair, that he regarded their movement as the grandest and most comprehensive of the age. It was for the people peaceably to take possession of their own,—the peaceable marshalling of the voters toward remodelling the industrial and saving civilization of the day. This movement was, first, the movement of humanity to protect itself; second, it was the assurance of peace; and, third, it was the guaranty against the destruction of capital. Mr. Phillips then presented the following resolutions, which were unanimously adopted. They may be said to be a "full body of faith," and they show just where Mr. Phillips stood for the last thirteen years of his life:

PLATFORM.

We affirm, as a fundamental principle, that labor, the creator of wealth, is entitled to all it creates.

Affirming this, we avow ourselves willing to accept the final results of the operation of a principle so radical, such as the overthrow of the whole profit-making system, the extinction of all monopolies, the abolition of privileged classes, universal education and fraternity, perfect freedom of exchange, and, best and grandest of all, the final obliteration of that foul stigma upon our so-called Christian civilization, the poverty of the masses. Holding principles as radical as these, and having before our minds an ideal condition so noble, we are still aware that our goal cannot be reached at a single leap. We take into account the ignorance, selfishness, prejudice, corruption, and demoralization of the leaders of the people, and, to a large extent, of the people themselves; but still, we demand that some steps be taken in this direction: therefore,—

Resolved, That we declare war with the wages system, which demoralizes alike the hirer and the hired, cheats both, and enslaves the workingman; war with the present system of finance, which robs labor, and gorges capital, makes the rich richer, and the poor poorer, and turns a republic into an aristocracy of capital; war with these lavish grants of the public lands to speculating companies, and, whenever in power, we pledge ourselves to use every just and legal means to resume all such grants heretofore made; war with the system of enriching capitalists by the creation and increase of public interest-bearing debts. We demand that every facility, and all encouragement, shall be given by law to co-operation in all branches of industry and trade, and that the same aid be given to co-operative efforts that has heretofore been given to railroads and other enterprises. We demand a ten-hour day for factory-work as a first step, and that eight hours be the working-day of all persons thus employed hereafter. We demand, that, whenever women are employed at public expense to do the same kind and amount of work as men perform, they shall receive the same wages. We demand that all public debts be paid at once in accordance with the terms of the contract, and that no more debts be created. Viewing the contract importation of coolies as only another form of the slave-trade, we demand that all contracts made relative thereto be void in this country, and that no public ship, and no steamship which receives public subsidy, shall aid in such importation.

Wendell Phillips, in presenting this platform, enforced its far-reaching principles in a speech from which the following passages are taken: —

"I regard the movement with which this convention is connected as the grandest and most comprehensive movement of the age. [Applause.] And I choose my epithets deliberately; for I can hardly name the idea in which humanity is interested, which

I do not consider locked up in the success of this movement of the people to take possession of their own. [Applause.]

"All over the world, in every civilized land, every man can see, no matter how thoughtless, that the great movement of the masses, in some shape or other, has begun. Humanity goes by logical steps, and centuries ago the masses claimed emancipation from actual chains. It was citizenship, nothing else. When that was gained, they claimed the ballot; and, when our fathers won that, then the road was opened, the field was clear for this last movement, toward which the age can't be said to grope, as we used to phrase it, but toward which the age lifts itself all over the world.

"If there is any one feature which we can distinguish in all Christendom, under different names, trades-unions, co-operation, Crispins and Internationals, under all flags, there is one great movement. It is for the people peaceably to take possession of their own. No more riots in the streets; no more disorder and revolution; no more arming of different bands; no cannon loaded to the lips. To-day the people have chosen a wiser method: they have got the ballot in their right hands; and they say, 'We come to take possession of the governments of the earth.' In the interests of peace I welcome this movement, — the peaceable marshalling of all voters toward remodelling the industrial and political civilization of the day. I have not a word to utter — far be it from me! — against the grandest declaration of popular indignation which Paris wrote on the pages of history in fire and blood. I honor Paris as the vanguard of the internationals of the world. [Loud applause.] When kings wake at night, startled and aghast, they don't dream of Germany and its orderly array of forces. Aristocracy wakes up aghast at the memory of France; and, when I want to find the vanguard of the people, I look to the uneasy dreams of an aristocracy, and find what they dread most. [Applause.] And to-day the conspiracy of emperors is to put down — what? Not the Czar, not the Emperor William, not the armies of United Germany; but, when the emperors come together in the centre of Europe, what plot do they lay? To annihilate the Internationals, and France is the soul of the Internationals. I, for one, honor Paris: but in the name of Heaven, and with the ballot in our right hands, we shall not need to write our record in fire and blood; we write it in the orderly majorities at the ballot-box. [Applause.]

"If any man asks me, therefore, what value I place first upon this movement, I should say it was the movement of humanity to protect itself; and secondly, it is the insurance of peace; and thirdly, it is a guaranty against the destruction of capital. We all know that there is no war between labor and capital, — that they are partners, not enemies, — and their true interests on any just basis are identical. And this movement of ballot-bearing millions is to avoid the unnecessary waste of capital.

"Well, gentlemen, I say so much to justify myself in styling this the grandest and most comprehensive movement of the age. [Applause.]

. . . .

"You don't kill a hundred millions of corporate capital, you don't destroy the virus of incorporate wealth, by any one election. The capitalists of Massachusetts are neither fools nor cowards; and you will have to whip them three times, and bury them under a monument weightier than Bunker Hill, before they will believe they are whipped. Now, gentlemen, the inference from that statement is this: The first duty resting on this convention, which rises above all candidates and all platforms, is, that it should keep the labor-party religiously together."

In the summer of 1871 Mr. Phillips informed an "interviewer" from New York, that, to his knowledge,

Gen. Butler intended to run for governor "on a joint Republican and labor platform." The platform which the general finally laid down was just this; and hence the information imparted by one who always had his confidence, was, nearly six months before, substantially correct.

Having been led into the campaign at the earnest solicitation of his friends, Gen. Butler made his first speech at Springfield on the 24th of August; his main topics for discussion being the labor-question and the question of the sale of liquors. He spoke subsequently at numerous other places in the State. His competitors in the field were George B. Loring of Salem, Alexander H. Rice of Boston, Mr. Speaker Jewell, and William B. Washburn of Greenfield. But, at the start, Gen. Butler appeared to be foremost in the contest.

On the 13th of September Mr. Phillips addressed a large gathering at Salisbury Beach, "of all parties and all classes of men." It was a speech in favor of Gen. Butler's candidature, honestly conceived, and earnestly uttered. Mr. Phillips had known Gen. Butler since the latter's boyhood, and was, therefore, fully competent to express an opinion of his fitness or unfitness for office. Very naturally, his words, which were not mincing, and which cut to the quick, gave great offence to Butler's opponents. There were not wanting many persons who believed that Mr. Phillips had himself "lost his head," or "was gone crazy." But the great orator was used to such aspersions and insinuations. But we will now quote from his speech: —

"Gentlemen, within the last twenty years Massachusetts has conferred honor whenever she has conferred office. She has not received any. And I have to say, that, among the worthy men whom for fifty years Massachusetts has chosen to put into her governor's chair, there is not one that will do more credit to the State than he who has just left this platform, and to whose voice you have just listened. [Applause.] I know the long list of the governors; I know all that can be said for Brooks, Briggs, Andrew, or any one else that may be your favorite; but, when history comes to record the great names and the great services Massachusetts has rendered to the nation and to the age, she will write the name of BENJAMIN F. BUTLER as high, if not higher, than any of those men who have filled the governor's chair for fifty years. I know what I assert ; and, though I do not choose to name any one of the long catalogue of candidates this year, yet I ask every one of you, no matter to what party you belong, or what name you worship, Show me a name in that long list which has been offered for your votes this fall, show me one, who represents *an idea*. Show me the man among these candidates, who, if he died to-morrow, any great progressive idea or movement would lose a champion. You know, every one of you, that death, in its mysterious interposition, might sweep from the stage of human affairs all these worthy gentlemen, and the cause of humanity and progress would not be the poorer."

He thus alluded to the labor-question : —

"The great question of the future is money against legislation. My friends, you and I shall be in our graves long before that battle is ended ; and, unless our children have more patience and courage than saved this country from slavery, Republican institutions will go down before moneyed corporations. Rich men die; but banks are immortal, and railroad corporations never have any diseases. In the long run with the Legislatures, they are sure to win.

"Now, this great battle which Gen. Butler represents, is the battle of labor. And I came here to say that I hope Gen. Butler will be governor, because he represents that element of disturbance in the Republican party; and, the moment he don't represent it, the great labor element that clasps hands from Moscow to San Francisco will trample him under its feet.

"There is one thing that the masses of this country and Europe are determined upon; and it is, that no future government shall be tested by the protection it gives to money, but to men. This question is a great deal riper in Europe than it is here, because the slave-question has lately absorbed all the attention. It shook this country as God shook the four corners of the sheet in the Acts of the Apostles. Now that it is settled, this great question will now fill the arena."

He concluded his address by saying, —

"I think Gen. Butler has been charged with about every sin that can be imagined; but there is one thing (I watched very carefully, — I put my ear down to the earth, like an Indian listening) he never has been charged, even since 1861, of not doing what he said he would do. You cannot find a newspaper correspondent so utterly reckless that he will charge Butler with having broken his promise.

"For one, I have nothing against him. He has done a great many things that I should not have done; he has done a great many things that I would ask him to do differently; but I will tell you a secret, friends. If I were Pope to-day, there is not a man among all the candidates, Butler included, whom I would make a saint of, — not one. If I were Pope to-morrow, there has not been a governor for fifty years that I would make a saint of. The difficulty is, saints do not come very often; and, when they do come, it is the hardest thing in the world to get them into politics. I don't believe, that if you could import a saint, brand-new and spotless, from heaven, that he could get a majority in the State of Massachusetts for any office that has a salary.

"And now I say, that this name that we present to you to-day, stands as high, as illustrious, as honored, and as historical, represents as much ability and as much will to work, as any one that has been named for governor; and I, for one, if I hear, in November, as I hope to hear, that from Barnstable to Berkshire the *people* of the Commonwealth have strangled the press with one hand, and the moneyed corporations with the other, and made Benjamin F. Butler governor of Massachusetts, I shall say, 'Amen, so be it!'"

A few days later, Senator Sumner and Senator Wilson "authorized" one of the newspapers to say that they "deeply regretted and deplored the extraordinary canvass which Gen. Butler had precipitated upon the Commonwealth; and that, in their opinion, his nomination as governor would be hostile to the best interests of the Commonwealth and of the Republican party." Gen. Butler called at Senator Sumner's rooms in the Coolidge House, Boston, and found the senator "chatting with his colleague."

Taking the morning-paper from his pocket, the general read the paragraph above quoted. "This purports to be by authority: is it true?" he inquired.

"Yes, general," replied Senator Sumner.

"Did *you* concur, sir?"

"I did," responded Senator Wilson.

The general then remarked, that there was a time when Senator Sumner was lying upon his bed, struck down, and suffering. "I called upon you, sir," he added, "to express my sympathy; and now you are co-operating with one,[1] who, at that time, sat down to supper with your assailant. And now you strike *me* a blow on the head."

"You are figurative, general," said Senator Sumner. "I have struck you no blow on the head, but have simply stated to the people what I think of your present course. Had you allowed your name to go before the people, as other candidates do, according to our usage, I should have quietly waited the action of the convention. But you have come forward, a self-seeker, attacking the Republican party and the existing State Government, making war on them for the purpose of elevating yourself. I do not think this is a good example. You are demoralizing the people. Such a system, carried out, as it might be, by all candidates for office, would be Bedlam again, besides the spoils system, with a vengeance."

The general retorted by saying that his speeches were not correctly reported, and added, —

---

[1] George B. Loring.

NEARING THE END. 273

"This all comes of your hostility to Grant. I am for him, and you are against him. I have foreseen this, but thought it would not come before May; but I am ready for it. You have always been against Grant, and every measure of his administration."

"Ah!" said Senator Sumner: "every measure? Be good enough, general, to name one."

"The San-Domingo Treaty."

"Waiving the question whether this was an administration measure, be good enough to name another."

There was no response.

"You are silent, general: please mention one other."

Still no answer.

"You are still silent, Gen. Butler. You mention only the San-Domingo Treaty, and yet you allege that I have been against every measure of the administration. I ask again for an answer. Now, general, have you not been against the treaty? So that, in opposition to the administration, we are even."

Gen. Butler then proceeded to quote certain language, which, he alleged, Mr. Sumner had used in disparagement of the President, adding, "I have an affidavit of it."

The senator remarked, that this matter of obtaining affidavits seemed a little too much according to the practice of the criminal courts. "But, general," said he, "to be frank, do you think any better of Grant than I do?"

No response.

"You are silent, general: you do not answer me. I ask you again: Do you think any better of Grant than I do? I know you do not. This I know."

At this point Senator Wilson joined in the conversation, which then ceased to have any interest for posterity.

On the 26th of September the delegates rallied at Worcester. Messrs. Rice and Loring had previously withdrawn; and, when the votes were called, it was found that Mr. Washburn had received 643, Gen. Butler 464, and that 9 were "scattered." Thus ended one of the most famous gubernatorial contests in Massachusetts, characterized by much bitterness on both sides. A prominent political writer of the day, "Warrington," voiced the opinions of the opposition by declaring Gen. Butler "a representative of nothing but himself, and some of the worst tendencies of modern politics." Later on he changed his mind in this regard, and regretted what he had said and written.

In November, before the election, Mr. Phillips spoke frequently on the labor-problem. In one of his lectures, he stated that his ideal of civilization was the New-England village of fifty years ago, and argued that owners of property ought not to have any consideration on account of its increase in value.

On the 7th of December Mr. Phillips addressed an audience in Steinway Hall, New-York City. The following passages are here quoted: —

"As I look down the years that are coming, and descry the harvests of our own institutions in their growth, I feel very gravely the vast importance — I might almost say the terrible significance — of this labor-question. You ask me to speak to you on the relations of capital and labor. I am a capitalist. Why do I come here? Because I am gravely dissatisfied with the civilization around me. I shrink from so large a word as that. Civilization is, in seeming, large and generous in some of its results; but, at the same time, hidden within are ulcers that confront social science, and leave it aghast. The students of social science, in every meeting that gathers itself, in every debate and discussion, confess themselves at their wits' end in dealing with the great social evils of the day. Nobody that looks into the subject but recognizes the fact that the disease is very grave and deep. The superficial observer does not know of the leak in the very body of the ship, but the captain and crew are suffering the anticipation of approaching ruin.

"Stretch out your gaze over all the civilized world. There are, perhaps, in Christendom, two or three hundred millions of people; and one-half of them never have enough to eat. Even in this country, one-half of the people have never enjoyed the resources of this life. All over the world one-half of Christendom starves, either bodily or mentally. That is no exaggeration. Take your city, and go down into the very slums of existence, where human beings by the thousand live, year in and year out, in dwellings which no man in Fifth Avenue would trust his horses in for twelve hours. [Applause.] I have known men who were intemperate in Boston, cured by being sent to Paris. Why? Because in the brighter life, the more generous stimulant, the great variety of interest in the European capital, he found something that called out his nobler nature, starved out his appetites. So it is with the intemperance of a nation; and, to cure it, you must supplement their life with the stimulus of the soul. [Applause.] will take the social spectre that confronts social science the worl over, — prostitution, the social ulcer that eats into the nineteent century. Everybody who studies the subject will confess that th root from which it grows is that the poverty of one class makes the victim of the wealth of another. [Applause.]

"I take the thermometer of the price of English wheat for th last century, and place beside it the thermometer of crime; and find, as the wheat goes up or down, the crime increases or dimi ishes. [Applause.] The great majority of the human race stan just on the edge of necessity. Has the classic genius of Greece an Rome, and the common sense of the Saxon race, given us nothir better than these apples of Sodom for the golden fruit of Paradis One-quarter of the human race lives in ease; and the other thre fourths contribute to it, without sharing it. If that is the end human existence, let us sit down, and blaspheme the God w made us. [Applause.]

"I am ashamed of the civilization which makes five thousar needy men dependent on one. The system which develops this faulty in its very foundation. [Applause.]

"You say, Why find fault with civilization? To-night is a co night, and you will go home to parlors and chambers warmed wi the coal of Pennsylvania. Why don't you have coal here for tv or three dollars a ton? Why don't you have it here at an advan of one dollar over what it costs at the mouth of the pit? Becau of the gigantic corporations, and vast organizations of wealt The capitalists gather three or four millions of tons in your ci — sell it when they please, at such rates as they please; and t poor man struggling for his bread is the sufferer.

"A rich man is careful: he won't put his foot in any farth than allows of its being pulled back. If he heard a groan fro the people at something he did, he would withdraw his inve ment; for nothing is more timid than wealth. But let that man make $100,000 or so, and put it in with nine others, and make a corporation with a capital of $1,000,000 : then he is as bold as Julius Cæsar. He will starve out 13,000 coal-miners. The London 'Spectator' says that the colossal strength of Britain has reason to dread the jointure of $456,000,000 of railroad capital. How much more should America have reason to dread such combinations, when Britain has more than ten times our wealth!

"Now, gentlemen, you say to me, What do you intend to do? Every man has a different theory, but I have no panacea. My theory is only this: I know that a wrong system exists, and that the only method in these States of turning the brains of the country to our side, is to bring on a conflict, and organize a party. [Applause.] If I should ask one of your editors to-night to let me indite an article on labor and capital, very likely he would refuse me; or, if he granted it, it might be because a fanatic like me would sell a copy or two. But if you will give me fifty thousand votes on our side, and the balance impartially divided between your Fentons and Conklings and Seymours, I will show you every journal in the city of New York discussing the question with me. Labor is too poor to own a New-York journal; but, when it comes in the shape of votes, then those same journals cannot afford to disregard it. Now, let us organize it.

"The ultimate thing which we aim at is co-operation, where there is no labor as such, and no capital as such, — where every man is interested proportionately in the results. How will you reach it? Only by grappling with the present organizations of power in the nation. It is money that rivets the chains of labor. If I could, I would abolish every moneyed corporation in the thirty States. Yet I am not certain that this would be a wise measure, because it seems that the business of the nineteenth century can hardly be carried on without corporations; but, if it be true that facility and cheapness of production are solely to be reached by the machinery of corporations, then I say, gentlemen, that the statesmanship of the generation is called upon to devise some method by which wealth may be incorporated, and liberty saved. [Applause.] Pennsylvania has got to find out some method by which Harrisburg may exist without being the tail to the kite of the Pennsylvania Central.

"I think, in the first place, we ought to graduate taxes. If a man has a thousand dollars a year, and pays a hundred, the man who has ten thousand a year ought to pay five hundred. I would have a millionnaire with forty millions of dollars taxed so highly, that he would only have enough to live comfortably upon. In Japan, when a man dies, his land is let to the state. Do you not think that is a wiser plan than ours? The land becomes more valuable through the labor of the whole country, and not by that of the man who eats off of it.

"Our great hope for the future is in the education of the masses, for they will yet be our rulers. New York stood aghast at the defalcation of millions of dollars, but will you submit to be robbed of hundreds of millions by monopolists? Fifth Avenue cannot afford to let the Five Points exist. You cannot get wealth enough to fortify you against discontent within your reach." [Applause.]

Towards the close of the year, Mr. Phillips delivered a lecture on "Courts and Jails," in which he also touched upon the subject of the treatment of the insane at some length. He made this assertion in closing: —

"We must bring our insane-asylums within the girth of the nineteenth century. We must make our insane-doctors study

Blackstone; and, until then, Massachusetts will never be a decent State to live in. A few years ago this very community threatened with an insane-asylum men who had strange ideas about the right of owning human flesh and blood. General courtesy, alone, saved them from their fate."

In the following January, 1872, Mr. Phillips again spoke in Boston, on the "Labor Movement," in his usual manner and eloquence; also in February on "Temperance," from the Park-street platform. In April he addressed a meeting of the International Grand Lodge of Crispins, in Boston. His speech on this occasion is, perhaps, the most noteworthy which he ever uttered on the "Labor Problem."[1]

The presidential canvass of 1872 found Mr. Phillips an ardent supporter of Gen. Grant and his Southern policy. In the month of August he addressed a letter to the colored citizens of Boston, upon their political duties. Of the many effusions which the anomalous character of the canvass induced, none exceeded this in incisiveness of statement, comprehension of the gravity of the occasion, and thorough analysis of the political character of the nominees. No one ever dissected Horace Greeley with more truthfulness and justice, and yet Mr. Phillips's letter had the merit of candor and fairness to all sides. Here is the correspondence in full: —

---

[1] See Phillips's Speeches, 2d Series,

Boston, Mass., 7th Aug., 1872

WENDELL PHILLIPS, *Esq.*

Dear Sir, — The undersigned, honoring you for your lifelong devotion to the cause of human rights, request you to address the citizens of Boston and vicinity on the political issues of the day, at such early date as may suit your convenience. With great respect we are,

Yours, very truly, —

ALEXANDER ELLIS,
LEWIS HAYDEN,
C. L. MITCHELL,
B. D. JACKSON,
CHARLES L. REMOND,
J. S. SIDNEY,
JAMES D. RUFFIN,
BUELL SMITH,
ELIJAH W. SMITH,
JAMES T. STILL,
JOHNNY WOLF,
S. B. JOHNSON,
E. GEORGE BIDDLE,
ROBERT JOHNSON,
PETER L. BALDWIN,
JOHN H. COKER,
J. P. SHREEVES,
GEORGE L. RUFFIN,
J. R. ANDREWS,
J. R. WATSON,
JAMES M. TROTTER,
J. M. CLARKE,
PETER H. NOTT,
RICHARD S. BROWN,
WILLIAM C. NELL,
THOMAS DOWNING,
S. A. HANCOCK,
NATHANIEL SPRINGFIELD,
DARIUS M. HARRIS,
H. L. SMITH,
JAMES McFARLYN,
ABRAHAM HUGHES,
G. F. GRANT.

SWAMPSCOTT, Aug. 9, 1872.

GENTLEMEN, — You ask me to address you on the questions involved in the canvass between President Grant and Mr. Greeley. I thank you for the confidence implied in your request. Among you, I see many who have been workers with me in the anti-slavery cause for years.

My residence here makes it inconvenient for me to attend a public meeting in Boston; and, indeed, I think I can state my views more satisfactorily in a letter than in a public address. If you please, therefore, I will communicate with you in this way, rather than in the one you suggest.

Of course the first thought that occurs to you and me just now is, that one of your best, ablest, and most watchful friends, Mr. Senator Sumner, advises you to vote for Horace Greeley, and believes that your rights will be safe only in his keeping. I touch with reverent hand every thing from Mr. Sumner. I can never forget his measureless services to the anti-slavery cause and to your race. Whenever I read his words, I read them overshadowed by the memory of his early and entire consecration to the service of impartial liberty; of that zeal which has never flagged; that watchfulness which has seldom been deceived; of that devotion which has so rarely shrunk from any sacrifice, which no opposition could tire, and no danger appall. From such a counsellor, I venture to differ with great reluctance, and only after mature deliberation. I should hesitate to publish my dissent if I were not sure that I was right, and that he was wrong; that the occasion was very important, and his mistake one which leads to fatal results.

My judgment is the exact opposite of Mr. Sumner's. I think every loyal man, and especially every colored man, should vote for Gen. Grant, and that the nation and your race are safe only in the hands of the old, regular Republican party.

Some may ask how I come to think thus, when I was one of the few loyal men who protested, in 1868, against Grant's nomination, and seeing that I have so often affirmed that the Republican party had outlived its usefulness.

Gentlemen, the reasons which lead me to my present opinion, in spite of my former views, ought to give my judgment more weight with you. I am forced by late developments to my present position.

You remember, that, in 1868, I emphatically denied Gen. Grant's fitness for the presidency. Derided by the Republican press, I went from city to city protesting against his election. In private, with Mr. Sumner and others, I argued long and earnestly against the risk of putting such a man into such an office. At that time they saw only his great merits, and supported him heartily. The defects of his administration are no surprise to me. I may say, without boasting, that I prophesied those defects. I do not wish to hide them to-day. I entirely agree with Mr. Sumner as to the grave fault and intolerable insolence of the administration in the San-Domingo matter. I think the frequent putting of relatives into office highly objectionable, and the sad career of Webster is warning enough against any man in public life venturing to accept gifts from living men. These and other defects are no surprise to me. The eminent merits of Gen. Grant's administration are, I confess, a surprise to me.

His truly original, statesmanlike, and Christian policy toward the Indians is admirable, and, standing alone, is enough to mark him a statesman. His patience amid innumerable difficulties in our foreign relations is wonderful in one bred a soldier. The aid the administration has given to the industrial and financial prosperity of the country is a great merit. Gen. Grant's prompt interference for justice to workingmen in defiance of those about him, relative to the execution of the eight-hour law, I shall always remember. The crime of the Republican party in tolerating the Ku-Klux is flagrant. But the President and his immediate friends deserve our gratitude for their efforts and success in that matter. His services to the fifteenth amendment, I shall never forget. When some, even of the foremost abolitionists, doubted, and were lukewarm, I wrote to Senator Wilson, asking him to urge Gen. Grant to put three lines into his first message commending that measure to Congress and the country. The answer came

NEARING THE END. 283

back, "You are too late. Gen. Grant's message was finished before your note arrived, and the recommendation you wish *is in it*." It still remains lamentably true, that the colored man has no full recognition at the North, and no adequate protection in the South — shame to the administration and to the Republican party! But their friends may fairly claim, that, during the last three years, the negro has steadily gained in the safe exercise and quiet enjoyment of his rights.

I know the defects of Gen. Grant's administration as well as any man. I think, distrustful as I was of him, I am able to see the good service he has unexpectedly rendered the nation.

But no matter for those defects. At the most they are not fatal, and events have lifted President Grant into being to-day the symbol and representative of loyalty. The conspiracy between Southern secessionists and Northern copperheads, of which, very naturally, Mr. Greeley is the tool, and, unfortunately, Mr. Sumner is the indorser, and, I think, the dupe, leaves room for but two parties, — those who are for the nation, and those who are against it. I bate no jot of my brotherly regard and sincere esteem for Mr. Sumner in thus holding him deceived. The entire faith I have in his honesty of purpose obliges me to think him duped. The only wonder is, how this is possible when the South is so insolent and shameless in proclaiming her intentions. The South has long seen her mistake, and often confessed it. "The Tribune" itself makes this statement as late as June, 1871. That mistake was, to contend for her ideas with *muskets*, and *outside the Union*, — leaving us the government, and taking herself the part of a rebel. She has often announced, — in the last instance by the lips of Jefferson Davis, — that the cause was not lost, and must be won by getting possession of the government, and leaving us in the opposition. Such is the present plot. That Mr. Greeley sees it, would never prevent his aiding it. That Mr. Sumner does not see it, is to me matter of profound astonishment. At such a moment the regular Republican party becomes again the accepted and only instrument of resistance, and Grant represents loyalty as Lincoln did in 1861. I do not care for his defects, were they ten times greater. Chatham and Junius rightfully forgot even the infamy of Wilkes, when he stood the representative and symbol of the rights of a British subject. Even if I accepted Mr. Sumner's portrait of Gen. Grant, — which in some sense is true, but in no sense is the whole truth, — I should still vote for him against a rebellion at the ballot-box, to which disloyalty gives all the strength, and childish credulity all the character.

To stop now for criticism of such faults as those of Gen. Grant, is like blaming a man's awkwardness when he is defending you against an assassin.

In proof that the conspiracy I charge is real, and no fiction, I need not cite Jefferson Davis's last speech, or the confession of Mr. Greeley's adherents. Every impartial man who comes to us from the South bears witness that the mass of Southern whites are wholly unchanged in opinion, and ready for another revolt whenever the way opens. The wide-spread organization of the Ku-Klux shows the same thing. That organization existed, only because public opinion there cheered it on; and, in suppressing it, our government had no tittle of help from the former rebels. All this was to be expected. It would be contrary to history and experience were it otherwise. To put the slightest faith in the protestations of copperheads and secessionists, made only to get office, is building on a quicksand. With the exception of Mr. Sumner, no leading Republican does really put any faith in those protestations. Theirs is not a case of delusion. They are hypocrites, not dupes. They know well the plot, and, for the sake of office, are willing to help it, and risk the consequences. They know that Mr. Greeley's election means the negro surrendered to the hate of the Southern States, with no interference from the nation in his behalf; that it means the Constitutional amendments neutralized by a copperhead Congress, our debt tampered with, and our bonds fallen twenty per cent in every market. The Democratic millionaire who is willing to risk this has already "hedged." He holds millions of Confederate bonds, and is plotting to make on them more than enough to pay four times over for all he loses on the national securities, and then safely laugh at the small bondholders he has duped.

Observe that I count as Mr. Greeley's allies only the copperheads of the Democratic party. It is loose talk to say he has joined the Democrats: such a statement is an insult to the Democracy. The exact truth is, he has joined the copperhead wing of the Democracy, its worst element. They are his reliance.

I know some honest war-Democrats wish to change their base, and accept heartily the result of the war. All honor to them! But their place is not with Greeley, but with Grant. They fought at his side: there they should stand to-day. I know it is hard to confess mistakes, but I practise what I preach.

If Gen. Grant is set aside, who is offered us in his place? Horace Greeley. I need not tell you, my friends, what Horace Greeley is: we abolitionists knew him only too well in the weary years of our struggle. He had enough of clear, moral vision to see the justice of our cause; but he never had courage to confess his faith. If events had ever given him the courage, he never would have had principle enough to risk any thing for an idea. A trimmer by nature and purpose, he has abused even an American politician's privilege of trading principles for success. But for lack of ability he would have been the chief time-server of his age. I never knew till now any of his eulogists so heedless and undiscriminating as even to claim that he was a sincere man. As for his honesty — for twenty years it has been a byword with us that it would be safe to leave your open purse in the same room with him; but, as for any other honesty, no one was ever witless enough to connect the idea with his name.

Mr. Sumner trusts him as "a lifetime abolitionist." This is certainly news to you and me. You and I know well, when *abolitionist* was a term of reproach, how timidly he held up his skirts about him, careful to put a wide distance between himself and us. You will find few working abolitionists, who stood in the trenches from 1840 to 1860, willing to trust the negro race to Horace Greeley. I can remember the day when he and his fellow-Republicans quoted our criticisms upon them as certificates that they were no abolitionists. We can give him just such a certificate now, with a clear conscience. Judged by the files of "The Tribune" itself, there never was an hour when Horace Greeley could have been trusted with the care of the black man's rights.

No man has known better than he, how to manufacture political and pecuniary success out of the convictions of other men. For himself he never had a conviction. Men contrast his former praise of Gen. Grant with his fault-finding now. Neither his praise nor his blame is of any account. Neither comes from the heart. Both are measured and weighed out with shrewd calculation for effect. Examine the files of "The Tribune," and you will see, that, whenever men's convictions on any subject got a keen edge, Mr. Greeley was always ready to blunt them with a compromise. He is only acting now the part he has always played. Men laugh when some stirring and loyal sentence is quoted from "The Tribune" of 1862 or 1864, and Horace Greeley immediately proves that he did not write it. But you and I always knew that three-quarters of the loyalty of "The Tribune" was smuggled into it in his absence, or in spite of him. If his letters and communications to Lincoln, during the dark years of 1862 and 1863, are ever published, the world will see what you and I have always known, that he could hardly have aided the Confederacy more, unless he had enlisted in its ranks, or taken a seat in its cabinet.

If, as Mr. Sumner says, Mr. Greeley is a "lifetime abolitionist," how comes it, that, till within three years, Mr. Sumner hardly ever got a kind word, and never had any hearty support, from "The Tribune"? How often have Mr. Sumner's friends heard him expatiate at length on this point! On the floor of Congress he has stood, for many a year, the incarnation of the anti-slavery movement. But he has again and again complained, that, instead of giving him any support, "The Tribune" has constantly belittled his efforts, and put obstacles in his way; cheering his opponents, and carping at his measures, or, at best, damning them with faint praise. My recollection of these well-grounded complaints is so fresh, that I look at Mr. Sumner's picture of Mr. Greeley with unfeigned astonishment. Even the supposed conversion of the Southern rebels is not so wonderful as that of "The Tribune" into a supporter of Charles Sumner.

Doubtless we could find a man who would, even if elected by rebels, still use them for his own purposes. And it is possible, that, in rare moments of exceptional courage or virtue, Mr. Greeley may dream of doing so. But, in cool and sane moments, he knows he is their tool, and is contented to be so. Every man of common sense sees, that of course, if copperheads and secessionists lift Mr. Greeley into the White House, they will claim — and it is now understood that they shall have — their full share in shaping the policy, and filling the offices, of the administration. They are no bunglers, but shrewd at a bargain, and sure to get good security for a promise. The corner-stone of their policy is, to repudiate our debt, or assume their own. We shall surely hear that advocated. We shall probably see Jefferson Davis in the Senate, and certainly have his agents in the cabinet. No doubt he will be consulted in the construction of the cabinet. This is to put in peril all the war has gained. I am not ready for such an experiment. An old friend now residing in Georgia, who stood, rifle in hand, in Kansas all through that fight, told me, just after the Cincinnati convention, —

"Sir, before Grant arrested those twenty Ku-Klux in North Carolina, I never slept without a loaded musket at my bed-head, and never ventured into the village unless fully armed. Since that stern interference in North Carolina, I, *even afar off in Georgia*, sleep and walk about as safe, careless, and free as you do here."

"If Greeley is elected, I suppose," said I, "you'll load those revolvers again."

"Never. I know, by Southern boast, what that election means. I'll never risk living in Georgia under Greeley. I'll sell out, and come North."

Such is the testimony of a loyal man in the South! That is how it looks in Georgia!

Gentlemen, I have another interest in Grant's re-election. The anti-slavery cause was only a portion of the great struggle between capital and labor. Capital undertook to own the laborer. We have broken that up. If Grant is elected, that dispute, and all questions connected with it, sink out of sight. All the issues of the war are put beyond debate, and a clear field is left for the discussion of the labor-movement. I do not count much on the recognition of that movement by the Republican convention, though I gratefully appreciate it. But I see in the bare success itself, of Gen. Grant, the retiring of old issues, and the securing of a place for new ones.

If Greeley is elected, we shall spend the next four years in fighting over the war-quarrels, constitutional amendments, negroes' rights, State rights, repudiation, and Southern debts. And we shall have besides a contemptuous ignoring of the labor-question. Its friends were at Cincinnati. The convention scorned their appeals, and Mr. Schurz himself affirmed that labor was "not a live issue." President Grant means peace, and opportunity to agitate the great industrial questions of the day. President Greeley means the scandal and wrangle of Andy Johnson's years over again, with secession encamped in Washington.

The saddest line, to me, of Mr. Sumner's letter, was, where he warns you colored men not "to band together in a hostile camp, and keep alive the separation of races"! The negro, robbed, tortured, murdered, trodden under foot, defenceless in unresisting submission — who has the heart to charge him with an iota of the guilt of "keeping alive the separation of races"? Surely this lamb has never shown any hate, or any undue prejudice, against the wolf. The senator used to think all the fault was on the other side.

"We put aside, with the scorn it deserves, the insult implied in preaching to us forgiveness and conciliation. Andersonville and Libby Prison are still living horrors. Besides the thousands who were starved there, hundreds still drag out weary lives in our streets, poisoned all through by that dread cruelty. The graves of seven white, native Georgian loyal men, ruthlessly shot down in the streets, are hardly yet covered. The first-born of a hundred thousand households are still freshly mourned. Till within a year, throughout half the South, the negro was robbed, tortured, and murdered with impunity; the Southern press glorying in the atrocities. Meanwhile — thanks to the unparalleled mercy, the unutterable generosity, of the nation — ninety-nine out of every hundred Confederate soldiers enjoy to-day all the rights they had before the war. Jefferson Davis and his fellow-assassins, the *real jailers* of Andersonville and Libby, —

> "Shame on those cruel eyes,
> That bore to look on torture,
> And dared not look on war!"

still live, unharmed, in peaceful possession of every right the law can give, except that of lifting their hands against the government which has spared them. I dare not affix the epithet I think fitting to that mood of mind, which deems it necessary and becoming to preach to such a community the duty of forgiveness!

We do forgive. We have forgiven. But duty to the dead and to the negro, forbids us to *trust* power to any hands, without undoubted, indubitable certainty that such hands are *trustworthy*. If we fail in this caution, we shall only have decoyed the negro into danger, and left him doubly defenceless. I wish my voice could be heard by every colored man down to the Gulf, — not because they need my advice. No: they understand and see the danger. But I should like to rally them to help us, a second time, to save the nation. I should say to them, "Vote, every one of you, for Grant, as you value property, life, wife, or child. If Greeley is elected, arm, concentrate, conceal your property, but organize for defence. You will need it soon, and sadly."

Workingmen, rally now, to save your great question from being crowded out, and postponed another four years.

Soldiers, at the roll-call in November, let no loyal man fail to answer to his name. We decorate our loyal graves with worse than empty ceremonies, if, over them, we clasp hands with still revengeful enemies. When parties and politicians betray us, do you rally, as you did before, and under the *same great captain*, save the State.

If Grant is defeated, I am not sure we shall see traitors in the Capitol, parting the nation's raiment, and casting lots for its flag. But we are sure to see Congress full of traitors, and in the White House their tool. Let every man who would avert that danger vote for Grant.

WENDELL PHILLIPS.

In September Mr. Phillips followed Gen. Butler in

a speech at Lynn, Mass., and again advocated the election of Grant. He began, —

"I shall not weary you, ladies and gentlemen. I shall not run any risk of wearying you, even by detaining you; because there is one element in Gen. Butler's oratory to which every one of you will bear witness now, — that he does not leave any thing for his successor to say. On the platform as in the camp, he cleans up so thoroughly and economically that there is nothing left to the general that comes after him. There was one general once that undertook to rule New Orleans after he had left it, and the record says he made a botch of it. I do not propose to follow in the footsteps of my illustrious predecessor. I do not propose to add an appendix to that earnest, sincere, eloquent, exhaustive, and, I think, unanswerable, argument. Why, then, you may ask, are you here? I am not a Republican. I never found myself before on a Republican platform. When I came here to-night, as some of you know full well, I came to the Republican platform at a moment when the greatest, the oldest, and most honored friend (Gen. Butler) of my life has quitted it. Why do I come here? I owe nothing to the Republican party: I ask nothing of it individually. I came here honestly, sincerely, from a full heart, because I think that to-day the great conflict is safe nowhere but in the Republican party. If I thought there were a question, if I thought it a matter upon which to an honest man there could be an honest difference of opinion, you would not see me here.

"You know me, some of you, for more than thirty years; for in your presence I have carried my heart on my sleeve, known and read of all men. You never heard me preach a rash confidence in a President: you never heard me ask you to put confidence in a political party. If I have had any mission in the thirty years of my Arab life, — my hand against every man, and every man's hand against me, — it was to preach the doctrine of the safety of distrust. I came to-night, to say to my fellow-citizens, Pour out your hearts like water, and hold up your hands, for Gen. Grant. He represents loyalty to-day, and salvation after that. It is not the man: I am not going to enumerate his faults; I know them: I am not going to catalogue his defects, for they are patent. I know all that can be said as a laboring man, as a temperance man, as an abolitionist, as a business man, of petty criticism against the government. I know Grant was said to have been drunk years ago, but so was Gratz Brown this year: and I know that Horace is said to be a teetotaler; so is Henry. It is, after all, six of one, and half a dozen of the other. As a temperance man, if there were time to note the difference between the two tickets, I think it would take a Philadelphia lawyer and a microscope of six million times magnifying power to find it out. It is not a matter of individual fault to-day.

"If Greeley, with all his faults, with all his nonsense, with all his weakness, — a bit of wet brown paper instead of a man, — had been nominated by the loyal party of these States; if the men that went up to Philadelphia representing peace, honesty in the payment of the debt, protection for every citizen, the law from Portland to New Orleans and San Francisco, had chosen to nominate Mr. Greeley, — I should have said, 'You run a great risk to take a blind pilot on stormy night; but go ahead, gentlemen; I trust the good ship. believe, even with him, we shall weather the storm.' But when party gathers together made up of every element that the country has had reason to dread for the last twenty years past, with a man at its head who never knew his own mind six days consecutively, I do not believe it. I do not look at the man. I see behind him the elements, the representatives of all the country has reason to dread. Now, if I were telling you of the two men, I should go back to two words of Old English which common men use very clumsily

NEARING THE END. 293

and loosely. You hear a man talking sometimes, who has heard that his brother has found a million dollars; and he says, 'I am very much disappointed.' He means he is surprised. You hear another, who has heard that a noted criminal has been arrested; and he says he is surprised. Now, when he is disappointed, it means that a man falls below his expectations. To be surprised means that a man gives you thought.

"I have known Mr. Greeley for forty years, and in every six months of those forty years I have been horribly disappointed in him. Failure after failure to meet the crises that have summoned him to manhood did not grind out faith in him, in my foolish confidence. I still continued in the crazy hope that a point would be reached by and by where the man would be found to have a principle. It never has been. Our friend Greeley has sacrificed all his life to save the remainder. He stands to-day the representative of every principle he has denounced: no man can deny it. On the contrary, I acknowledge I am the same man who came here in 1869, and lectured here, — "After Grant, what?" — and, every hour since, I have not been disappointed in Gen. Grant: I have been surprised. As Gen. Butler has said, it is not a question of men. The question is the last, perhaps — and I am not sure it is that — but one of the last struggles of a defeated section to place itself at the head of the government. Now, if I have studied any thing in my life, it is the temper and character of the Southern political leaders, and the Democratic leaders that followed with them at the North. If I know any thing, I pretend to know that; for I summered it and wintered it with all the intellect God gave me ever since I have been a man: and I say, as my judgment — with no honesty in the mere politics of the Republican party — I say that no sane man can say that this is not an attempt, with the sanction of Horace Greeley, of the Southern States, to do exactly what they did in the time of Andy Johnson, — to get back in disguise, and get control of the government. I know what a converted Democrat is. We had one of them. Andrew Johnson was a converted Democrat. Do you want another? We did not lose four years with him. We lost the golden hour of the rebellion: we lost the harvest of victory.

"The South outwitted us: she showed the greater statesmanship. When the question was confiscation, when the question was arrangement on the basis of security, when in the generous impulse of a triumphant moment the American people were ready to forgive, she foisted a converted Democrat upon us; and in those four years we lost fifty per cent of the value which the hundred thousand fresh-born graves and the three thousand millions of dollars had earned. I know what a converted Democrat is. I do not call my friend the general [Gen. Butler] a converted Democrat. I call him a sifted Democrat; since 1861 was the great sieve that took the promiscuous mass of the Democratic party, and sifted it, the pure flour from the chaff. Every man that answered to that bugle-call of national necessity, every true bit of metal that the magnet of the nation's danger drew out of the mass, like Gen. Dix and Gen. Butler, is a sifted Democrat. That was a thorough sifting. There is nothing but chaff left in what was the Democracy after that. There would be no use in having a second sifting, — none whatever. You know that the copperhead of your neighborhood is not any different now from last year. You would not trust him with the care of your martyred dead: you would not absent yourselves from the polls, and put into his hand the national debt. You know that as well as I do. Multiply that man by five or six millions, and he is the Democratic party that went up to Cincinnati. A man with half an eye open can see it, just as he could see that Mr. Greeley was their candidate before the convention was held. As long ago as the 12th of May, I said that Horace Greeley was the secession candidate. 'The Tribune' laughed at me: some of the newspapers said, 'That is one of Phillips's follies.' But it turned out to be so, and the disguise that was used was of the very slimmest."

After a brief reference to Gen. Butler's efforts to pass the Ku-klux bill through Congress, Mr. Phillips continued, —

"Gentlemen, this is a very serious generation to live in. There is no boys' play left for us. God laid on this generation the burden of weeding out the slave-system. They did it with the sacrifice of wealth and blood such as no nation has seen. He lays upon us now the burden of watchfulness. Mr. Sumner has said that revolutions never go back. That is true indeed of centuries, but it is terribly false of a dozen years. Poor, sad, overburdened France! Why, revolutions have been going back and back for years and years. Does any man suppose that Horace Greeley is foolish enough to imagine, that, if the Democratic party lift him into the White House, they will not dictate his cabinet? Who elects him? Liberal Republicans? Where are they? I venture to say, and no man says it with a sadder heart, that the great, the honored name of the Democratic candidate for the governorship of this State, with all its undoubted honesty, will not take a thousand votes from the Republican party next November. If there is any difference in the number of Democratic votes that lift him into notice, it will be similar to the one that lifted Jack Adams into his place last year. Liberal Republicanism is nothing but Ku-Kluxism disguised; and behind it is Jeff Davis, Banks, and other men, who miscalculated their chances. There is one man, however, who, if elected to the presidency, would have strength of will to resist the demands of the Democracy. I believe the Democratic candidate for the governorship is so thoroughly persuaded they are all Liberal Republicans who would support him, that, if he were to be placed in the White House, he would, in the sublime serenity of his content, imagine that he owed nothing to the Democratic party. He would not allow a point in very strength or weakness; but, from the unalterable conviction that the State of Massachusetts owed him the chair, he would pursue the even tenor of his way undisturbed by petty calls."

Mr. Phillips paid a high tribute to the pertinacity and watchfulness of the South, bade Republicans be on their guard, for secession never slept, and concluded as follows: —

"The reason why I support the Republican party, is that to my utter surprise, to my unutterable surprise, to my indescribable delight, to my relief, I have at last found a party that is willing to execute all the laws that are given them. It is for that reason that I say, Long live Ulysses Grant! May he continue to be President of the United States until every white man over forty years of age who lives south of Mason and Dixon's line has been forever put into the ground!"

The occasions on which Mr. Phillips manifested his sympathy for the Irish cause are so numerous, that volume after volume could be filled with his speeches upon that theme alone. Like the true friend, he ever appeared at the time his services were most needed. When, in 1873, James Anthony Froude came over from England to slur the Irish name, and destroy Irish influence, he was met by the clear, ringing replies of Mr. Phillips at the very threshold; and his calumnies were hurled back upon him with fearful force.

Speaking of Froude's visit to this country, and answering the falsehoods of that apologizer of England's crimes, Mr. Phillips said, —

"I think Mr. Froude's arrival, and his course in this country, have had one very beneficial effect: they have lifted the Irish question into full notice, and into far juster appreciation among the American people. Mr. Froude's arrival has led the American journals and public men to ask, 'Why does an English scholar refer this question to us?' There was great surprise expressed that he had not chosen some other topic. If he is a historian, as men claim; if he is a brilliant scholar, as certainly he is, — why not choose, from the abundant treasure-house of English subjects, something of deeper interest, and of greater importance. Men said to the American people, 'What have we to do with the relations of Great Britain and Ireland?' Well, I was never surprised for a moment that Mr. Froude chose this special question to lay before the grand jury of the American people. I was never surprised that any Englishman solicitous for the good name of his country, or any patriotic man desirous of wiping away the eclipse on the good fame of England, should clutch the opportunity to explain to the world, through an appeal to the grand jury of the American people, the relations between his own country and Ireland, and the reason why England, up to this moment, has failed in doing any thing noticeable in the way of justice or statesmanship toward the sister island.

"Just look at it. Two years ago, there was a great war in Europe. France was ground to powder under the heel of a military power. What does France represent? She represents ideas: she represents the democratic instinct and progress of Europe. Ever since the days of Thomas Jefferson she has inspired the democracy of Europe; and it would hardly be an exaggeration to say, that, when that great American penned the Declaration of Independence, he borrowed the inspiration of it from France. Ever since, she has occupied the van in Europe in the war of men against institutions, of brains against military power. What does Prussia represent? She represents the re-organized feudal system of the nineteenth century. She is a power marshalled into form by the one purpose of court and soldiers. She is not a nation: she is an army. Her great public schools and all her civil life have a great, if not primary, purpose in the design to make men soldiers. Every man of the population — banker, mechanic, tradesman, or scholar, — every thing but the pulpit — goes, for the three appointed years, into the camp, to be disciplined to arms; and Prussia's policy is an effort to drag the world back three hundred years. She is the great military outgrowth, the abnormal monstrosity, of the nineteenth century. And still, for the moment, — for the present hour, — she has ground France, the representative of ideas, to powder under her foot. It was a crisis, not so much between two nations as between two civilizations. It was an awful struggle, pregnant with most enormous results to Europe. Where was England?

"When Bismarck smote her contemptuously in the face, in the presence of all Europe, why did she not draw her sword? She never had been reluctant to draw the sword. She had been the great intermeddler for the last three centuries. There could not be a crisis in the remotest corner of the globe, about the most insignificant motive in the world, that England did not put in her mailed hand. Palmerston's laurels were all won from meddling in other people's messes. If China wished to give up opium, England wished it to be there. If Portugal and Spain differed, Canning must send his fleet to watch over the safety of Lisbon. She never knew a war that she could leave alone. Why did she break the great historic precedent of two hundred years in this single instance?

"Seven years ago I was hissed in the Cooper Institute for saying that England was a second-rate power, and that she no longer dared to take a place among the first-class powers of Europe. Now, in my view, the reason why she did not draw the sword is twofold. One is, that she can hardly trust her own masses; but the larger and closer reason is, that the English statesmen know right well that the first cannon-shot they dare to aim at any first-rate power, Ireland stabs them in the back.

"Seven hundred years of oppression have earned the traditional right of opposition, whose creation is four millions of men, every one of whom hates England with right good cause. And English statesmanship knows that either France, Germany, or Russia has only to land twenty thousand men, one hundred and fifty thousand stand of arms, and ten millions of pounds, in Ireland, and England is checkmated: she cannot move hand or foot.

"Mr. Froude said, with great truth and epigrammatic terseness, that, 'No matter how long God waited, the wickedness of one generation was sure to be punished by the weakness of another.' How true it is, that the wickedness of the Edwards, the Henrys, the Elizabeths, and the Stuarts is punished to-day, in the face of Europe, by the weakness of Victoria, checkmated on her throne. I do not wonder at all that the thoughtful Englishman should long to explain to the world, if he can, how the steps by which his country has been brought to this state have been inevitable; that by no wit of statesmanship, by no generosity of high-toned and magnanimous honor, could she have avoided the path in which she is treading. If Mr. Froude could make out that proposition; if he could convince the world through the American people that England accepted the inevitable fate which the geographical proximity of Ireland had entailed upon her, — it would have gone half way to wipe out the blots on his country's fame. I do not wonder he should make the attempt. I believe, that instead of England's having conquered Ireland, in the true, essential statement of the case, as it stands to-day, Ireland has conquered England! She has summoned her before the bar of the civilized world, to answer and plead for the justice of her legislation; she has checkmated her as a power on the chess-board of Europe; she has monopolized the attention of her statesmen; she has made her own island the pivot upon which the destiny of England turns; and her last great statesmen and present Prime Minister, Mr. Gladstone, owes whatever fame he has, to the supposition that at last he has devised a way by which he can conciliate Ireland, and *save* his own country.

"I thank Mr. Froude that he has painted the Irishman as a chronic rebel. It shows that at least the race knew that they were oppressed, and gathered together all the strength that God had given them to resist. They never rested contented. It is by no means, therefore, a surprise that a patriotic Englishman, looking back on the last three centuries, should long to justify his nation and his own race, after having conceited that it has all the brains, and two-thirds of the heart, of the world. It volunteered to be the guardian of this obstinate Ireland. It volunteered to furnish a government to the distracted, ignorant, poverty-stricken, demoralized millions of Ireland. It has been three hundred years at the experiment; and Mr. Froude told us the other evening, that, rather than let Ireland go, — weary of their long failure, — rather than let Ireland go, they would exterminate the Irish race! What a confession of statesmanship! 'We have tried for seven hundred years to manufacture a government, and at the end of it our alternative is extermination!'

"Well, you see, the world asks, whence comes this result? Was the English race incapable? Did it lack courage? Did it lack brains? Did it lack care? Did it lack common sense? Did it lack that discriminating sagacity which knows time and place?

NEARING THE END.

What is the reason of the failure? And, of course, the only answer of an Englishman who is unwilling to tear down the great splendor of his flag, is, to find the cause in the dogged incapacity of Ireland, and not in any lack of his own country. Mr. Froude is obliged to prove that the Irish were left by God *unfinished*, and that you cannot, by any wit of man, manufacture a citizen out of an Irishman. He is shut up to this argument: for, unless he proves the Irishman a knave, he is obliged, from the facts of the case, to confess England a fool; and that is the grand alternative. They have had time enough, power enough, and opportunity enough, and why have they not created a government? Why have they not conciliated Ireland? Why have they not satisfied the citizens of the world that the task has been accomplished? Why does Europe cry out 'Shame,' until within a dozen years? Suppose that we should remain with the South in our right hand, — passive and powerless as she is to-day, — that we should remain in that attitude for one hundred years, and that, at the end of it, the South was just as defiant, just as demoralized, just as hostile, and just as lacking in good government, and the mechanism of industrial prosperity, as she is to-day, what would be the fact, patent on that showing? Why, that we were incapable of the task we had assumed.

"That is where Mr. Froude finds England: and he is shut up — logically speaking — shut up to the necessity of proving that Ireland lacks the elements — that the Celtic race lacks the elements — that go to make up self-government, statesmanship, and a law-abiding community; that they are unwilling to associate with the great movements of the British race. He comes, therefore, to us with that purpose. He comes to excuse England on the ground of Irish incapacity. Well, it was a marvellously bad choice of a jury: for, in the first place, there were a number of logical, middle-aged gentlemen, who met in Philadelphia, on the fourth day of

July, 1776, and asserted that God created every man fit to be a citizen; that he did not leave any race so half made up and half finished, that they were to travel through the cycle of seven hundred years under the guardianship of any power. And, on that fourth day of July, they established the corner-stone of American political faith, that all men are capable of self-government; while the whole substratum of this course of lectures, by this eloquent British scholar, was the fact that God left Ireland so unfinished that a merciful despotism was necessary."

This address was received with unbounded applause, and deserves to be read by all students of Irish wrongs.

Mr. Phillips with his family spent the summer of 1873 at Swámpscott. For several months he gave no public utterance, except upon certain local improvements about Boston, and before purely lyceum audiences. As a lecturer, his services were always in demand.

On the 15th of December of this year, the New-England Woman-suffrage Association had a celebration at Faneuil Hall. Never was a finer-appearing or more intelligent company of ladies and gentlemen assembled in "the old Cradle." Col. Higginson presided; and addresses were made by Mr. Phillips, Mrs. Livermore, James Freeman Clarke, Fred Douglass, Mr. Garrison, Mrs. Lucy Stone, and others. The following resolution was unanimously adopted: —

"Whereas, a bill has just been introduced into the Senate of the United States by Mr. Frelinghuysen to disfranchise the women of Utah, and subject them to the proscriptions of the common law of England; therefore, be it

"*Resolved*, That this assembly of men and women of New England, as convened in Faneuil Hall to celebrate the enfranchisement of the Boston Tea Party, unite in calling upon Congress to modify or defeat the bill."

On Tuesday evening the "ladies' tea-party" came off in the hall, Josiah Quincy presiding. Speeches were made by several of Boston's favorites, and Mr. Emerson read a characteristic poem.

In the spring of 1874 Mr. Phillips lectured several times on the subject of temperance. At Tremont Temple he began by saying, —

"This is the largest audience that I have seen within these walls for fourteen years, since the outbreak of the great Rebellion; and I hope it foretells the outbreak of a greater rebellion still, — of the people of New-England against the tyranny of the grog-shop."

Mr. Phillips spoke very frequently on this important theme, and argued, with great force, against license, and for a complete closing of the rum-shops. He believed that alcohol was the cause, not only in great part of poverty among the laboring-classes, but also of corruption in high places, especially in the governments of large cities.

On the 22d of July Mr. Phillips addressed the following letter to George J. Holyoake, on the "Labor Problem." It shows that its author thought deeply, and was continually studying this great question.

Boston, July 22, 1874.

To G. J. HOLYOAKE.

My dear Sir, — I ought long ago to have thanked you for sending me copies of your pamphlets, and with so kind and partial a recognition of my co-operation with you in your great cause. That on Mill was due certainly to a just estimate of him, but how sad that human jackals should make it necessary! Those on co-operation I read again and again, welcoming the light you throw on it; for it is one of my most hopeful stepping-stones to a higher future. Thank you for the lesson: it cleared one or two dark places — not the first I owe you, by any means; for I've read every thing of yours I could lay my hands on. There was one small volume on rhetoric, "Methods of address, hints towards effective speech," etc., which I studied faithfully, until some one, to whom I had praised it and loaned it, acting, probably, on something like Coleridge's rule, that books belong to those who most need them, never returned me my well-thumbed essay, to my keen regret. Probably you never knew that we pirated your book. This was an American reprint, wholly exhausted, — proof that it did good service. We reprinted, some ten years ago, one of your wisest tracts, "The *difficulties* that obstruct co-operation." It did us yeomanly service.

I wish I could have an hour's talk with you on this labor and capital question, — one, perhaps, to have as angry an agitation as slavery caused. Wealth, with you, governs; but its power is, I suppose, somewhat masked, sometimes countervailed or checked by other forces. With us it rules, bare, naked, shameless, undisguised. Our *incorporated* wealth, often wielded by a single hand, is fearful with direct, and still more with indirect, power. We have single men who wield four hundred million dollars, so shaped that towns, counties, States, are its vassals. Two or three united railways (*one* president) will subject a State to their will. Vanderbilt is reported to say, "It is cheaper and surer to buy Legislatures than voters." This is the peril of universal suffrage. Then, rum rules our great cities whenever it chooses to exert its power. The sadness of the whole thing is, one hardly sees whence the cure is to come. I *believe* I don't *see* Truly our movements demand a most patient faith. I never expected to see any success of our anti-slavery struggle. Fortified in church, state, and capital, the system would have outlived this generation, and perhaps the next, with ordinary shrewdness on the part of its friends The gods made them mad on their way to destruction, and so hastened it.

Neither shall I live long enough to see any marked result of our labor-movement here, though it is true that our masses ripen marvellously quick; but, as you've said, the cliques, jealousies, distrust, and ignorance of workingmen are our chief obstacles. Indeed, we sometimes get better help from open-hearted capitalists. Your ranks are infinitely better trained than ours to stand together on some one demand just long enough to be counted, and so insure that respect which numbers always command in politics where universal suffrage obtains. Then we'd have all the *brains* of the land, our servants, and soon gain that *attention* which is *here* half of success. But I suppose all this is familiar to you, as well as the strength we expect from related questions, — finances, mode of taxation, land, tenure, etc. There'll never be, I believe and trust, a class-party here, labor against capital, the lines are so indefinite, like dove's-neck colors. Three-fourths of our population are to some extent capitalists; and, again, all see that there is really, and ought always to be, alliance, not struggle, between them. So we lean chiefly on related questions for growth : limitation of hours is almost the only special measure. But enough.

"I shall beg you to accept a volume of old speeches, printed long ago, because it includes my only attempt to criticise you, which you probably never saw I will put, when I mail it, the last and best photograph of Sumner; and, if you exchange, I will add one of

>Yours, faithfully and ever,

>>WENDELL PHILLIPS.

The exact and definite statement of Gen. Sheridan, and the moderate and conclusive message of President Grant to Congress, relative to the disorders and the action of the military in Louisiana, in the winter of 1874–75, wrought a wonderful effect upon public sentiment, causing the sustainers of the administration to be prouder than ever of the promptitude, decision, and humanity of their officers, while it forced the hasty and inconsiderate critics in the Republican ranks to take the defensive, and at least taught them a lesson to beware of alliances with their opponents.

The evidence is conclusive, that the tactics of the white Leaguers, on the 4th of January, at New Orleans, was the commencement of a plot to revolutionize the State. Fortunately it was nipped in the bud by the promptness of De Trobriand and Sheridan. Whatever may be said of Gen. Sheridan's characterization of the "white rebels" of Louisiana, he held the city of New Orleans in perfect order from the time when he first entered its streets. Gen. Butler was the city's first "monster:" Gen. Sheridan proved to be the second.

The decisive action of Gen. Sheridan put all the rebellious element of the country into a ferment; and many worthy men who voted for Greeley, or who did not approve all the measures of President Grant, were too ready to be panic-stricken by their effervescence. Not a few public meetings were held to "rebuke the administration."

In New York one such meeting was held at the Academy of Music, at which William Cullen Bryant and William M. Evarts were the only conspicuous Republicans participating. The Democracy were present in full force, and were profuse in their resolutions of censure.

In Boston the gathering was held on Jan. 15, at Faneuil Hall. The call was stimulated by Democrats, and a larger proportion of nominal Republicans than was the case in New York. The petition to the city government for the use of the hall had one hundred names, a large proportion written in one hand, and many of the alleged subscribers with no residence in Boston, though professing to be legal voters in the metropolis. The gathering, save so far as the Democratic element went, was virtually a failure, the speaking tame, the interruptions quite suggestive. The marked characteristic was the absence of a goodly portion of those who placed their names to the call.

The most remarkable fact to be recorded, however, is, that the meeting was turned against its projectors by its attendants, who insisted on hearing from Wendell Phillips, who, quietly standing in the gallery, was watching the development of the plot to play into the hands of the rebels at the South, and rebel sympathizers at the North; and who, with masterly logic and eloquence, carried an undoubted majority of his listeners with him. This was shown by the responses to his various points, but more particularly by the vote on the resolution thanking Grant and Sheridan, where the volume of affirmative voices was equal to the negative, though the latter were given with more explosive force than is possible with the sibilant "yes." Mr. Phillips's argument is worthy of being read and re-read by all students of the history of that period.[1]

At two of the meetings of the financial department of the American Social Science Association in March, Mr. Phillips gave his views of the financial problem. His plan for bettering the state of affairs was, to, 1st, take from the national banks all right to issue bills; 2d, to let the nation itself supply a currency ample for all public needs; 3d, to reduce the rate of interest. He objected to any attempt to secure a specie basis as injurious. Time and circumstances alone, he thought, would make greenbacks equal to gold, — yes, better than gold. To take from national banks all right to issue bills, and to oblige them to return what bills they had within a reasonable time, would, he claimed, put greenbacks on a par with gold, and would secure the

---

[1] See Phillips's Speeches, etc., 2d series.

government enough gold to meet its obligations until that happened. Mr. Phillips would allow any person to do what banks were then allowed to do, — that is, to deposit national bonds, and receive from the nation greenbacks in exchange, with this difference, however, that such depositor should receive the full amount of the bond, and pay for the use of such greenbacks three or four per cent per annum. Why, he asked, should not an individual be allowed to borrow greenbacks on a bond, as well as banks? Why should either of them be allowed this privilege without paying for it? Mr. Phillips argued that the high rate of interest was the cause of business depression, and only by its reduction could the laboring and trading classes prosper.

On the 6th of August, 1875, the centennial of the birth of the Irish patriot, Daniel O'Connell, a grand celebration was held in the Boston Music Hall. By request, Mr. Phillips delivered an oration on the great Irishman. It was a wonderfully eloquent production, and showed the orator's powers at their best. It has already become a historic document, as one of the best and most truthful analyses of the agitator's character that has ever yet received the honor of print. One cannot but admire, in reading it, the faithfulness of Mr. Phillips to his convictions, as, before that audience of Irishmen, Roman Catholics, and Democrats, as nearly all of them were, he elevated the character of Martin Luther, securing rapturous applause for that great reformer, and equally did justice to the anti-slavery cause as exemplified alike by O'Connell in past days, and the colored workmen (who sent a telegram to the meeting) in these.

It is such orations as these, filled with pregnant thought, and eulogistic of men who have unselfishly served their country, that the young men of to-day should study for proper fitting for the responsibilities of the future.[1]

During the years 1876–77, the life of Mr. Phillips was chiefly that of a public lecturer. During the season he travelled far and wide, and spoke before many audiences. To chronicle his whereabouts in these months would be a task without a purpose. In many places his voice was raised in behalf of the cause of Temperance, — a theme of which he never wearied. At other times he spoke in favor of preserving the "Old South Meeting-house" in Boston, which many persons of severe business tact were desirous of seeing razed to the ground. Again, he recalled before several audiences the life and achievements of Daniel O'Connell; spoke on education, on various political questions of the time; and delivered eulogies, before public and private assemblies, on Charles Sumner, and other contemporaries who had passed away.

In the month of May, 1877, he delivered, at the Old

---

[1] See Phillips's Speeches and Lectures, 2d series.

South, for the first time, his exceedingly eloquent and entertaining lecture on Sir Harry Vane. It was repeated before numerous audiences in Boston and elsewhere, and with the exception of that on "The Lost Arts," and that on O'Connell, was, perhaps, the most brilliant effort of the sort ever prepared by the orator. Mr. Phillips was a great admirer of Vane, and made many allusions to him and his accomplishments in his public speaking. He referred to him notably in his famous Phi Beta Kappa oration of 1881, and held him up as a bright and shining example for youth. "It is a pity," said Mr. Phillips to the present writer one day, "that we have no readable biography of Sir Harry Vane! Of all lives, that of Vane, the first Republican, most merits the attention and study of young Americans."

During the autumn of 1877 a slight effort was made to induce Mr. Phillips to accept a nomination for governor of the State. Several letters were printed in the newspapers on the subject, but the effort progressed no farther. We give one as a sample, which contains some features of interest: —

"*Editor 'Commonwealth,'* — Were it not for the habit of Mr. Phillips of allowing his name to be used by Tom, Dick, and Harry, and *his* sister, we verily believe he might be elected governor this fall. There is no other difficulty in the way whatever, and this may itself be to many voters a strong recommendation. It is well known that Mr. Phillips deliberately throws his weight into the scale of the weakest side, provided it be deserving, without much care for himself. Thus he has come to be considered a woman-suffragist, prohibitionist, labor-reformer, and soft-money man, without satisfactory grounds. On the currency question alone has he been more than usually explicit; and yet it cannot be shown that he differs, in any sensible degree, from the majority of those whose interests are not involved as shippers or importers, or as agents for foreign houses. Until our people have definitely acted upon the pending question, as to whether the government greenback shall or shall not be retained, no fault can be found with Mr. Phillips. He thinks it *ought* to be. So do we, and so do many thousands more. He thinks it ought to be kept close up to par: so does everybody. But in arguing in favor of such an augmentation of volume as may not be inconsistent therewith, under the stress of increasing business and population, he is, as usual, a little in advance of the rest of us — that is all. It may transpire that he has caught hold of the tail-end of a largish-sized fish, which some one else will have to help bring to land. As a provision against our old-fashioned periodical panics, it is the only one that has been proposed, so far as we know; and, indeed, it seems hardly to have been thought of.

"What the views of Mr. Phillips may be on these and other matters is wholly immaterial. As governor he could neither give us greenbacks nor prohibition if he desired so to do. It is simply a complimentary position to which he is richly entitled. We should have no fear of placing Wendell *anywhere*. What he may *say*, in the character of advocate, is one thing: what he would *do*, as a sitting magistrate, is quite another. We would like to see Wendell elected any way. It is not quite safe to say, that, in the ensuing quadrangular fight, he may not be. Certain it is, that, if every man in the Commonwealth who is friendly to Mr. Phillips should vote for him, he would carry the position by storm.

"Devotee."

NEARING THE END. 313

In the autumn of this year the famous Grant-Sumner controversy came again prominently before the public. The facts in the case are now too well known to be rehearsed. The subject is here brought forward for the purpose of placing Mr. Phillips's "statement" on record. In a lecture which he delivered in Newton, Mass., he said, —

"Gen. Grant has thrown the weight of his name against Mr. Sumner. I have a great respect for Gen. Grant. I have been a Grant man when Faneuil Hall hissed me for it. I acknowledge his merits. I have no doubt of his sincere patriotism. But Gen. Grant must remember, that, when he impeaches history and the loftiest patriotism, there are blows to take as well as to give, and it is himself that provoked the quarrel. I have always known Mr. Sumner as the most methodical, laborious, painstaking, and business-like member of the Senate. The only members of Congress, in my day, who have had a regular ledger, or docket, of public employment and engagements, were Gen. B. F. Butler and Mr. Charles Sumner. They were the only two members of Congress that I ever knew to do business on business principles, and I felt great surprise and indignation when the charge of negligence of public business was made by Gen. Grant against Mr. Sumner. It was only outdone by the intimation that Charles Sumner had told a falsehood. As Schurz says in his eulogy, he was so direct, he could not carry any thing by a flank movement. His nature was incapable of concealment. He had none of the usual tact of men who push their plans in the world. He made up for it by superhuman energy, with which he bore down all opposition.

"The case to which Gen. Grant refers is the removal of Mr. Sumner from the chairmanship of the Committee on Foreign Relations, which he says was proper and justifiable, because Mr. Sumner was negligent of public duty, and the confirmation of the act is found in the charge that Mr. Sumner had been detected in a falsehood. You remember Mr. Sumner's singular fitness for that chairmanship. Carl Schurz says no chairman ever came to the office so eminently fitted for it. This is the man removed for negligence, for leaving his pigeon-holes full of treaties. You remember the position of Mr. Fish when Sumner was deposed. You remember that the whole North surged with hot indignation. When did Gen. Grant first find this out against Sumner? Why did they not think of this before? Why never utter it till now? If the opposition papers had known that Mr. Sumner was negligent, would they not have told of it? No: this charge is an after-thought. If it had been true, we should have heard of it from every chamber of types in the country. Go to the Republican papers and the anti-Grant papers: they never heard of these charges.

"But Gen. Grant says that Mr. Sumner lied. I remember the occasion. Pardon me if I recite it. Mr. Sumner received from the hands of Gen. Grant the treaty of San Domingo, — from Gen. Grant, who drove up to his door while he was sitting with some friends at dinner-table. He said to the President, 'I will look at the bill. I trust I shall have the pleasure of supporting the administration.' They were words of politeness, of courtesy merely, without having examined the instrument. When he went home, and examined it, he found the dark treachery to the black race. The next day he found Gen. Grant, and took back even the courteous words. He pointed out the objections to the treaty, laid before him the impossibility of his supporting it, and urged a reconsideration of the action of the administration. Gen. Grant listened in silence, — perhaps I might say sullen silence. There was present a gentleman who has been in Washington for forty years, and he came away with Mr. Sumner. As they came down the stairs of the executive mansion, the gentleman remarked,

'What is the matter with the President? Do you think he understands you?'—'I should think he might,' replied Sumner. 'No, he doesn't,' was the response: 'he is in no state to understand any thing.' If Grant never heard that Sumner took back that courteous pledge in the chamber of the White House, it was because his brain refused to perform its office. He is no judge of the veracity of the senator from Massachusetts.

"Gen. Grant also refers to the action of Mr. Sumner in vindication of his friend, Mr. Motley. The case is a grave one. It concerns one of the noblest Americans who upheld our fame abroad. Gen. Grant intimates that he was no American. I knew Lothrop Motley from boyhood. It is very true, that, in his earlier European life, he drank too deep of the foreign spirit. In 1838 and 1840, he was largely European. But at his return to this country, ten years before the war, he told me, 'This is the greatest country in the world. This is a noble nation to work for. It is the noblest people. I have come back from Europe, and have relearned the value of America; have come home one of the humblest laborers, to make justice and liberty prosper.' It came from his heart. He was made over into a most enthusiastic American. I was not surprised when he sprang to the helm in the columns of the London 'Times.' It was an echo of the old talks on the sidewalks. When Grant appointed him to England, he appointed the warmest American heart that ever beat.

"Now, when the senator has been in Mount Auburn for three years, when his pen cannot write a denial, nor his lips utter a rebuke, now, from a foreign shore, bearing a lie on its lips, comes this accusation, that this senator, who never was absent from the Senate one hour (Mr. Sumner told me, in the last year of his life, 'I never was absent one hour till the last twelvemonth'), that this senator was removed for negligence. Find me one other man who has not lost weeks, or even months, by absence. Mr. Sumner refused opportunities to make hundreds of dollars by lecturing, because he was bound by his duties in the Senate.

"In the quarrel with Mr. Motley, the records in the State department, in black and white, prove that the administration stooped to a falsehood. Mr. Fish exhorted Mr. Sumner to take the British mission, — told him he ought to go to London. Six months later the minister was recalled, on the ground that he had leaned too much upon the opinion of a great Northern senator. Mr. Sumner's indignant exclamation to Mr. Fish was, 'If Mr. Motley's leaning was an unpardonable sin, by what right did you sit in my study six months ago, and urge me to go to England, and press my views on the Alabama claims?' He said then and there, 'Sir, you are a tool of the President for base purposes; and this removal is out of spite.' And it is true. The testimony is on the files of the diplomatic service itself."

Ex-secretary of state, Hon. Hamilton Fish, subsequently affirmed that Mr. Sumner, while chairman of the Foreign-Affairs Committee, was exceedingly negligent of the duties of his office; that the "reasons" for the removal of Mr. Sumner from the chairmanship "never existed;" that Mr. Sumner was not removed from his position, but that his time "simply expired." He said further, the statement that President Grant placed the San-Domingo treaty in Mr. Sumner's hands, as related by Mr. Phillips, was "ridiculously untrue;" that the President never had the treaty-papers in his possession; that Mr. Sumner favored the treaty until the selection of a commissioner came up for settlement, and that, when he found that J. M. Ashley of Ohio was not to be the nominee, he then all at once lost interest in the treaty, and finally placed himself in direct opposition to it. The conversation between the President and Mr. Sumner on the subject took place toward the last of December, 1869; and, in February following, Mr. Fish says, two senators (Carl Schurz, and Mr. Stewart of Nevada), gentlemen of opposite political views, canvassed the Senate, and found that the treaty could not pass that body, — that it was dead. Upon the meeting of the new Congress in 1871, Mr. Sumner failed of being re-appointed to the chairmanship. Mr. Fish thought that there were good reasons for his being left off the committee at that time. He was not on speaking-terms with either the President or the secretary of state, — a most unpleasant condition of affairs, thought Mr. Fish, to exist between the holder of so important a position as Mr. Sumner filled, and the first officers of the administration.

Mr. Fish's statement of the case called forth many responses, nearly all of them in opposition. In a lecture before an audience in Cambridge, Mass., Mr. Phillips replied to Mr. Fish's allegations in language from which we quote as follows: —

"Mr. Fish guessed that the reason Mr. Sumner did not vote for the project was because Ashley of Ohio — a favorite of Sumner's — was refused a place on the commission. This is as false as the claim of Mr. Grant. Mr. Sumner's opposition to it was bitter, and he opposed it to the fullest extent. It was to do that very thing that he went to the United-States Senate. Was it not devotion to the principle he illustrated which characterized his whole life? The policy of duty urged him on in one direction during his whole public career, and he never departed from it a hair's-breadth. The matter of Ashley's appointment to the San-Domingo commission had nothing to do with Sumner's opposition. You have but to examine records and documents to see, that while the matter was being discussed, and before the commission had been thought of, Mr. Sumner denounced the project in deep accents as the road to hell. The annexation, he said, would lead to the wreck of the two governments, — one in reputation, and one in the matter of its very existence. Those who know Mr. Sumner, know that it was not Ashley's disappointment which fired the great heart. It is not a question of the statement of Mr. Fish, and the silent refutation of Senator Sumner dead. We do not need to judge the likelihood of the truth of the allegation by the dead senator's sincerity of purpose, veracity of utterance, purity of mind. There are dates, and there is the ineffaceable evidence in black and white. Every word he spoke in public, every letter he sent or received, is still recorded: every place he went to is marked. This evidence we will submit. Mr. Sumner was always found in the right place saying the right thing."

In February, 1880, Mr. Phillips addressed a "plain talk" to a committee at the State House, in Boston, on the license system. He said, —

"I confess that I have no satisfaction whatever in addressing the Legislature or its committee on this subject of reform. We might as well address masks. Not a member of any political party has the courage to act as he thinks. The Legislature and the city government are an organized hypocrisy. They have all the light they want upon the subject now, but do not dare to pass a prohibitory law, for rum rules the government. It is simply a question of public agitation. You know well enough, that any law you may pass will not be enforced; and you only give it to us as a blind. The police are in league with the rum-sellers, and point out to passers-by the side-doors where they may enter, if they do not know where they are. The shop which the policeman searches, he knows contains no liquor, — that it is in the next cellar. There is an organized arrangement between the police and the rum-sellers. If there were any law or purpose in the Commonwealth, the mayor of Boston could put forth his hand, and crush these illegal sellers. Neither the mayor nor any alderman dares raise his hand against them. The police do not try to enforce the law; but, as one of the captains of the police stated, if the chief will allow them to execute the law, they could do it. The city officials know it would be suicide for any individual alderman or candidate for the mayoralty to take a pronounced and decided ground on the side of temperance. I have been told, in regard to other laws placed upon your statute-books, that they were placed there to cheat, — notably the law relative to colored school-children. This liquor-law is placed there to cheat. Liquor-drinking costs the country six or seven hundred millions of dollars. It is being said that universal suffrage cannot be continued. Universal suffrage is the highest element of civilization. When we were willing to risk the experiment of trusting the government into the hands of the people, we made the greatest stride that history recalls. When State Street looks down into a baby's cradle, it knows, if that baby is not educated in morality, its own house is not safe. And yet it cannot be denied that the mayor and aldermen for forty years have been any more than a standing-committee of the grog-shops. Some say, 'Surrender!' I say, 'Fight it!' Something can be found by Yankee ingenuity to meet and overthrow this curse. We know what we want. We want the sale prohibited. We don't care what a man does in his own parlor. He may drink his champagne or whiskey, and we don't care. But the moment a man opens his shop, and sells, we will interfere. The moment he undertakes to sell liquor, the State has an absolute and unlimited right to step in. The question demands the extreme use of this power. Every man familiar with the execution of the law knows that three-fourths of crime is due to rum, which fills your prisons and almshouses, and burdens your gallows. In every case in Great Britain and this country where the rum-shops have been closed, freedom from crime, freedom from taxation, follows. The law is unchanging: no liquor, no crime; no liquor, no tax. Wherever the English blood flows, it would seem that the stimulus of the stomach had supreme power. There are over two hundred laws of this Legislature endeavoring to curb this devil, but every one knows that we have never succeeded in curbing it for a moment. All over the State you will find whole towns that have been sold for a rum-debt. There was no law in the city on that sunny afternoon in October when Garrison was trampled underfoot. So it is to-day. There has not been a mayor for forty years who would enforce a liquor-law, and there won't be for forty years to come. There is not a Republican to-day who can look into another Republican's face, and think of the license-law, without laughing. It is but the tub thrown to the whale. A gentleman told me, that, though he could not open his door without looking upon hell, he did not wish to complain of the patrolman; for he was a good friend of his. He explained to me clearer than ordinary fiction, how the policeman was dependent upon the rum-seller for his baton. When you passed the civil-damage bill last year, you struck the traffic a dire blow. The boot is on the other leg when damages are left with juries, and not with mayors and aldermen. The law rests on a logical basis, on a moral basis. If intemperance impoverishes the country, what the devil do you want a license-law for? Prohibition means something. License has been tried in every shape. As long ago as 1837 the fifteen-gallon law was tried, and numerous other devices have been tried since; but we have never gained a point. Every man who walks the street, knows, that, whenever we have had a prohibitory law, there has been an immediate change in the amount of drinking. Under the license-law, sometimes less arrests are reported; but there is nothing so easy to make lie as figures. If a poor man get his wheel caught in a rut, there will seven policemen rush to his rescue; but let there be a drunken row, you won't find a policeman within forty rods. There are four thousand rum-shops in Boston; and taking these four thousand, and their four thousand best customers, you will have eight thousand votes, — a larger number than decides any election. You can't execute a license-law. If you enact another license-law, I shall say you are hiding behind your political responsibility."

In his discussion of the liquor-question, Mr. Phillips did not address himself wholly to the "fathers" at the State House. With the opening of the spring season, he became intensely wrought up on the subject of rum and its kindred poisons, and gave full vent to his feelings and opinions in the following address to the liberal clergy of Boston, and to Rev. Dr. C. A. Bartol in particular: —

PHILLIPS TO BARTOL.

THE LIBERAL CLERGY AND THE INTERESTS OF RUM.

It seems a little disrespectful to Dr. Bartol for us temperance-men not to notice his struggles with the whispers of his own conscience. I would cheerfully reply to him if I could see any thing to answer; but in all seriousness, and with no intention of sarcasm or disrespect, I can find nothing in his sermons worthy of notice. The statement he makes in one sentence, he takes back in the following one; and the objection which one paragraph notices, he himself disposes of the next moment. Outside of what Dr. Miner has made way with, all is trifling and immaterial, with one exception. In his second discourse he asserted that the temperance lodges were the nests and "hiding-places of nameless vice." am not a member of any temperance-lodge, and have nothing to do with this accusation; but, if the members of those lodges sit down silent under such a public charge, we are at liberty to believe them guilty. I presume Dr. Bartol would not make so grave an accusation without having in his possession what he thinks ample evidence of its truth. If the members of such lodges should claim of him to prove or retract it, of course he is man enough to do so. In the mean time I wish to offer the public two pictures:—

My first is the West-church pulpit in 1826. Rev. Dr. Charles Lowell fills it, the father of the poet, Russell Lowell; but Dr. Lowell need borrow no lustre from his illustrious son. Boston honored and loved him as few of his contemporaries were loved and honored. In his diary the late Samuel J. May records,—

"In May, 1826, I attended the anniversaries in Boston. Among them I attended the annual meeting of the Massachusetts Society for the Suppression of Intemperance, and afterward a meeting ministers called together in the vestry of the First Church,—the Chauncy-place Church,—to consider what was our special duty ministers. Several things were said that moved me deeply. At length Dr. Lowell rose, and, having added a few words in further delineation of the frightful ravages of intemperance, said, with sweet solemnity of manner, 'We can at least do one thing,— we can ourselves set a good, yes, a perfect, example. Let us abstain wholly from the use of whatever can intoxicate. If such example should be generally followed, we may be sure the evil deprecate would be extirpated from the communities in which we live. I know not that this can be done by any other means. This expedient is proposed: let us try it faithfully, at any expense of discomfort, at any sacrifice.' I have not probably reported exactly his words: the above was the meaning of what he said. My determination was formed at the close of his speech, and total abstinence was then established as a rule of my household."

My second picture is the West-church pulpit, in 1880. Dr. Bartol occupies it; and this is the "aid and comfort" he gives to those "that tarry long at the wine; . . . that go to seek mixed wine," who love to "look . . . upon the wine when it is red, when it giveth his color in the cup," though "at the last it biteth like a serpent, and stingeth like an adder:" —

"I am not sure there is any demonstration that the taking of wine or beer occasionally, not as a healing-drug, but for pleasure and good cheer, and because, in the language of David and Ecclesiastes, it 'maketh glad and merry the heart of man,' is to be quite condemned as malfeasance now, if moderation presides at the feast. I know not whether we can or ought to destroy alcohol from the face of the earth. It will, in some form and measure, continue to be used. It is not true that it is a duty for every man to abstain from all use of intoxicating liquor, for the sake of others who are liable to be overcome by their appetite for drink. It is not true that total abstinence is requisite universally, either for self-protection or for example's sake. It may be necessary to such as, like Mr. Gough, have been once long and thoroughly steeped, like a naturalist's preserved specimen, in alcohol. 'Touch not, taste not, handle not,' and smell not, may be the rule for them. As well abstain from cabbage and cauliflower on such a plea. But he who cannot resist the cravings for drink, which participation in the service of communion might cause, is not fit to participate it, and should refrain."

So, it seems, partaking of the communion is not so important as keeping open a grog-shop at every street-corner, to create appetite, and then to tempt men of weak resolution.

"Total abstinence is not the equivalent or synonyme of temperance. Temperance is composure. Strong drink is called the foe of our civilization, but how extravagant and erroneous it is to say this! Let the body, too, have its dues, and not be macerated or crucified to no end, and the soul will be all the better for its mortal companion's good estate! Stringent laws often court defiance; and it is the confession and lamentation of the friends of temperance, that the consumption of wine, beer, ale, cider, and stronger liquors is not prevented, or apparently reduced, in Maine and Massachusetts; but it is only for the viciously inclined to be somewhat regulated and kept within decent bounds by restrictive laws."

The preacher next commented upon prohibition, claiming that the strict facts are not adhered to in what is said by prohibitionists about it.

Will Dr. Bartol — this claimant that strict facts be adhered to — please state when and where any respectable temperance man or journal has ever "confessed" or "lamented" that the consumption of liquor was not *reduced* in Maine?

"Gentlemen will suffer no Legislature to dictate their habits by any sumptuary decree as to what they shall eat or drink at their boards."

Will the "strict adherent to facts" please state when any temperance body ever asked the Legislature to do this? Prohibition asks only to shut up grog-shops to prevent the public sale of drink.

"Shall this freedom be the monopoly of the gentlemen? Will the laboring-classes make over and assign to the leisurely and luxurious upper ones their share of this prize of personal option which was politically wrenched one hundred years ago from the British tyrant, and vindicated and rescued from the despotism of American bondage so recently again? We are Republican or Democrat in this land. Let us have no law that does not bear alike on high and low! Aristocracy, however plumed with benevolence, is not the form of mercy fit for our folk! It pleases God to make us free; with liberty to what marvellous and perilous, but shall we say injurious, extent? Can we go back on our Creator, or get before him, or complain of his construction of the world? This continent is consecrated to equal rights. If a man undertakes to dragoon me by menace, and word of mouth, into a philanthropic position," etc.

Does not this sound just a wee bit like a New-York Democrat haranguing a crowd of roughs?

" A man is intemperate, who, with sumptuary laws of any sort, would tyrannically override his neighbor, or cramp him in the freedom he discreetly employs. Ought I to inculcate total abstinence from hammers, screwdrivers, and chisels for all mechanics, because certain burglars handle them at midnight to unrighteous ends? But I so respect earnestness, that I unwillingly take offence at fanaticism, save for its injury to any worthy cause. Yet those who would enforce total abstinence have unquestionably set up a new inquisition among us, and one more intrusive than the old ones of Germany and Spain; as it is for people's habits as well as for their beliefs. Instead of a temperance movement, we have an intemperance movement now, which will not tolerate facts. One of the best and most temperate of men in my parish-round has, by the medical use of rock-candy in whiskey, been withdrawn, for new years of usefulness, from the brink of the grave."

Is it exactly in keeping with fair discussion and a " strict adherence to facts " thus to insinuate that we temperance-men should have bid that " best and most temperate of men " die before consenting to use alcohol as medicine? That convenient epithet, " fanatic," has been flung at every reformer, whose arguments could not be answered, for eighteen hundred and fifty years. I am sorry to see Dr. Bartol resorting to this disingenuous artifice of the helpless conservative and the demagogue.

"Excite a nobler thirst, fill the vacuum of the mind with a satisfaction more lofty and pure, and feed it with beauty and truth. Let me accordingly suggest to all engaged in the temperance reform, that their main business, as it is the solemn obligation of us all, is, to stir in ourselves, and waken in our fellows, the cravings, whose satisfaction is the soul's salvation."

Is this, in very truth, the "*main business*" of temperance reformers? Well, then, they will succeed when, mightier than Shakspeare, "they can charm ache with air, and agony with words." But let me remind Dr. Bartol of the words of the MASTER, "This kind goeth not out but by prayer and FASTING."

I wonder if the present generation of West-church sheep are intelligent enough to perceive the difference between these two pulpits. And, if so, which do they look up to with the better satisfaction?

Some temperance-men are surprised and indignant at what they consider Dr. Bartol's prostitution of the Liberal pulpit. Such men forget the history of the temperance movement in Boston. When Rev. John Pierpont, forty years ago, returned from the East, he stated, in his pulpit in Hollis Street, that the first thing he saw there (in Smyrna, I believe) was a barrel of New-England rum,— N.E. RUM burned into its head in large capitals. He made this the text for an earnest and eloquent agitation of the temperance question. The richest parishioners were rum-makers and rum-sellers: their rum was then stored, I think, in the very cellar of his church. I will not mention their names: their children continue the manufacture and the traffic. They set to work, by reducing his salary, refusing to pay one dollar of it, mortgaging the church for heavy debt, and by every means, to drive Pierpont from the pulpit. Finding this ineffectual, they announced their determination to buy up every pew that could be had, and thus, securing a majority of votes, dismiss him from his charge. *Francis Jackson*, a name always to be written by Bostonians in letters of gold, and the late venerable Samuel May, led the temperance-men in resisting this plot. They succeeded *in form;* they vindicated Mr. Pierpont on every trial, leaving no smell of fire on his garments; but they could not "hold the fort." *In fact*, rum triumphed. The wealthy rum-sellers of the city, whether attending the Hollis Street or not, bought pews there, — pews they never used, — and finally obliged Mr. Pierpont to agree to vacate his pulpit. During the seven years of this hard-fought battle between the penniless, eloquent, and devoted apostle in the pulpit and the wealthy rum-sellers in the pews, the Unitarian clergy of Suffolk County gave the public to understand that they renounced all ministerial fellowship with Mr. Pierpont, never exchanged with him, or extended to him professional recognition or courtesy. With two or three exceptions (Rev. J. T. Sargent, Dr. Gannett, and one or two others — Mr. Theodore Parker was not then preaching in Boston), all the Liberal clergy shut him from their pulpits. In their last letter to Mr. Pierpont, the rum-sellers taunted him with the fact that hardly one of his clerical brethren in Boston would exchange with him. And, in his letter of farewell to the Unitarian Association, Mr. Pierpont refers to this desertion, and affirms that this repudiation of him by his brother clergymen was *the special thing* which made it impossible for him to remain in the Hollis-street pulpit; and, further, his certain knowledge that this course of conduct toward him was adopted, on their part, *on purpose, and with the intention*, to drive him from that pulpit.

Mr. Bartol, therefore, does not prostitute the Liberal pulpit; although one might sigh for the purer gospel Lowell preached in the West Church. Judged by the example and conduct of the vast majority of the Liberal clergy of Boston for the last forty years, such sermons as Dr. Bartol has of late delivered are just the preaching for which the Liberal pulpit was created and is sustained.

WENDELL PHILLIPS.

Dr. Bartol sent the following "note" to the editors of "The Boston Daily Advertiser:" —

TO THE EDITORS OF "THE BOSTON DAILY ADVERTISER:" —

You will excuse me from replying to Mr. Phillips; and he will be glad to have me state, first, in regard to Mr. Pierpont, that the West Church took no part in his trial; and I was, I think, the last Boston minister, not long before he left his pulpit, to exchange with him. We were on terms of friendship, fellowship, and mutual confidence to the end. Secondly, I referred, under the head of "nameless vice," only to certain rural gatherings, or meetings, of "lodges;" and several persons assure me, that such facts as I had in mind have existed, as they have, perhaps, more often, in churches, and at camp-meetings too. For the Masons and Odd Fellows, as a body, I have a profound respect. Thirdly, Dr. Lowell, my ever dear and honored colleague, was not what is called a total abstainer; but he was, in speech and act and habit, a thoroughly temperate man.

C. A. BARTOL.

On the 24th of January, 1881, the Tremont Temple in Boston was filled to overflowing with an audience desirous of hearing Mr. Phillips's review of Dr. Howard Crosby's recent anti-total-abstinence discourse. The lecture was in the orator's best vein, although he deadened his usual brilliancy of delivery by reading (contrary to his custom) his address from a manuscript.

Mr. Phillips thoroughly examined Dr. Crosby's argumentation, and answered all his points, as will be seen by a reading of the following sketch: —

"'Dr. Crosby's lecture was noticeable for lack of novelty, or weight of argument, and of correctness in his statements. I dissent from Dr. Crosby's remark that we "cannot conscientiously object to the means employed by others unless they contain an immorality," and say that Dr. Crosby should have studied the history of the temperance movement. I may sum up Dr. Crosby's lecture as follows: —

"'1. Dr. Crosby objects to the total-abstinence theory and movement, and it insults the example of Jesus; that its advocates undermine and despise the Bible, while they strain and wrench it to serve their purpose; and he asserts that the Bible, correctly interpreted, repudiates total abstinence, and such a temperance crusade as has existed here for the last fifty years.

"'2. Dr. Crosby objects to this movement as immoral and unchristian; the total-abstinence system is "contrary to revealed religion," and "doing unmeasured harm to the community;" he considered it as the special and direct cause of the "growth of drunkenness in our land, and of a general demoralization among religious communities;" asserts that it is exactly the kind of movement that rum-sellers enjoy, and that it ought not to succeed, never will, and never can.

"'3. The pledge is unmanly, and kills character and self-respect.

"'4. The assertion that moderate drinking leads to drunkenness is untrue.

"'5. The total abstainers bully and intimidate the community, and disgust all good, sensible men.

"'6. That what is needed to unite sensible men, in a movement sure to succeed, is a license system recognizing the distinction between moderation and excess, between harmless wines and beer and strong drink. Such a system, "free from taint of prejudice and instinct, with practical wisdom, will establish order and peace, and save us from a moral slough."

"'The looseness of these statements is noticeable. Total abstinence is abstaining from intoxicating drinks ourselves, and agreeing with others to do so. No one pretends that he can cite a biblical text which forbids total abstinence. Dr. Crosby's argument is, that Jesus drank intoxicating wine, and allowed it to others. There is no proof that he ever did drink intoxicating wine; but let that pass, and suppose, for the sake of the argument, that he did. What then? To do what Jesus never did, or to refuse to do what he did, are such acts *necessarily* "contrary to revealed religion"? Let us see. Jesus rode upon an ass's colt: we ride upon railways. Are they contrary to revealed religion? Jesus never married. Is marriage contrary to revealed religion?

"'Now, there is a class of biblical scholars and interpreters who do assert, that, wherever wine is referred to in the Bible with approbation, it is unfermented wine. Of this class of men Dr. Crosby says, "Their learned ignorance is splendid;" they are "inventors of a theory of magnificent daring;" they "use false texts" and "deceptive arguments;" "deal dishonestly with the Scriptures;" "beg the question, and build on air;" their theory is a "fable" born of "falsehoods," supported by "Scripture twisting and wriggling;" their arguments are "cobwebs," and their zeal outstrips their judgment, and they plan to "undermine the Bible." Who are these daring, ridiculous, and illogical sinners? As I call them up in my memory, the first one who comes to me is Moses Stuart of Andover, whose lifelong study of the Bible, and profound critical knowledge of both its languages, place him easily at the head of all American commentators. "Moses Stuart's Scripture View of the Wine Question" was the ablest contribution, thirty years ago, to this claim about unfermented wine, and still holds its place unanswered and unanswerable. By his side stands Dr. Nott, the head of Union College, with the snows of ninety winters on his brow. Around them gather scores of scholars and divines, on both sides of the Atlantic. In our day Taylor Lewis gives to the American public, with his scholarly indorsement, the exhaustive commentary by Dr. Lees on every text in the Bible which speaks of wine, — a work of sound learning, the widest research, and fairest argument. The ripe scholarship, long study of the Bible, and critical ability of these men, entitle them to be considered experts on this question. In a matter of Scripture interpretation, it would be empty compliment to say that Dr. Crosby is worthy to loose the latchet of their shoes. Now, the truth is, the only "castle built in the air" in this matter, is the baseless idea that the temperance movement uses dishonest arguments, or wrests the Scripture, because it maintains, that, where the drinking of wine as an article of diet is mentioned in the Bible with approbation, *unfermented* wine is meant. The fact is, there are scholars of repute on both sides of the question. But we do not claim too much when we say that the weight of scholarly authority is on our side, and not on that of the doctor.'

"Mr. Phillips devoted further attention to the scriptural argument, saying that once the Bible was thrown in the way of the abolition of slavery just as it is now thrown in the way of the total-abstinence movement. He said, 'I see your lecturer last week closed his eloquent and able address by triumphantly claiming that the gospel abolished slavery — which is true, only he should have stated that it was the gospel of Jesus Christ, and not the gospel of the church of that day. Hence I am not impatient nor distrustful. I rest quiet in serene assurance that by and by, when our temperance cause is a little stronger, men will blush to think they ever belittled and dishonored the Bible by such claims and arguments as these. At that time ninety-nine out of every hundred Christians will look askance upon you, and suspect your orthodoxy, unless you believe Jesus never drank any fermented wine, and that the Bible's precepts touching wine-drinking can only be reconciled with each other, or with its claim as a revealed religion, by recognizing the distinction between fermented and unfermented wines. In my active life of fifty years I have seen more men made infidels by these attempts to prove the Bible an upholder of slavery, than I ever saw misled by the followers of Paine; and I think this sad exhibition of New-York partisanship will have the same result. The misled men to whom I refer were not ignorant, careless-minded, or unprincipled, but men of conscientious earnestness, purpose, good culture, and blameless lives. The Bible is a divine book, a strong proof of which is, that it has outlived even the foolish praises and misrepresentations of its narrow and bigoted friends. The New Testament is a small book, and may be read in an hour. It is not a code of laws, but the example of a life and a suggestion of principles. It would be idle to suppose that it could describe in detail, specifically meet every possible question, and solve every difficulty that the changing and broadening life of two or three thousand years might bring forth. The progressive spirit of each age has found in it just the inspiration and help it sought. But when timid, narrow, and short-sighted men claimed such exclusive ownership in it that they refused to their growing fellows the use of its broad, underlying principles, and thus demanded to have new wine put into old bottles, of course the bottles burst, and their narrow-surface Bible became discredited; but the real Bible soared upward, and led the world onward still, as the soul rises to broader and higher life when the burden of a narrow and mortal body falls away.'

"Signing the total-abstinence pledge was the next subject taken up by Mr. Phillips, and the general principles which are at the basis of promises were stated as follows: 'Dr. Crosby is undoubtedly a member of a church. Does he mean to say, that when his church demanded his signature to its creed, and its pledge to obey its discipline, it asked what it was "unmanly" in him to grant? He only objects to a temperance pledge, not to a church one. The husband pledges himself to his wife, and she to him, for life. Is the marriage ceremony, then, a curse, a hinderance to virtue and progress? Society rests, in all its transactions, on the idea that a solemn promise, pledge, or assertion, strengthens and assures the act. The witness on the stand gives solemn promise to tell the truth; the officer about to assume place for one year or ten, or for life, pledges his word and oath; the grantor in a deed binds himself for all time by record; churches, societies, universities, accept funds on pledge to appropriate them to certain purposes, and no other: these and a score more of instances can be cited. In any final analysis, all these rest on the same principle as the temperance pledge. No man ever denounced them as unmanly. I sent this month a legacy to a literary institution on certain conditions, and received in return its pledge that the money should ever be sacredly used as directed. The doctor's principle would unsettle society; and, if one proposed to apply it to any cause but temperance, practical men would quietly put him aside as out of his head. These cobweb theories, born of isolated cloister-life, do not bear exposure to the mid-day sun, or the rude winds of practical life. This is not a matter of theory. Thousands and tens of thousands attest the value of the pledge. It never degraded, it only lifted them to a higher life. We who never lost our clear eyesight or level balance over books, but who stand mixed up and jostled in daily life, hardly deem any man's sentimental and fastidious criticism of the pledge worth answering. Every active worker in the temperance cause can recall hundreds of instances where it has been a man's salvation.'

"Moderate drinking and Dr. Crosby's defence of it were next handled; Mr. Phillips saying, 'Dr. Crosby says it is false our constant assertion that moderate drinking makes drunkards. Will he please tell us where, then, the drunkards come from? Certainly teetotalers do not recruit these swelling ranks. Will he please account for the million-times repeated story of the broken-hearted and despairing sot, or the reformed man, that "moderate drinking lulled them to a false security until the chain was too strong for them to break?" Will he please explain that confession forced from old Sam Johnson, and repeated hundreds of times since by men of seemingly strong resolve, "I can abstain: I can't be moderate"? Do not the Bible, the writers of fiction, the master dramatists of ancient and modern times, the philosopher, the moralist, the man of affairs, — do not all these bear witness how insidiously the habits of sensual indulgence creep on their victim until he wakes to find himself in chains of iron, his very will destroyed?'

"Mr. Phillips then answered, with some sarcasm, the remark that the rum-sellers are pleased with the enactment of a prohibitory law, and that such a law is an injury to the cause of temperance. He could prove Christianity a failure by the same reasoning which proves the temperance reform to be a failure. Mr. Phillips drew a graphic sketch of the progress of the temperance movement in the last fifty years. 'Dr. Crosby then had,' said he, 'every man, lay and clerical, on his side in construing the Bible; whereas now we are in a healthy majority: then a few scattered temperance-tracts, like rockets in a night, only betrayed how utterly the world was in the desert on this subject; now a temperance literature crowded with facts, strong in argument, filled with testimonies from men of the first eminence in every walk of life, in every department of science and literature, challenges and defies all canvass: then the idea of total abstinence was not so much denied as wholly unknown; now, if New England were polled to-day, our majority would be overwhelming: then all men held liquors to be healthy and useful; now seventy men out of a hundred, whatever their practice, deny that claim, and the upper classes, well-informed, and careful of health, lead the way in giving up the use: then the medical profession waded in the same slough of indulgence and ignorance as their patients; now the verdict of the profession is undoubtedly and immeasurably against the use of intoxicating drinks at all in health, and but seldom in favor of it in disease. We have driven the indulgence in drink into hiding-places, and for the first time the Legislature is obliged and willing to prohibit the use of screens to hide rum-drinkers from the public view they dread.'

"The State of Maine was cited as a proof of the possibility of the enforcement of a prohibitory law. License was denounced. 'The statute-books in forty States are filled with the abortions of thousands of license-laws that were never executed, and most of them were never intended to be. We have as good a license-law in this State as was ever devised; and yet it leaves such an amount of defiant, unblushing grog-selling as discourages Dr. Crosby, and leads him to think nothing has been done at all. His own city, with license-laws, is yet so ruled and plundered by rum, that timid statesmen advise giving up republicanism, and borrowing a leaf from Bismarck to help us. License has been tried on the most favorable circumstances, and with the best backing for centuries, — ten or twelve, at least. Yet Dr. Crosby stands confounded before the result. We have never been allowed to try prohibition except in one State, and in some small circuits. Wherever it has been tried, it has succeeded. Friends who know, claim this: enemies who have been for a dozen years ruining teeth by biting files, confess it by their lack of argument, and lack of facts except when they invent them.'

"REMARKS OF GOV. LONG.

"After Mr. Phillips finished, Gov. Long was introduced with hearty applause, and spoke as follows: —

"'LADIES AND GENTLEMEN, — I came, as you did, to listen, and not to speak. Men may come, and men may go. Dr. Crosby may attack, and Mr. Phillips defend. You may belittle, if you will allow me to say so, the character and teachings of Jesus Christ by quoting him upon the topic on which he never expressed himself (I say it reverently), and on which he is no more to be quoted as an authority than upon the question of the tariff. But for myself I want no better test than I find when I go to the moral and intelligent conscience of the great body of the people of a Commonwealth like this, whose representatives you men and women gathered here in this audience are. [Applause.] And I find in this matter of temperance, and the crusade against intoxicating liquors, as in every other great moral reform, that the standard must be put infinitely higher up in the plane of conscience itself, — infinitely higher than the cold framework of any moral system of logic. [Applause.] I believe that the votaries and advocates of total abstinence, who are doing something for the growth and self-respect and character of the work in so many a noble channel in cities and villages, through the forces of moral influences for the good of their fellow-men, will still increase more and more the moral sentiment and encouragement and help of every true Christian and true philanthropist.'"

In February Mr. Phillips, who had often before expressed his opinions on the subject of Irish agitation, again spoke on "The Crisis in Irish Affairs" at a Land-League meeting held in Somerville, Mass. He said, —

"The Irish question is a riddle which English statesmanship

has tried for more than a century to solve. It is made up of hatred of race, hatred of creed, and intense adherence to certain old-time prejudices in regard to land tenure; and these three strands make a cable which it is almost impossible to break. Charles James Fox, the great English statesman one hundred years ago, died with the confession, 'I have tried to solve the Irish question; I have been unable to do it; and I confess I do not see how anybody can ever solve it.' He meant, the difficulties are so inherent, so profound, so radical, that he saw no possibility of ever reconciling the feelings and the interests of the two islands by any arrangement, any policy of conciliation that he could devise; and if you had asked him, in the closing years of his great life, what solution can be possibly made of this quarrel of the centuries, he would have answered, 'There is none except the separation of the two islands, and giving Ireland to the Irish.' [Applause.] It may look like a wild dream; and wise men have thought, that, among the colossal monarchies of Europe, an island of only eight million or twelve million of people would be so small a State, that it could not vindicate its own existence. Undoubtedly it would be an exception to the general law of European kingdoms; but so great are the difficulties in the way of a union between the two islands, that that seems the only door out of the great difficulty which has beset land-locked England for more than one hundred years.

"I said it was a riddle which English statesmanship has tried to solve for one hundred years. They tried with intense earnestness. They had all the most selfish motives to solve this Irish difficulty. For if there be any one cause that has reduced England from a first-rate Continental power to a third, or, at least, second, rate on the chess-board of Europe, it was the fact that the immeasurable and the irreconcilable hate of Ireland reduced her moral and military power. The Continental nations of Europe know to-day that England is checkmated, to a great extent, by this

Irish question. The ranks of the English army are more than half recruited from the Irish race, and England knows that that army is inefficient. It may turn any moment against them. Why did Bismarck smite them in the face ten years ago in the matter of the Danish parties, insolently, in the presence of all Europe? Because the great German knew, that if any one put a regiment in the field, or pointed a cannon, against English power, Ireland stood ready to stab her in the back. [Applause.] It was exactly the weakness which came over our government during the existence of the press-hatred of the civil war. English statesmanship, recognizing this fact, has tried, with intense earnestness, to solve the great trouble. Pitt and Fox, and every great statesman since down to Gladstone and Beaconsfield, have devoted their most earnest energy, and Irish genius has added its contribution. Burke and Grattan and Emmet and Curran, and all your great names down to O'Connell and Parnell, have laid on the altar of a solution of this riddle their grandest energy. And still it confronts us unsolved and doubly pointed to-day.

"There is, on every side, a resemblance point by point to the negro question with which America grappled. Gladstone's position, at the present time, is this: he has the wolf by the ears, and he can neither hold him nor let him go. [Applause.] If he ever thanks God on his bended knees, he probably thanks him earnestly that that jury in Dublin disagreed. If they had agreed, and condemned the Land-Leaguers, he would have had an elephant on his hands too big to handle. There was no prison that could have held them, and there was no public opinion that would have sustained him; whereas, if the jury had acquitted them, the government would have stood ridiculous in the face of the world for having made an issue on which the usual tribunals of the country wrote 'Shame!' [Applause.] The grand danger and great difficulty of the Irish question to-day is one that is made by civilization itself. We stand in an epoch of change in the whole conditions of the world. It is like the discovery of America, which changed the kingdoms of Europe. It is ten times greater than the discovery of golden California, which revolutionized the commerce of the world. There are certain great waves beating against the present systems of industry and commerce, which have brought this Irish question to confront us. Parnell is merely doing what O'Connell did before him. He is using England's adversity as Ireland's opportunity. Gladstone seems verging to a point from which nothing can extricate him but force. When a government, in this age, reaches that point, it dies. Brains rule now, not bayonets. If Gladstone is driven to the point of resting the government on force, it is only the beginning of the end; and, if he had not neared the fatal emergency, he never would have stooped to the indescribable meanness of having arrested Davitt, whose single crime was that he was making a great moral agitation in behalf of the race to which he belonged."

Mr. Phillips closed his address by a peroration, in which he reminded his audience that the time for Ireland's friends to act had come. England being distracted on every side, she could spare no troops for Ireland. If they let this opportunity slip by, such another might not arise in this generation. A burst of applause followed his sitting down.

On the 30th of June, of this year, Mr. Phillips delivered his remarkable address, entitled "The Scholar in a Republic," at the centennial anniversary of the Phi Beta Kappa of Harvard College. The following exceedingly interesting recollections of this memorable occasion are given by Dr. James Freeman Clarke of Boston: —

"Listening to Wendell Phillips at Cambridge," says Dr. Clarke, "and seeing him at last among his literary peers, and returned for one day to stand in the halls of Harvard, I thought the event so historic as to be worth some reflections. I compared it with another historical Phi Beta Kappa oration, given in the same place forty-four years ago. I was present at the delivery of the oration, in 1837, by Ralph Waldo Emerson. He had then just entered on the career which has since been so brilliant and so triumphant, but at that time he was an unpopular and suspected man in the literary circles of Boston. His philosophy was transcendentalism, and transcendentalism had a dark and ominous sound to the ears of Boston people. It was supposed to be some mysterious infidelity, dangerous to the order of the State. At all events, it meant rebellion to the established ways of thought and speech. Mr. Emerson's language was dark and mysterious. He did not use the old commonplaces of New-England rhetoric. His style was plainly not Addisonian. Many eminent persons triumphantly declared his sayings wholly unintelligible. One *mot*, very current at that period, was attributed to a very learned lawyer of the Suffolk bar, who, having been seen at one of Mr. Emerson's lectures, and asked if he understood him, replied, 'No, I do not; but my daughters do.' But Mr. Emerson had a very earnest body of admirers, who, like Mr. Mason's daughters, thought that they understood him. They were those who loved, and did not fear, his originality of thought and expression. They loved to be taken away from the endless repetition of the school of John Locke, and to catch some fresh breezes from a higher mountain load of thought. Mr. Emerson fed their souls with bread which seemed to have come down from heaven. He, again, introduced immediate vision of truth and reality. He opened the way into untrodden domains of spiritual thought. Those who had listened with joy to Channing, who had been made glad by Wordsworth and Coleridge, came to hear Emerson whenever he spoke. You always saw nearly the same audience at his lectures, — the same men and women.

"Thus it came to pass, that, when it was known that Emerson was to give the Phi Beta Kappa oration, the old church in Cambridge contained two wholly distinct bodies of hearers. On the platform, on each side of the speaker, sat the dignitaries, the old leaders of opinion, who were there because that was their place. These were the men of eminent gravity, of marked influence, — governors and ex-governors, judges and magistrates, the Boston ministers, members of Congress, professors and physicians. To them what Mr. Emerson said on that day was plainly distasteful. They held down their heads, and looked mortified, as people look who are hearing things they don't like. Meantime the other audience in front, consisting of Emerson's friends and admirers, listened with very different feelings to the charmed speech of this admirable thinker. They leaned forward, their eyes full of animation, their features radiant with delight. They applauded with rapture, while the platform remained silent and unmoved. It was very curious and very amusing to see brought together in one place the representatives of the past and of the future. It marked a turning-point in the movement of thought. Something like this, but different from it, was the scene of Thursday week.

"When I knew that Wendell Phillips was to give the Phi Beta Kappa oration at Cambridge, I was very curious to know what course he would take. I said, 'He has two opportunities, neither of which he has ever had before. He has always spoken to the people. Now he is invited to address scholars. He has an opportunity to deliver a grand academic discourse, and to show, that, when he chooses to do it, he can be the peer of Everett or Sumner on their own platform of high culture. He can leave behind personalities, forget for the hour his hatreds and enmities, and meet all his old opponents peacefully, in the still air of delightful studies. This is an opportunity he has never had before, and probably will never have again.'

"'But there is another and different opportunity now offered him. Now, for the first and only time, he will have face to face before him the representatives of that

Cambridge culture which has had little sympathy with his past labors. He can tell them how backward they were in the old anti-slavery contest, and how reluctant to take part in any later reforms. If he has been bitter before, he can be ten times as bitter now. He can make this the day of judgment for the sins of half a century. This opportunity, also, is unique. It will never come again. Can he resist this temptation, or not?'

"It never occurred to me that he would accept and use both opportunities, but he did so. He gave an oration of great power and beauty, full of strong thoughts and happy illustrations, not unworthy of any university platform or academic scholar. It was nearly, though not wholly, free from personalities; but it was also one long rebuke for the recreant scholarship of Cambridge. It arraigned and condemned all scholarship as essentially timid, selfish, and unheroic. It gave a list of the leading reforms of the last forty years, in none of which Cambridge scholarship had taken any share, — anti-slavery, woman's rights, the wrongs of Ireland, reform in criminal legislation, — and wound up the catalogue by denouncing as disgusting cant all condemnation of Russian Nihilism and its methods. He admitted, that, in a land where speech and the press are free, recourse to assassination is criminal, but defended 'dynamite and the dagger' as the only methods of reform open in Russia.

"Thus the theme which he elaborated for scholars was the essential cowardice of scholarship.

"The courage of the oration, and its honesty, were both apparent. I think that it was not without an effort that Phillips brought these charges. I have no doubt it was done as a duty. He wished to be faithful there, as elsewhere, to his real convictions; not to waste his time on any mere subject of idle literature, but to talk only of what seemed to him of chief importance, whether men would hear, or whether they would forbear. From this point of view, his position was dignified and honorable.

"But the temper of the audience was finer still. There were no two audiences present, as in the case of Emerson. The whole body of his hearers was one in respect and good will. They honored Phillips for his long services in the cause of freedom, and took every occasion to applaud his own sentiments and career. They listened in silence to his paradoxes, his denunciations of scholarship, his defence of Nihilism. Their disapproval of many of his opinions was marked and apparent. It was evident that they approved of the man, and disapproved of most of his opinions. There was one striking incident when Phillips (quoting the words of Garrison) described the man who would not equivocate, would not retreat an inch, and at last would be heard. Phillips was thinking of Garrison, but the audience applied it to himself. They received the sentence with repeated thunders of applause. This touched him deeply; and, when he spoke again, there were (as the French say) 'tears in his voice.' The body of hearers, in their silent condemnation and their hearty sympathy, seemed to me larger and more just to the orator than the orator was to them. For, after all, it was a one-sided argument. Scholarship may be very conservative; but it is no more so than commerce, labor, wealth, journalism. Every working-element in society sticks to its own principles, and is not easily diverted into new channels.

"It seemed to me that Phillips was unjust to Cambridge scholarship in remembering only its lapses, and forgetting its examples of courage. He remembered Everett, and forgot Sumner. He condemned John Pierpont for one action, and said nothing of his long career of courageous, self-sacrificing devotion to reform. Though he quoted Lowell, he did not mention him as an exception to his censure. He forgot to remember the combined scholarship and courage of Theodore Parker, equally eminent as a reformer and as a man of learning. When we recollect that Cambridge has given to the work of reform such scholars as Channing, Emerson, Horace Mann, Theodore Parker, Charles Sumner, Samuel J. May, James Russell Lowell, John Gorham Palfrey, John Quincy Adams, Josiah Quincy, we see that there is another side to the question.

"Wendell Phillips had a great opportunity, and used

it well. No one sympathized with the extravagances of his statements. It was unfortunate that he should have defended assassination in Russia by the argument of necessity, — 'necessity, the tyrant's plea,' — an argument which every assassin can use, from his own point of view, with equal force. If it seems necessary to the Nihilists to assassinate the emperor, because they have no other method, so it seemed necessary to Wilkes Booth to assassinate Lincoln, as the only way left to do any thing for the Lost Cause. And even the lunatic Guiteau, using the same argument, claims that his murderous act was done from 'a political necessity.'

"But, after all abatements, this Phi Beta Kappa oration will be remembered as a great effort of intellectual and moral power. Its delivery, and the way it was received, constitute an important event in the history of American thought."

The venerable Parker Pillsbury, in a letter to the editor of "The Boston Commonwealth," thus alluded to Mr. Phillips's oration at Cambridge: —

My article would be too long should I say half that I would on the oration. Mr. Phillips would have died too soon, had he departed without pronouncing it. It will be worth to the college, officers, and students, all the teachings of the last four years. His title henceforth should be "D.C.," Doctor of Colleges. You, Mr. Editor, may do it up in the customary Latin if you think best. I began to be a little mad at him for using the words "universal suffrage," as though we had it. But his magnificent demand for woman's equality toward the close made all perfectly right. His tribute to the French Revolution was super-excellent and just. His mistake about Voltaire, if it be a mistake, I trust Mr. Parton will be able to correct.

PARKER PILLSBURY.

CONCORD, N.H., July 14, 1881.

Mr. George William Curtis, speaking at Brown University, in June, 1882, paid the following compliments to Mr. Phillips and his Phi Beta Kappa oration of the previous year: —

"A year ago I sat with my brethren of the Phi Beta Kappa at Cambridge, and seemed to catch echoes of Edmund Burke's resounding impeachment of Warren Hastings, in the sparkling denunciation of the timidity of American scholarship. Under the spell of Burke's burning words, Hastings half believed himself to be the villain he heard described. But the scholarly audience of the scholarly orator of the Phi Beta Kappa, with an exquisite sense of relief, felt every count of his stinging indictment recoil upon himself. He was the glowing refutation of his own argument. Gentleman, scholar, orator, his is the courage that never quailed; his, the white plume of Navarre that flashed meteor-like in the front of battle; his, the Amphion music of an eloquence that levelled the more than Theban walls of American slavery. At once judge, accuser, and culprit, in the noble record of his own life he and his class are triumphantly acquitted."

Mr. Phillips, as is well known, was an ardent supporter of the Irish cause. All through the Land-League campaign, he addressed meeting after meeting. When the Gladstone government turned on the leaders, and imprisoned every active man in Ireland, he was the one man whom it was thought could fill the void.

In the faint hope that he might have strength left to face the ocean and the enemy, he was the object of an appeal. But it could not be made possible for him to accept, as the following correspondence will show: —

OFFICE OF "THE IRISH WORLD,"
NEW YORK, Oct. 31, 1881.

WENDELL PHILLIPS, *Boston.*

I have just received the following cable from Mr. Egan, Land-League treasurer, Paris: —

"Will Wendell Phillips come to Ireland, to advocate No Rent during the suspension of Constitutional liberties? The League will pay all expenses. Reply. PATRICK EGAN."

I beg you, Mr. Phillips, to hearken to this as an inspiration and a call from God himself. You are the one man in America fitted for the glorious mission. All Ireland will rise to its feet to bless and cheer you. Never did Cæsar receive such an ovation. Civilization will look on in admiring wonder. The good which your heroic act will effect is incalculable; and your name, consecrated in the memory of a grateful people, will live whilst time endures.

PATRICK FORD.

To this invitation Mr. Phillips sent the following reply, under cover of a note to Mr. Ford: —

BOSTON, 2d Nov., 1881.

Sir, — I receive with humility the summons you send me, well knowing, that, in any circumstances, I could not do a tenth part of what your partiality makes you think I could.

But, in this case, humanity, civil liberty, constitutional government, and civilization itself claim his best service of every man.

THE ESSEX-STREET HOUSE

Ireland to-day leads the van in the struggle for right, justice, and freedom.

England has forfeited her right to rule, if she ever had any, by a three hundred years' exhibition of her unfitness and inability to do so. The failure is confessed by all her statesmen of both parties for the last hundred years.

Discontent, poverty, famine, and death are her accusers.

Her rulers cannot plead ignorance. Their own shameless confessions, repeated over and over again, admit that England's rule has been unjust, selfish, and cruel. She has planned that Ireland should starve, hoping she would then be too weak to resist.

To-day, while her government tramples under foot every principle in English history that makes men honor it, the world waits in sure and glad expectation of her defeat, confident that her overthrow will be the triumph of right, justice, and civilization.

The three thousand miles of ocean that separate us from her shores, enable us to judge her course as dispassionately as posterity will judge it a hundred years hence; and we see the mad blunders of her government as posterity will see them.

Let Ireland only persevere, and her victory is certain.

With unbroken front, let her assault despotism in its central point, RENT. Ireland owes none to-day, — certainly not to a class whose government is the prison and the bayonet.

How cheerfully would I do my part! How gladly would I share in the honors of such a struggle! But the state of my health obliges me to give up public speaking. I can only bid you God-speed, and pray for your speedy and complete success.

Yours very respectfully,

WENDELL PHILLIPS.

For many years Mr. Phillips's home was in Essex Street, Boston, a quiet street, now almost wholly devoted to business. Near by, in Exeter Place, lived Theodore Parker, the neighbor and bosom-friend of Phillips. Although socially attached to one another, in theology these genial spirits never agreed, for the reason that Mr. Phillips was born and bred, and always remained, a Calvinist. This fact, however, did not interfere with their friendship. But, while Parker was fully informed of the secret plans of John Brown in 1858, it was not until 1859, and then not fully, that Brown saw fit to communicate them to Phillips, who probably knew of them but generally. Yet, after Brown's death, Mr. Phillips, who spoke at his funeral in North Elba, brought thence the correspondence between Brown and his Boston friends, which would have made a great stir had it fallen into the hands of his opponents. These papers Phillips deposited with John A. Andrew; and from him, in the winter of 1859–60, the correspondents got back their dangerous epistles.

To allude again to the old home: it was a brick house, rather narrow, of three stories and a half. Painted on the door, in black letters on a dark ground, was the name —

```
PHILLIPS.
```

Two or three servants looked after the domestic details of the house; and, long before there was any talking about servant-girls' rights, he was quietly granting them, both in the form of greater leisure and higher wages. When a stranger appeared at the door, and asked for Mr. Phillips, a servant never falsified: she said, "Yes" or "No," or "Yes, but he is engaged." Mr. Phillips was never guilty of the meanness of compelling his servants, not only to work for their wages, but to tell lies for his convenience, — one of the cowardly customs America has borrowed from European domestic despotism.

The house was *not* elegantly furnished. On passing the doorway, the stranger found himself in a narrow entry, not hall, with a door to the left, opening into a dining-room, and at the bottom of a flight of stairs with a well-worn, cheap carpet on them. The stairs had old-fashioned banisters, of the "mould-candle" style. The walls of the entry were covered with a dark, greenish paper, that had been there for more than a quarter of a century. Instead of the inartistic or upholstered hat-tree, there was a high, old-time hat-rack, with wooden pegs, painted white long ago. On the floor was a well-worn oilcloth. Every thing was as neat and clean as it could be kept.

At the top of the stairs was a narrow passage, opening into a front room. This was the parlor and reception room, the width of the house, and rather low-studded. The walls were painted a yellowish white. There was an old, cheap, but neat and not gaudy, reddish carpet on the floor. The furniture was old-fashioned, and made chiefly of mahogany. Beneath the large, old-time mirror, between the windows, stood a table covered with books, papers, and magazines. The books were chiefly of political economy and political philosophy, and were all in English. In the centre of the room was a large mahogany table, with side-leaves; and it, too, was covered with books, papers, etc., and with perhaps hundreds of letters, manuscripts, and the like. On the left-hand side, as one entered the room, was a large, heavy sofa; near the window a bust of Bowditch on a wooden pedestal made from the rafter of his house, or some of his furniture. Near the door was a tall, old-fashioned what-not, with books on every shelf, and Brackett's bust of John Brown on the top. Opposite, on the mantel-piece over the fireplace, there was a French clock, small statuettes of Theodore Parker and John Knox, and a few tasteful ornaments. A folding-door, always closed, led into a dark room, where Mr. Phillips kept his library, by no means an extensive one. Between this folding-door and the door of entrance was another small table, with books, and a photographic portrait of John Brown. In the farther corner of the room stood Martin Milmore's masterpiece, a bust of Phillips. There were no pictures on the walls; and, such as it was, it was the best room in the house. With the rest of this modest home, the public has no concern.

For forty years and more, Phillips, with his wife, and part of the time his adopted daughter (now the wife of Mr. G. W. Smalley of London, England), lived here. In 1882 came the summons from the city government of Boston to quit. The exigencies of trade, and other projects, compelled an alteration in the thoroughfare; and Mr. Phillips's house was doomed to be razed to the ground. In sorrow, which he keenly felt, he removed his household gods into a still smaller and equally unattractive house, located in Common Street, near the corner of Tremont. From that day his heart failed him; he began to grow old fast; there he died.

At the time of his removal from his Essex-street home, Mr. Phillips made a disposition of the larger portion of his library; having, as he thought, no further use for it. The following letter, dated Aug. 16, 1882, and addressed to Mr. Aaron M. Powell, formerly editor of "The American Anti-slavery Standard," discloses what was done with his valuable collection of books: —

"You ought to know what I did with my anti-slavery library. Did I tell you? I sent a complete file of 'The Standard,' from 1840 to 1872, to Mr. Spofford, for the Congressional Library; also three volumes of 'The Liberator,' to fill up his gaps, which are not now many. I sent the Astor Library a complete file of 'The Liberator.' It had all 'The Standards.' I sent the Boston Public Library a complete file of 'The Standard' (it had almost perfect 'Liberator'), also all my reports, pamphlets, and surplus numbers of newspapers, bound and unbound, 'Emancipators' and 'Herald of Freedom,' they agreeing to distribute. I had none to fill up the reports you needed; but, if you find any at the Boston Public Library, they were told of your prior right. Swarthmore College I could not help, not having enough, and deeming the Astor, Boston, and Washington Libraries more important. offered Cornell Library, vols. iii., iv., and v. of 'The Liberator,' to help its file. So, you see, I have acted as my own executor, to get rid of twenty-five hundred volumes."

The unveiling exercises over Miss Anne Whitney's statue of Harriet Martineau were held in the Old South Meeting-house, Dec. 26, 1883. A large audience were present, the most of them being ladies. After the applause attending the unveiling had subsided addresses were made by Mrs. Mary A. Livermore, who presided on the occasion, William L. Garrison, jun., and Wendell Phillips. As Mr. Phillips advanced to the front of the stage, he was greeted with a hearty welcome. He then began, and continued as follows:—

"Webster once said, that 'In war there are no Sundays.' So in moral questions there are no nations. Intellect and morals transcend all limits. When a moral issue is stirred, then there is no American, no German. We are all men and women. And that is the reason why I think we should indorse this memorial of the city to Harriet Martineau, because her service transcends nationality. There would be nothing inappropriate if we raised memorial to Wickliffe, or if the common-school system of New England raised a memorial to Calvin; for they rendered the greatest of services. So with Harriet Martineau, we might fairly render a monument to the grandest woman of her day, we, the heirs of the same language, and one in the same civilization; for steam and the telegraph have made, not many nations, but one, in perfect unity in the world of thought, purpose, and intellect. And there could be no fault found in thus recognizing this counsellor of princes, and adviser of ministers, this woman who has done more for beneficial changes in the English world than any ten men in Great Britain. In an epoch fertile of great genius among women, it may be said of Miss Martineau, that she was the peer of the noblest, and that her influence on the progress of the age was more than equal to that of all the others combined. She has the great honor of having always seen truth one generation ahead; and so consistent was she, so keen of insight, that there is no need of going back to explain by circumstances in order to justify the actions of her life. This can hardly be said of any great Englishman, even by their admirers. We place the statue here in Boston because she has made herself an American. She passed through this city on the very day when the father of my honored friend was mobbed on State Street. Her friends feared to tell her the truth when she asked what the immense crowd were doing, and dissimulated by saying it was post-time, and the throng were hurrying to the office for the mail. Afterward, when she heard of the mob and its action, horror-struck, she turned to her host, the honored president of a neighboring university; and even he was American enough to assure her that no harm could come from such a gathering; said it was not a mob, it was a collection, or gathering. Harriet Martineau had been welcomed all over America. She had been received by Calhoun in South Carolina, the chief justice of Virginia had welcomed her at his mansion. But she went through the South concealing no repugnance, making her obeisance to no idol. She never bowed anywhere to the aristocracy of accident. This brave head and heart held its own throughout that journey. She came here to gain a personal knowledge of the abolitionists, and her first experience was with the mob on State Street. Of course she expressed all the horror which a gallant soul would feel. You may speak of the magnanimity and courage of Harriet Martineau; but the first element is her rectitude of purpose, by which was born that true instinct which saw through all things. We have had Englishmen come here, who were clear-sighted enough to say true words after they returned home; but this was a woman who was welcomed by crowds in the South, and about whom a glamour was thrown to prevent her from seeing the truth. It is easy to be independent when all behind you agree with you, but the difficulty comes when nine hundred and ninety-nine of your friends think you wrong. Then it is the brave soul who stands up, one among a thousand, but remembering that one with God makes a majority. This was Harriet Martineau. She was surrounded by doctors of divinity, who were hedging her about with their theories and beliefs. What do some of these later travellers who have been here know of the real New England, when they have been seated in sealed houses, and gorged with the glittering banquets of social societies? Harriet Martineau, instead of lingering in the camps of the Philistines, could, with courage, declare, 'I'll go among the abolitionists, and see for myself.' Shortly after the time of the State-street mob, she came to Cambridge; and her hosts there begged her not to put her hand into their quarrels. The abolitionists held a meeting there. The only hall of that day open to them was owned by infidels. Think of that, ye friends of Christianity. And yet the infidelity of that day is the Christianity of to-day. To this meeting in this hall Miss Martineau went, to express her entire sympathy with the occasion. As a result of her words and deeds, such was the lawlessness of that time, that she had to turn back from her intended journey to the West, and was assured that she would be lynched if she dared set foot in Ohio. She gave up her journey, but not her principles.

"Harriet Martineau saw, not merely the question of free speech,

NEARING THE END. 357

but the grandeur of the great movement just then opened. This great movement is second only to the Reformation in the history of the English and the German race. In time to come, when the grandeur of this movement is set forth in history, you will see its grand and beneficial results. Harriet Martineau saw it fifty years ago, and after that she was one of us. She was always the friend of the poor. Prisoner, slave, worn out by toil in the mill, no matter who the sufferer, there was always one person who could influence Tory and Liberal to listen. Americans, I ask you to welcome to Boston this statue of Harriet Martineau, because she was the greatest American abolitionist. We want our children to see the woman who came to observe, and remained to work, and, having once put her hand to the plough, persevered until she was allowed to live where the pæan of the emancipated four millions went up to heaven, showing the attainment of her great desire."

How many that listened to these noble words dreamed that they were to be the last which Wendell Phillips, the defender of equal rights and equal burdens for all men and women under the law, would ever utter in public? The heart that had so long beat for others, the silvery voice that had so long spoken for the suffering and oppressed, the perfect manhood that had so long existed for the good of all humanity, now felt the weight of years, and were already weakening beneath the pressure.

The new year came; but it brought only misgivings, the full meaning of which Mr. Phillips seems now to have interpreted rightly. On Saturday evening, Feb.

2, at quarter-past six o'clock, the great orator passed from earth.

He had been seriously ill, only since the Saturday of the previous week. On the morning of that day he was seized with an attack of heart disease. A physician was promptly summoned, who pronounced the trouble to be *angina pectoris*, — the same malady which had brought Charles Sumner to his grave, and which, having caused the death of Mr. Phillips's father and three brothers, was greatly dreaded by the friends and relatives of the orator.

The disease made rapid progress. He was confined to his bed on Sunday, suffering terrible pains; and his physician, Dr. Thayer, was called to the house no less than four times. By well-directed efforts the patient appeared to rally, and hopes were entertained of his recovery. But on Wednesday came a relapse, so serious in its nature that constant medical attendance became necessary. On Thursday, the 31st inst., Mr. Phillips's condition was exceedingly critical; and at midnight it was thought that he would not survive until morning. Again he rallied, however, but with only temporary relief. The exertion of moving in bed taxed him severely, and renewed paroxysms of pain, which necessitated the employment of anæsthetics.

No one now doubted that the end was approaching: even the patient realized this fact. When the doctor told him the probable result, he replied, —

THE COMMON-STREET HOUSE

"I have no fear of death. I am as ready to die to-day as at any time."

Still, he expressed a desire to outlive Mrs. Phillips, that he might care for her. In fact, during all the agony of his illness, when racked with pain, his thoughts invariably centred on his invalid wife.

On Friday, Mr. Phillips being no better, a consultation of physicians was held; but all agreed as to the condition of the patient. He grew easier during the forenoon, and was comfortable at noon. Friday evening the pain returned, but afterward passed away; and the attending physician, who remained with him, said that he passed a comfortable night.

On Saturday he suffered but little pain until about four o'clock in the afternoon, when he attempted to rise; but the exertion proved too much for him, and he fainted. He was laid back in the bed, when a severe pain seized him. Anæsthetics were applied, and quiet followed their administration. The loving wife and sisters, and other relatives, gathered around the bedside, watching the slow but certain passage through the dark valley. The last hour of life was one of perfect peace; and, as though reposing in the slumber of a little child, Mr. Phillips passed from life to eternity without a struggle. Bravely facing death, thankful for the slightest attention, thinking naught of himself, but of the loved one with whom and for whom he had lived so many years, he died as he had lived, ready to make any sacrifice for others.

Wendell Phillips was dead: the perfect orator was no more. The eloquent lips were silenced. The tidings were borne far and wide, and it was hard to believe them true. It was a time for memories and for tributes. The former were unsealed, the latter were forthcoming.

In every home in Boston, the death of Mr. Phillips was discussed on Sunday; and clergymen alluded to it from the pulpits. On Monday a public meeting was held at the Tremont House, under the auspices of the Labor-Reformers; and arrangements were made for a public memorial meeting on the following evening at Faneuil Hall. On the same day a special meeting of the City Council was called, to take appropriate action; and for the same purpose a committee was appointed in the State Legislature. The public press everywhere referred to his death as though it were a national bereavement. By public or private speech, by letter, by the telegraph, or by the cable, from far and wide, everybody expressed kind words and feeling tributes for the dead. In at least two instances, the eulogies were not only true, but epigrammatic. Said Joseph Cook, "Fifty years hence it will not be asked, 'What did Boston think of Wendell Phillips?' but, 'What did Wendell Phillips think of Boston?'" Said O'Donovan Rossa, "Wendell Phillips, of America, is dead in Boston."

The very atmosphere, full of Phillips as he died, and

articulating itself in thousand-fold manner, more than any or all particular written or spoken eulogies, seemed to commemorate a man not to be spared from American history, and without whom this country could not have done.

A service over the remains was held on Wednesday forenoon, the 6th inst., in the Hollis-street Church. Long before the hour appointed for the beginning of the exercises, people had assembled in the vicinity of the church; and, when the doors were open, such seats as were not reserved were quickly filled. The two races to whom Mr. Phillips had been a conspicuous friend were well represented in the throng, and appeared deeply touched as the preachers uttered affectionate words over the form that had been near and dear to them.

As the old clock in the belfry struck the hour of eleven, the remains were borne up the centre aisle to a resting-place in front of the pulpit. Judge Sewell, Dr. Holmes, Theodore D. Weld, Hon. John M. Forbes, W. P. Garrison, Lewis Hayden, W. I. Bowditch, Charles K. Whipple, Richard Hallowell, and Edward M. Davis were the pall-bearers. The casket was covered with broadcloth, and on the plate was inscribed, --

---

WENDELL PHILLIPS.
DIED FEB. 2, 1884.
AGED 72 YEARS.

The casket was closed; and at its head lay a miniature sheaf of ripened wheat, and a wreath of ivy-leaves bound with purple ribbon.

As the funeral procession moved forward, the organist, Mr. John A. Preston of St. Paul's Church, played Chopin's "Funeral March." The choir then chanted Longfellow's "Angels of Consolation." Rev. Samuel Longfellow read parts of the Scripture, and offered a prayer of much fervor. A few remarks and a prayer by Rev. Mr. May concluded the exercises at the church.

After the casket had been borne out, and placed in the hearse, a procession was formed to Faneuil Hall. Along the whole route, the sidewalks were lined with spectators; and nearly every window was crowded with people.

At a quarter past twelve the funeral *cortége*, to the music of two muffled drums, arrived at the eastern entrance to Faneuil Hall; Company M of the Sixth Regiment, and the Shaw Veterans, in command of Major Watkins, forming the guard of honor. The entire military escort was thus most fittingly composed of colored men. When the procession came to a halt, the remains were lifted from the funeral-car, and borne to the hall, by four white men, and the same number of colored soldiers from the guard of honor. Directly in front of the platform, from which so many times the stirring voice of the great abolitionist had been heard, was placed his body, that the thousands might take one last look at his face. In the centre of the hall was an enclosed space, containing a platoon of police, around which the throng passed during the afternoon.

The floral tributes were few, but beautiful in the extreme. On the centre of the platform was a mound of flowers about three by four feet. In the centre of it was the word "Humanity," in fresh violets on a bed of carnations. Around the carnations were wreaths composed of Niphetos roses, shamrock, hyacinths, pansies, and smilax. This beautiful tribute was presented by the Irish National League of Boston. On the easterly end of the platform was a harp four feet in height, composed of ivy-leaves, dotted with japonica blossoms and pansies. On the base of the harp was the word "Ireland," in violets on a bed of carnations; and around the base were numerous calla lilies. The strings of the harp were of silver, and one of them was broken, emblematical of a life departed. This was presented by the Irish-American societies of Boston.

On the westerly end of the platform was the tribute presented by Ex-Governor Butler. It was a crown of ivy, about two feet in height, dotted with Niphetos roses, japonicas, and pansies. On the coffin was a wreath of laurel and a sheaf of wheat, the latter tied with lavender ribbon, presented by George E. Hosler.

After the relatives and friends, who followed the dead to the hall in carriages, had taken a last look at all that was mortal of the departed, the military companies marched in, and stacked arms on one side of the hall. A body-guard was detailed, to stand watch over the remains; and sentinels were posted at various points, to assist the police-officers in managing the crowd. At one corner of the platform the battle-flag of the old Fifty-fourth Regiment, which is now in the possession of the Shaw Veterans, was borne. Opposite were the colors recently presented to the same association.

The assemblage in front of the Cradle of Liberty seemed to grow larger as the hours went on. Orderly and intent upon their mission as the great gathering proved, it was no small task for the officers of the police and the guard of honor to guide them aright. Nearly a quarter of an hour after the procession arrived at the hall, the doors were opened to the public. The police arrangements were admirably made, to preclude the possibility of any confusion. The incoming crowd was given entrance through the eastern portal of the hall; while those who had looked upon the face of the dead, made their departure through the other broad doorway.

The throng was emphatically a gathering of all sorts and conditions of men and women. Old anti-slavery workers, such as John W. Hutchinson, who sang the cause of freedom for the slave so effectively in early war-times, were there. The friends of the woman-suf-

IN FANEUIL HALL

frage cause took the opportunity afforded of a last look at the remains of their lost leader. It was fitting that men in their working-clothes, toilers who could afford no time for preparation, should be noted here and there in the line. Next to one of these, perhaps, would come a dignitary of State Street, or some merchant well-to-do, who had opposed the agitator all his life, but had yet respected all the while his absolute purity of motive and intensity of purpose. The crowd, adjured now and then to "Keep in line," "Keep moving, please," was as democratic, in truth, as such an occasion should have called together. Few words were spoken, but tears often gave keener expression to the thought of the great heart of Boston. Men of every race and of all walks in life, agitators of all names, people widely differing in their views on well-nigh every other subject, were as one in this purpose of honoring, so far as their presence could honor, the memory and the great work of the "silver-tongued" orator, whose voice can no more be heard among men.

White-haired old gentlemen, whose tottering footsteps showed declining strength and years, passed by with bowed head, and dropped a reverent "God bless him!" Aged women stood with tears in their eyes as they thought of their boys who had fought and died for the same cause that Wendell Phillips had so grandly espoused. Young men and women looked in sadness upon the features of him whom they had listened to with admiration in that very hall. Then, there were hundreds of boys and girls assembled, to obtain a single glance at one they had often heard of with pride. Occasionally a father would pass by with his child in his arms; and, as the tears flowed down his face, the little one would look as if dazed, and then burst into weeping. Children, whose heads barely reached above the casket, were lifted up, that they might look upon the face of him they had never heard, but whose addresses they will read and be thrilled by in the coming years.

The colored race, as a matter of course, was well represented in the long line of passers-by. In fact, it seemed as if the entire colored population of the city had assembled. They would gaze reverently upon the face of him whom they considered almost divine, and then, looking up at the battle-flag of the Fifty-fourth Regiment, would burst into tears as its tattered shreds brought vividly before them the scenes of their old bondage.

Many warm expressions of admiration for the deceased were heard on every side, but the colored people were the most demonstrative. "Bress de Lord! he am gone to de New Jerus'lem, shoah," said an old colored lady, as she reverently raised her hands, as if invoking a blessing. Another was heard to remark, feelingly, "He was de best fren' we ever hed. We owes him a heap."

NEARING THE END.

Many touching and expressive incidents and scenes happened during the afternoon. An old colored lady hesitated a moment, as if she would take one more glance at that face, and then as she turned away, with every feature expressing the deepest sorrow, murmured to herself, "Our Wendell Phillips has gone." Behind her came an old soldier. As he stood there for a second, he said, as if in deep thought, "We all fought for the same cause, and suffered alike."

On the platform, at half-past one o'clock, were seen the familiar face and form of Frederick Douglass. Many a glance from the passing multitude below was directed towards the tall figure, white-haired, of noble presence, evidently much affected by the scenes of the day. At his side stood the golden-haired wife whom he has so lately wedded, scarcely less moved than her husband by the scenes of the day. It was but a few moments before, that he had passed the casket of the dead. As he gazed at the features of Phillips, there seemed to be a pause for a moment in the current of humanity that had so steadily set toward the platform. Douglass was affected to tears, and bowed his head, saying brief words of regret and farewell to the leader so idolized by his race. Surrounded by some of the best colored citizens of Boston, Mr. Douglass said to a friend, "I came here not only to see the remains of my dear friend. I wanted to see this throng, and to see the hold that this man had upon the community. It is a wonderful tribute."

As the hours went by, with no sign of abatement in the number of pilgrims to the old hall, but a constant stream of people pressing to do honor to the dead, the great significance of the demonstration became more and more evident. It was a gathering long to be remembered, and but seldom equalled in numbers at any similar occasion of honor to the illustrious departed. At ten minutes after four the procession was stopped, and the doors closed; although thousands were still waiting outside, and were thus obliged to go away without obtaining a farewell glance at the familiar features of the "silver-tongued" orator.

After the doors of Faneuil Hall were closed in the afternoon, no more were admitted to see the face of Wendell Phillips. The crowd gathered about the door, and all the space around the hall was thronged with people. The hall was cleared of all but a few of the most intimate friends, one or two gentlemen necessarily present, and the guard. Before the kindly face of Mr. Phillips was covered forever by the casket-lid, a cast of the features was taken by Mr. P. A. Garey.

At about half-past four the guard filed out of the hall, and formed in line, facing the hearse, which stood at the door. The crowd in the mean time occupied every available inch of space on the steps of the lower market, in the windows and balconies of buildings facing the square, on the market-wagons standing in the street, and every place which commanded a view of the lower door of the hall. Here, as elsewhere, the number of colored persons in the crowd was unusual, and plainly indicated the affection which the negroes felt for Wendell Phillips, and their respect for his memory. After a considerable time, during which the crowd waited with no sign of breaking up, the casket was brought from the hall, and placed in the hearse; a guard of three from each of the military companies taking their places on each side, with arms reversed. The procession then formed, with Company M (Commander C. F. A. Francis) at the head, the Shaw Veteran Association, commanded by Major James B. Watkins, following, and immediately preceding the hearse, behind which came perhaps a dozen carriages, containing intimate friends. A vast crowd lining the streets, and following in a long procession behind the hearse, constituted the mourners. The line of march was through Merchants' Row to State Street, up State to Washington, Washington to School, School to Tremont, and so to the Old Granary Burying-ground, where, in the family-lot, hallowed to him by the ashes of his father and mother, Wendell Phillips was laid to rest. No words were spoken at the grave; and in a few moments the vast crowd had dispersed, having paid by its presence an honest tribute of respect to the memory of the dead.

CHAPTER XV.

PHILLIPS AS A PHILOSOPHER.

Origin of the "Radical Club." — Phillips's Views on Religion. — On the Christian Name. — On Heart in Religion. — Economic Laws. — Phillips on the Boston of To-day. — Phillips's Opinion of Jonathan Edwards.

"Christianity is a great moral power, the determining-force of our present civilization, as of past steps in the same direction."

"Unbelief has written books, but it never lifted a million men into a united struggle. The power that urged the world forward came from Christianity."

IN the spring of 1867 the Boston "Radical Club" had its origin in the growing desire of certain ministers and laymen for larger liberty of faith, fellowship, and communion. In this respect, it very closely resembled the Transcendentalist movement of an earlier date. It was designed to meet a demand for the freest investigation of all forms of religious thought and inquiry, and was composed of representatives of all denominations. At the first meeting of the club, thirty persons were present: at the closing sessions, in 1880, nearly two hundred were in regular attendance.

The meetings were held at No. 13 Chestnut Street; this being the residence of the Rev. John T. Sargent, whose childlike manner, earnest mood, and kindly heart, endeared him to all, high or low, rich or poor. In 1880 Mrs. John T. Sargent published her "Sketches and Reminiscences of the Radical Club," made up largely from notes and reports made of the meetings. Whatever is of worth and interest in the present chapter is culled mainly from this exceedingly pleasant and readable volume.

In May, 1867, Ralph Waldo Emerson read, at the club, his essay on "Religion." It was followed by a discussion, in which Mr. Sargent, Mrs. Julia Ward Howe, Col. Higginson, and others joined. We quote from Mr. Phillips's remarks: —

"He thought they ought not to fight windmills: they did sometimes fight shadows. He had never met a man of the old faith, — one worthy to be taken as a type of any thing, — who denied that the religious sentiment had found meet and valuable and admirable expression in the mythologies; and he thought that three-quarters of all the investigations which had been made into Oriental religions, translations of their books, inquiries into their history, and analyses of their faiths, had been made by so-called orthodox men. Yale College was as learned in all that matter as Harvard. He did not think, therefore, they could claim that the truth, as it appeared in those books and in those religions, had not been recognized by orthodox men. The point where they separated was not there, by any means. Of course, the old religions and mythologies grew out of an inspired religious consciousness, to a certain extent. He never knew a man who denied it. Every intelligent man that he ever met, of any sect, acknowledged the contributions to the literature of the West that had been made by many of the older faiths: they had not neglected, they had not depreciated, that development. On all this we agree. There is a great deal of astronomical speculation in the world, yet that does not interfere with the fact that there is a true astronomical method. Because a great many scholars had speculated about the stars, did that show that Copernicus and Sir Isaac Newton are not upon the right track? The question was, 'Is there any indication anywhere that we have touched, even slightly, on absolute truth in any of the mythologies?' When it was claimed that some parts of the New Testament could be found in Æschylus and Sophocles and Epictetus, he admitted it; but, when any man said that the New Testament could be found in Confucius and Buddha, he stopped, and demanded the proof. He did not *know* that any Jew by the name of Jesus Christ had said, 'Do unto others as ye would that others should do to you;' but he knew that the best scholarship of Europe had scrutinized every line of the record in the most exhaustive manner, until we know, if we know any thing, that, three hundred years after his death, he was supposed to have said it. So far they were on solid ground. It was said that Confucius, five hundred years before Christ, said, 'Do not do unto another as you would not have another do to you.' There was a remarkable similarity in the sentences, and very little probability that a Jew, in that narrow valley, ever heard of a Chinese. How did they know Confucius said it? All they knew about the Chinese was not older than three hundred and fifty years. If they could prove to him, that, three hundred years after the death of Confucius, he was supposed to have uttered those words, he would believe it, but not now; and he did not give any more weight to the legends about Buddha. No story, forty years old, could be relied upon without scrutiny.

"But suppose it was admitted that Confucius and Buddha did say just what Christ did? Steam and water were the same elements: but water would not move a locomotive; steam would. The Sermon on the Mount might be paralleled in Sophocles; they might find a great deal in Confucius: but one was water, the other steam; one had moved the world, the other had not. The proof that there was something unusual there, was seen in the results. India had all the intellectual brilliancy that Greece had; she touched all the problems, exhausted all the intellectual debate, thousands of years ago; and there she lies to-day. On the other hand, here was Europe. She had made marvellous progress; and, with the single exception of race, there was no element mixed in the European caldron to distinguish it from the Asiatic. Unless they were going to lay on this distinction of race the whole difference between European and Asiatic development, they had nothing but Christianity to account for it. It seemed to him that it was wiser to claim for Christianity the largest share in the merit of European civilization.

"Everybody knew that the Chinese had hospitals before Christ, if we are to trust history; everybody knew all about their progress in civilization; but they make no progress to-day. The bee could make an eight-sided cell better than Brunel could make it, but the bee can make nothing else. The Chinese had not advanced for a thousand years. They had every spring-board and fulcrum and motive-power to go ahead, and had not. Europe had constantly gone ahead. We had saved all we had got, and gained more. We had taken the classic and the Roman civilization, — taken their law, their ethics, their religious ideas, their idea of popular rights, — and we had carried them on. Europe was the hand and brain of the world to-day; the pioneer, the constructor, the administrator, of the world to-day; and there was nothing underlying her to make her so, except race and Christianity. Other portions of the world had had the same intellect. Tocqueville had told us, in his report to the French Institute, that there was no theory or dream of social science ever debated in Europe, that could not be found in the

Hindoo discussions. The difference was not caused by a lack of intellect. Here was a fact to be explained, and it could not be brushed away by saying this man and the other made a very near approach. No doubt that was so: nobody ever denied it. God never left any race, nor any man, nor any time, without himself; and these twilights, and approaches to noon, were seen everywhere in history. But they had got, at last, the Copernican theory; and no fact appeared that it did not explain. They had got, at last, the true chemical analysis; and that went down, and weighed the atoms. That explained all new combinations and all new discoveries. The reason why he believed in Sir Isaac Newton was, that he gave the key to every fact, discovered no matter where. Sir Thomas Browne could tell a great many beautiful dreams about astronomy, but they did not explain the facts. Christianity had faced the facts, and explained them. He claimed, therefore, that there was something essentially different in it from the religious experience of other races."

At another meeting, an essay on "The Christian Name" was read by William H. Channing. It called forth the following statements from Mr. Phillips:—

"'Christianity [said he] is a great moral power, the determining-force of our present civilization, as of past steps in the same direction. Jesus is the great religious genius who has given its peculiar type to the modern world. Speculations as to the why and the how may differ, but we see the fact. We cannot rub out history. Europe shows a type of human character not paralleled anywhere else. The intellect of Greece centred around power and beauty; that of Rome around legal justice. The civilization of modern Europe was inspired by a great moral purpose. Imperfect as it was, and limited in many ways, the religious element there had steadily carried those nations forward. The battle for human rights was finally fought on a Christian plane. Unbelief has written books, but it never lifted a million men into a united struggle. The power that urged the world forward came from Christianity. Mr. Channing has explained to us its origin. I look at its results, and they lead to the same conclusion. He claims to be Christian. So do I. The best part of the life of Europe may be traced to Christianity.

"'The religious literature of Asia has been compared with the Christian Scriptures. The comparison is not just. That literature has many merits, and contains scattered sayings and precepts of great excellence; but there are heaps of chaff in that, and in the writings of the early Christian Fathers; none in the Gospels and Epistles. Of the mediæval writings, one-half was useless. Of the boasted works of Confucius, seven-tenths must be winnowed out, to find what the average reason of mankind would respect.'"

At one of the meetings, "Heart in Religion" was the subject of an essay by the Rev. John Weiss.

When it came to the discussion, Mr. Phillips maintained that the character of Jesus was no mystery.

"'You need not analyze a lemon, to find out whether it is sour. You speculate as to whether Jesus was a masculine character. Look at the men who have learned of him most closely,— at Paul and Luther and Wesley. Were they effeminate? yet the disciple is but a faint reflection of his Master. The character from which came the force which has been doing battle ever since with wrong and falsehood and error was nothing less than masculine; but sentiment is the toughest thing in the world,— nothing else is iron. And, in spite of friend Wasson, Jesus was right in pitying the poor in pocket, the burden-bearers, the takers of other men's wages. Compulsory labor *is* a curse — always has been.'"

"Economic Laws" was a theme discussed at one of the sessions by the Hon. David A. Wells. It gave rise to a very earnest debate, which is here given as reported at the time:—

"Next was Mr. Wendell Phillips; and, before he ceased, the clash of opposing doctrines and the earnestness of positive natures made the discussion singularly entertaining. Mr. Phillips stated, first, his disbelief in the free-trade doctrine, though he held that creed fifteen years ago. He had been misled by the theoretical arguments in favor of free trade, but had been set right by hearing the facts as stated by Mr. Henry Cary, the patriarch of political economy, to whose judgment the world listens. He had heard Mr. Cary say, 'I had just finished a crushing reply to the New-England tariff men, — one that I thought demolished their whole structure of argument. I went to bed delighted with my success in stating my case. Somehow I could not help seeing, that, though the logic seemed perfect, it did not cover the facts. On paper it was all right: out in the world the facts were the other way. I lay awake all night, chewing on the contradiction, and arose the next morning a tariff man.' Any one who listened from Cary's lips to the stern facts which converted him in that night of anxious, honest thought, would never again be duped by free trade.

"Nations are large enough, Mr. Phillips thinks, to be considered separately from each other. Internal industry should be diversified. Under free-trade rule, our country would be wholly agricultural. Other elements must be considered besides the mere question of wealth. Should we lose our diversified occupations, we should suffer a great loss; though there might be a pecuniary gain. Nations might gain the whole world, — that is, half the material wealth of the world, — and yet lose their own souls, and most of their bodies too. Theories are pleasing things, and seem to get rid of all difficulties so very easily. One must begin with abstract principles, and study them. But wisdom consists in perceiving when human nature and this perverse world necessitate making exceptions to abstract truths. Any boy can see an abstract principle. Only threescore years and ten can discern precisely when and where it is well, necessary, and right to make an *exception* to it. That faculty is wisdom: all the rest is playing with counters. And this explains how the influx into politics of a shoal of college-boys, slenderly furnished with Greek and Latin, but steeped in marvellous and delightful ignorance of life and public affairs, is wrecking the Republican party.

"National lines — *artificial* lines — trip up fine theories sadly. If all the world were under one law, and every man raised to the level of the Sermon on the Mount, free trade would be so easy and so charming! But while nations study only how to cripple their enemies, that is, their neighbors, and while each trader strives to cheat his customer, and strangle the firm on the other side of the street, we must not expect the millennium.

"From this point, Mr. Phillips proceeded to state how he would get protection without the arbitrary laws which Mr. Wells denounced, and unfolded his well-known views upon paper currency, by which money enough for business can be borrowed for two or three per cent. Mr. Wells asked him how it is that interest here is now seven per cent; and Mr. Phillips promised to answer him a little farther on, and explained his theory of using the credit of the government as the basis of the currency.

"'The next presidential election [said Mr. Phillips] will turn, to a great extent, on the currency question. If the South can be broken into natural divisions, and brought to behave decently, the currency will be the *only* great question. The next step of the Democracy will be, to establish the greenback system.'

"'It will be worthy of it' [the Democracy], keenly interrupted Mr. Wasson; and his sally was received with laughter and applause by the unsympathizers.

"'Yes,' said Mr. Phillips, 'it *will* be the *first* work needed by a *true Democratic* party. For this greenback question only means whether we shall trust the Declaration of Independence, — that all men are equal in money matters, as in every thing else. Hitherto we have been Tories in money questions, and trusted the people only in other matters. July 4, 1776, said, "The sober second thought of the *people* is the safest and best guide in all civil affairs, — personal rights, property, marriage, crimes, and all; and we can devise machinery which will secure that sober second thought."

"'We have been living successfully and prosperously for a hundred years on that plan and platform, with one exception, — money matters. In those, capitalists, bank directors, and a select class, have been thought to be the only safe guides. The people now claim that they can and will decide these as wisely and honestly as they do all other matters. This is the last fight between wealth and the people, — not between noble

PHILLIPS AS A PHILOSOPHER. 381

and serf, but between money-bags and the workingmen; between the men who create wealth, and those who steal a living by the hocus-pocus of banking and the nonsense of coin. The people will now carry the Declaration of Independence into Wall Street, where it has never yet penetrated; and we shall have a more honest finance than the world has yet seen.'

"Mr. Wells retorted, 'We are the most dishonest nation on the face of the globe.'

"'No,' said Mr. Phillips, 'not the most dishonest *nation*. Perhaps ours has been of late as dishonest an administration as the world often sees, — not the fault of the masses, but of the capitalists. Three times within a dozen years, capitalists, with their knives on the throat of the government, have compelled it to cheat its largest creditor, the people, whose claim, Burke said, was the most sacred. First, the pledge that greenbacks should be exchangeable with bonds was broken. Secondly, debts originally payable in paper, as Sherman confessed in the Senate, were made payable in coin. Thirdly, silver was demonetized, and gold made the only tender. A thousand million dollars were thus stolen from the people. These are the crimes of capital: the people are honest enough if left to themselves.'

"To one who doubted this *popular* virtue, Mr. Phillips replied, 'Never expect heaven in Boston. I never said that a democracy was a *good* government.

A thing may be the *best* we can get, and yet not be *good*. Democracy is not a good government, but it is the best we can get while we have only this poor, rotten human nature to work with. Governments created by the people have always been more honest and less corrupt than those originating with the aristocracy, and revolutions made by the people have generally been more merciful and less bloody than the victories of the upper classes. No student of European history can fail to see this.'

"Mr. Phillips's enthusiastic advocacy of his scheme of abolishing all coin, and issuing two thousand million dollars (an amount equal to the national debt), based on the thirty thousand millions of property of the country, so that interest should never be more than five per cent, was welcomed with much good-natured laughter, which betrayed no sign of a new convert to greenbackism.

"Mr. Wells replied to the so-called facts of Henry Cary, that he had once looked upon Mr. Cary as his Gamaliel, had been very intimate with him, and was brought up as a protectionist; but he found Mr. Cary's facts were no facts, and he became a free-trader perforce. He has repeatedly challenged Mr. Cary to public discussion, and has received only abuse in reply. More sparks were struck from each side: and Mr. Wells declared he hoped the question would go into the next presidential campaign, as Mr. Phillips said it would;

and he wished that they two could meet in public discussion, and see which was right. He would be glad to meet Mr. Phillips on the platform.

" So the warfare of words raged bravely and profitably, if public discussion for popular enlightenment shall be the outcome. A few other gentlemen spoke briefly; and the company dispersed, after a sitting of more than two and a half hours."

In 1873 there was a club-reception given to Mr. Emerson. Among those who assembled on the last day of the year, to show their respect for the "Sage of Concord," were John G. Whittier, Henry W. Longfellow, Dr. Hedge, Mr. Phillips, Henry Wilson, and Henry James. A question whether the Boston of to-day would always act with the same spirit as it did a century ago, drew out various opinions. Mr. Phillips opened the discussion by saying, —

" 'I believe the pictures of that Boston, a hundred years ago, are very highly colored. That the word "caucus" has been even guessed to have taken its origin from the *Calkers*, betrays the popular notion and estimate of the rising Rebellion. John Hancock's scarlet coat becomes historic as being the only one which covered a rebel. That "brace of Adamses," whom Hutchinson has immortalized, were then men of no repute, vulgar fanatics, heading a crowd of working-men, scoffed at, and scorned, by the respectables of the day. The marvel is, that the middle, well-to-do, and commercial classes headed a rebellion which had no religion in it. That is explained by the fact, that every successful merchant in Boston was obliged to be a smuggler. England crippled our trade to save her own, as she has been doing with Ireland for the last century. So the traders, angered by self-interest, *calculated* it would pay to join the mob, and rise. But Toryism had the fashion, the old wealth, and the prestige, as it has always had.

"'As to our day rising as high even as that, I doubt. Not much if a reform-city is one which puts a rope round Garrison to hang him, which even yet hates Sumner; one whose Unitarian pulpit deserted and betrayed Pierpont for his temperance fidelity, and where there never has been, even to this day, a fashionable Orthodox church opened for an abolition meeting. Would any young enthusiast, on fire with a new reform idea, be crazy enough to go to State Street, Beacon Street, the Old South, or Harvard College for countenance? If so, he must be *very* young, and will soon learn better. The young patriots, who, when Sumter called, leaped to arms, ten years ago, were exceptions, not average specimens, by any means.'"

In the spring of 1880 Oliver Wendell Holmes read his essay on "Jonathan Edwards." The remarks upon it of Mr. Phillips must close this chapter.

"'The picture drawn by Dr. Holmes, though truthful and accurate so far as it goes, cannot be full or complete. As a whole, it cannot be just to Edwards: there must be other sides, which would soften and redeem it; other doctrines, that explain and fill out the full religious life and character, and justify the profound and loving respect our fathers had for him. Else how can we account for the great fact of New England, which is the outcome of his and similar pulpits?

"'No one doubts that a large majority of the New-England pulpits, one hundred years ago, sympathized with, and sustained, Edwards. These horrible doctrines, which Dr. Holmes shocked us with, were not Edwards's individual and singular views, but the common faith of New England. Now, religion and theological doctrines are great factors in forming character. If the pulpit of New England taught only, or mainly, these hateful, narrow, inhuman, and degrading doctrines, — if such was the *character* of its teaching, — whence came this generous, public-spirited, energetic, hopeful, broad, humane, self-respectful, independent, and free-thoughted New England, ready for every good work, and willing for every necessary sacrifice?

"'We must have a theory broad enough to cover all the facts. It used to be said, that "He who makes religion *twelve*, and the world *thirteen*, is no true New-Englander." His religion was three-quarters of a Yankee. What you gentlemen here call "free religion" and "liberal Christianity" is of very recent growth, and of still very narrow influence. But character is of slow growth. Any theory which narrows and degrades the New-England pulpit of the eighteenth century fails to account for the community which grew up under it.

"To one who suggested as an explanation, that our fathers never really believed such doctrines, Mr. Phillips replied, 'It will hardly do to maintain that the hard headed and practical Yankee, so keen and ready witted in affairs, so free and bold in civil life, the world's intellectual pioneer, did not know or understand what he believed, in — to him — the most important matter of all, his religion. Four generations passed over the stage, and left us this commonwealth, their creation, — sober, painstaking, serious, earnest men. We cannot accept the theory which represents their religion as carelessly taken up, loosely held, and only half understood. Great jurists, practical statesmen, profound scholars, liberal founders of academy, college, and hospital, boldly searching the world over for means to perfect institutions on which the world now models itself, — were these minds crippled by absurd dogmas, worldlings without faith, or hypocrites afraid to avow their real belief? True philosophy never accepts such theories to explain history. It is more natural and philosophical to suppose that the sketch we have listened to, admirable as it is, has not given all the sides of the picture.'

"Dr. Bartol suggested that Edwards's parish repudiated him: after twenty years listening to him, they voted against him ten to one.

"Mr. Phillips replied, 'That argument proves too much. We have just exhausted language in praising the eminent Christian spirit and untold influence of Dr. W. E. Channing. But we all know, that, after Channing had preached twenty years to men who idolized him, they mobbed him for his anti-slavery ideas, and refused him the use of his own church for the funeral services of the Abolitionist Follen, Channing's most intimate and valued friend. Channing failed as thoroughly, forty years ago, in teaching his church justice and humanity, as Edwards did, a hundred years ago, in bringing his hearers to relish the idea of infant damnation. It will not do for Unitarians in Boston to throw that Northampton vote in Edwards's face. Northampton never mobbed Edwards for his infant damnation, as Boston did Channing for his anti-slavery, in Faneuil Hall.'"

CHAPTER XVI.

EULOGIES AND TRIBUTES.

THE death of Wendell Phillips called forth many tokens of respect and admiration. In nearly every city and town in the country, east, west, north, and south, his name was mentioned, and his life-work reconsidered, from public platforms, from pulpits, or in social and literary gatherings. To reproduce in these pages even a tithe of what was said or written, would swell the size of the volume many fold. It becomes necessary, therefore, to limit the present chapter chiefly to the utterances that were publicly heard in the city which witnessed the birth and death of the great orator.

"A meeting to commemorate the name of Wendell Phillips was held in Faneuil Hall on the evening of Feb. 9. Mr. E. M. Chamberlain was the presiding officer; and the ruling spirits of labor reform, and other issues which Mr. Phillips espoused, were numerous upon the platform. Representatives of the colored race were also conspicuous. A lifelike and life-size bust of the dead orator was upon the platform, with its pedestal twined about with smilax. Among the people present were Mrs. Susan B. Anthony, George T. Downing, Dr. William Wells Brown, George H. Lowther, John M. Devine, Charles H. Litchman, T. C. Brophy, Gustavus B. Hutchinson, James H. Roberts, Mrs. Ednah D. Cheney, James N. Buffum, Samuel C. Fay, the Rev. Dr. Miner, A. B. Currier, Professor Twohey, James Tarone, and Joshua Whittemore.

"DETAILS OF THE MEETING.

"At half-past seven Mr. James Sumner of Milton called the meeting to order, and introduced Mr. George E. McNeill, formerly secretary of the Butler Independent Republican State Committee, as chairman of the meeting. He said that it was proposed to have Mr. E. M. Chamberlain as president; but, at the last moment, he had been called upon. With brief eulogy he referred to Mr. Phillips as a living protest against a false Christianity, against the disfranchisement of women, and against the oppression of the poor. He was the voice of the voiceless, the friend of the downtrodden and suffering everywhere. In conclusion, Mr. McNeill presented Mr. J. M. L. Babcock of Cambridge as the first speaker. In substance he said, —

"I am to speak of a man in whose career there was no error, and in whose character there was no defect. He needs no eulogy. Where are the anointed lips that can eulogize the perfect man? If we would name a career that would be worthily emulated, we have only to name Wendell Phillips. A great orator was defending one of the foulest murders of the time, when a young man, unknown to fame, flung himself upon the spear-points, to 'make way for liberty.' That scene tells the story of his life. The speaker said Phillips was made a prophet by his high, moral purpose, which kept his soul so pure that he could see where others could not. I am glad it has been said that Phillips was no politician. Politicians are a very low order of beings. [Applause.] He is praised to-day for that for which he was censured thirty years ago. From this, we may expect the success of every reform he has espoused. I should hesitate to doubt the success of any reform sanctified by the advocacy of his holy lips. Only ignorance can impute malice to Wendell Phillips. [Applause.] We cannot appreciate the greatness of his oratory, because we have no one with whom to compare him on either side of the water. Phillips found a Boston which said, 'Cursed be Canaan!' he left a Boston ready to say, 'Perish Bibles and constitutions that send young, trembling girls to the auction-block!' [Applause.] One thing we can do: we can erect on Boston Common a statue of Wendell Phillips, and so lead our young men to drink of the same moral fountains, and remove from our age the reproach of having no advocate of great reforms.

"The president announced James Sumner of Milton, as secretary, and then said, that, as Mr. E. M. Chamberlain had arrived, he would act as presiding officer for the remainder of the evening. Mr. Chamberlain eulogized, in measured periods, the many traits of Mr. Phillips. Said he, 'Phillips never separated the question of the black man from that of universal emancipation. We are approaching the greatest contest of all the ages. The heroic efforts of the race from Greece, America, and France will give place to a conflict in which all the civilized globe will unite, to which all other conflicts will be nothing. Phillips has well upheld the honor of Massachusetts. He was a noble successor to those disinterested patriots who have shed honor upon all mankind.' [Applause.]

"Mr. Chamberlain then introduced Mrs. Julia Ward Howe. Her eulogy was in these words:—

"'The loss which has fallen upon us is one which silence best expresses. Stricken hearts, losing forever the dear intimacy of a beloved friend, ask to make their sorrow so quiet, that no one shall hear it. But the swift issues of life forbid this silence. Another change of the glass, and we shall be, not only silent, but voiceless. So, in the very quick of our grief, we must speak, in order to give form and expression to our feeling and conviction. I am here to-night, with my small woman's voice, to speak the praises of this great friend. I am here as one of the weak, to praise the strength of the helper and deliverer. But I am here, too, in the strength which he helped me and others to find. A weak thing, with justice behind it, is strong. [Applause.] A strong thing, with justice opposed to it, is weak. [Applause.] Our champion knew this weakness and this strength. He has taught us and the world to know it better than we should have known it without him. The aid which Mr. Phillips gave to the cause of woman was characterized like all his work, by a great strength of purpose, and solidity of moral conviction. There was nothing airy, fanciful, or voluntary in his advocacy of woman suffrage. The solidity of Mr Phillips's belief was matched by the extension of his views. Some have spoken of him as having shown a failure of judgment in his later years. He was not infallible. But his view of justice was infallible, for it was founded upon the truth of God himself. [Applause.] His belief was, that the rights of the poorest and meanest are as sacred as the rights of the highest and greatest. The despised slave, the wronged Indian, the derided woman suffragists, the distrusted Irishman, — all of these were his clients. And we can commit his example to posterity, without fear or remorse, so deep are the foundations of right, so wide is the application of justice. Wendell Phillips would have thrown open to women the doors of every opportunity, of every career. He would have had them free as air in the streets, which he wished to see pure enough for the presence of angels, and which, we know, would only attain that purity when the angels of humanity should walk in them. But let no one think or say that this heart's desire of his involved the desertion of home and the neglect of its duties. His own devotion to the woman who was home to him shows us that he knew the value of the fireside, and of its dear and sacred intimacy At the funeral services, recently held at the Hollis-street Church, it was observable that those who spoke, spoke to God in prayers. The gulf between our noblest examples and the common level of our daily life sometimes seems so wide, that we can only cross it on the wings of prayer. The friends who on that day looked on Wendell Phillips, and the world around him, could only pray to God that the truth which made his life glorious might enter more and more into the heart and life of the community. I will add my voice to theirs, imploring the heavenly powers that the steadfast faith which Wendell Phillips kept may more and more prevail in the doubting hearts of his countrymen and countrywomen. May those who dare not receive the doctrine of the fathers, that all human creatures are born free and equal, and endowed by God with inalienable human rights, may they learn from the record of his life a deeper wisdom and a nobler courage! and may the women of our Commonwealth take counsel, not of men who have never grasped the largeness of moral principles, but of this great gentleman, who was free as well as forcible, tender as well as true, who believed in the instant help of God, and in the constant redemption of man!' [Applause.]

"Mr. John Hutchinson, of the Hutchinson family of singers, was introduced, to sing an original song upon Mr. Phillips. Prefacing his song with the statement, that for forty years his family, as a family, had been singing for the same causes as those for which Mr. Phillips had been speaking, he sang tender words, beginning, —

"'Close his eyes: his work is done.
What to him is friend or foeman!'

The closing stanza was, —

"'Lay him low, lay him low,
Under the clover, or under the snow:
How we loved him none, can know.
Lay him low.'

The music written for the words was plaintive, and fitting to the hour, and proved highly pleasing to the audience.

"The Rev. P. A. McKenna, the next speaker, said that Wendell Phillips was not only a lover of his kind and an advocate of the rights of women, but an ardent champion of the cause of Ireland. In the great heroes of the world, Faneuil Hall claimed her citizens and her inspiration. It was in Faneuil Hall that Phillips first spoke; in Faneuil Hall that he lifted up his voice for Ireland. He stood alone among the living in his greatness, and there was none to equal him in the awful company of the illustrious dead. When the great question called in Russia Nihilism, in Italy and Germany Socialism, in Ireland the agrarian question, in America the labor-question [applause], pressed for a solution, then it was that the agitator stepped to the front, and pushed aside the politician. The history of the wronged Irish race appealed to the mind of Wendell Phillips. The lesson of his life was the efficacy of constitutional agitation. This was the chief lesson to Irishmen. The reform of the suffrage, the repeal of the corn-laws, the disestablishment of the Irish Church, were not brought about by the dagger, but by agitation.

"The Rev. Dr. Miner was next introduced. 'If only those who could equal Phillips's eloquence,' he said, 'were allowed to speak, let all the world keep silent. But if all who had been lifted and helped to liberty could speak, let all the world raise its voice. Calumny is said to be the honor paid by contemporaries. If this is true, how highly has he been honored already! Did the motive remain, the enemies of Phillips would calumniate him, as they did in the days of slavery. Though there were four millions held in slavery, yet fifty millions in this country are held in the bonds of the liquor-traffic. [Applause.] He knew the shams in Boston in regard to enforcing the liquor-law. Mayor, aldermen, council, and police were doing all they could to nullify the prohibitory law.

[A voice, "No."] The legislative committee would sit as cowardly as craven dogs of war under his scathing sarcasm. But the world moves, and there will be no truce on Beacon Hill until the truth is organized into law. [Long applause.] In the causes of human rights, — purity of lives, and distribution of property, — there is equality of persons. A dozen men on Beacon Hill hold Massachusetts in their hands. It is for you who have ballots, to teach those men where they belong, and teach them to respect right and justice. It is said that he was foolish in the schemes of his later life; but, when the manufacture and use of liquors shall be prevented, then the temperance cause will rise to honor, with the name of Wendell Phillips. Dr. Miner then defended Mr. Phillips's well-known greenback views. 'The capitalist puts his money into government bonds, payable, principal and interest, in gold. But the poor soldier was set up, to be shot through and through, and driven into splinters, and was paid fifteen dollars a month, worth about five dollars. He was a soft-money man. [Voice, "That's true."] Yes, that's true in the light of justice. But he put the burden where it belonged, — on the whole people. Congress is as ignorant on money-matters as a boy unborn. [Laughter.] That is not a popular saying. I shall hear from it to-morrow.' [Applause.] Dr. Miner said he sympathized with these laborers, and laborers everywhere, in their struggles for equal distribution of property. [Applause.] He sympathized with the efforts for woman's enfranchisement. He sympathized with the efforts to redeem Ireland. [Applause.]

"Dr. William Wells Brown was next introduced. He said that he first met Mr. Phillips at an anti-slavery convention in 1842, and from that time down to his death was more intimately acquainted with him than any colored man in Massachusetts. On one occasion the speaker found seven colored men waiting to ask him for money for some Southern work or college. He gave to them all, shutting none out.

"James N. Buffum was introduced as a friend of Mr. Phillips, and one who had been a part of the troublous times contemporary with him. After describing the 'mobocracy' troubles in Boston, when Garrison was placed in Leverett-street jail to protect him from violence, when he took a part in thwarting their endeavors to harm him, he passed to the great meeting in Faneuil Hall, where Mr. Phillips first appeared as the champion of liberty. He said, 'And then it was that Rev. Dr. Channing, that venerable old man, joined with others to call a meeting in this hall, to protest against the mobocracy that so ruled in the country. By my side sat Wendell Phillips: in front there, Hancock and Adams, and those old heroes of the Revolution, were on the wall. Dr. Channing came forward with his beautiful, heavenly voice, and lifted it up in favor of humanity against the vice of the day; and he said, "Let my name be attached to it: let it go across the Atlantic, and be heard wherever I am known, that I have tried to do all I could to roll back this storm of mobocracy." Here sat Mr. Phillips; and, when Dr. Channing had closed, James T. Austin, who was then our State attorney, arose, and undertook to defend that act of murder. He said that "it was only in accordance with the Revolution: the throwing overboard of the tea was against law, the fight on Bunker Hill was nothing but a mob, and the people outraged would always resist it." He went on to say, "Dr. Channing has come down from a holy place, the pulpit, and has mingled in the strifes of the political arena." I listened to him throughout, for he was an eloquent man; and, when he closed, this young man (Mr. Phillips), twenty-six years of age, one of the handsomest men I ever saw, — his face beaming with excitement, his eye like an eagle's, — took the platform, and began in these words: "Mr. Chairman, I have lived to see the day when the old heroes of the Revolution have been compared to a mob. I have lived to see the day when those who fought on Bunker Hill have been compared to the murderers of Lovejoy!

I wonder," said he, "that those painted lips on yonder wall had not broken the silence of fifty years, and burst forth to rebuke this recreant son of America! I wonder, that in this old Cradle of Liberty, consecrated by the Adamses and Hancocks, the floor, upheaving, had not yawned to swallow him up." Those galleries were crowded: this hall was nothing but a sea of men, rolling backward and forward. And they cried out, "Take it back, recreant." Mr. Phillips stood with majesty and dignity; and, when the howling of the mob subsided, he said, "An abolitionist takes nothing back." They howled again; but he went on with such power, such beauty of expression, that he awed them into silence, and broke their power in this place. He continued, "Has it come to this? did God intend this country should be the burial-place of liberty? did he scoop out the Mississippi as her grave, and pile up the Rocky Mountains as her monument, or pour forth the Niagara for her requiem?"' And so on, in a rare address, combining his recollection of the scenes with a vivid portrayal of them, Mr. Buffum led the audience on and on, to a deeper interest in his reminiscences."

On Thursday evening, Feb. 28, a memorial meeting under the auspices of the Massachusetts Woman Suffrage Association was held in the Meionian, Boston. It was a most interesting and memorable occasion. Mrs. Julia Ward Howe called the meeting to order, and was the opening speaker. She was followed by William Lloyd Garrison, jun., who read a most beautiful address, the closing paragraphs of which are here quoted: —

"I cannot close with more appropriate words than those of Mr. Phillips himself, as applicable to his career as to that of Francis Jackson, at whose funeral they were pronounced: 'The pitiless storm of hate beat upon him for thirty years. Malice — personal, political, religious — watched his every act, dogged his every step; and yet no breath of suspicion ever touched his character. Out of that ordeal he comes, with no smell of fire on his garments: the boldest malice never gathered courage to invent an accusation. . . . No man ever suspected him of any thing but bravery, of holding opinions which all hated, and of acting them out at the risk of property and life, and the actual sacrifice of all common men love. How few have such an epitaph! We who knew him, when we read of Hampden resisting ship-money, or Sidney going to the block, feel that we have walked and lived with their fellow. . . . His best praise is our following his example, and each fearlessly obeying his own conscience, and doing with his might whatever his hand finds to do for his fellow-man. Let us so do him honor. And, as the great Englishman said of his friend, "There's none to make his place good: let us go to the next best," so of thee, dear comrade and leader of many years, thy place is sacred forever to thy memory. We go to the next best, till God gives us to see thee once again face to face.'"

Theodore D. Weld, the man who led in the anti-slavery agitation in Ohio in 1834, paid a most eloquent tribute to the memory of his old friend. He was followed by Judge Thomas Russell, Mrs. Ednah D. Cheney, Hon. Elizur Wright, Rev. Samuel May, Mrs. Lucy Stone, George W. Lowther, and others. Every word that was said by these speakers was well worthy of reproduction in these pages; but, unfortunately, the limits of our space will not permit even fragmentary selections.

The colored citizens of Boston and vicinity assembled in Tremont Temple on the evening of the 11th of April, to listen to a eulogy by Mr. Archibald H. Grimké of

Boston. No attempt at decoration of the hall was made, and nothing emblematic of mourning was visible; but a life-size portrait in oil of Mr. Phillips, half-buried within ferns and calla lilies, stood immediately in front of the organ. The seats upon the platform were fully occupied by ladies and gentlemen, all more or less identified with the struggle for the abolition of slavery, and the elevating of the colored race. Hon. George L. Ruffin introduced the orator of the evening in the following short address: —

"No other class of people can, with greater propriety, meet to pay a tribute to the memory of Wendell Phillips than the descendants and representatives of those for whose freedom he labored so long. During the latter part of his life he advocated other causes, and labored for other reforms; but the best years of his life, the period of his early manhood and middle age, were given wholly to the cause of the negro. And to-day his immediate colored constituents have gathered, to say some words of respect to his memory, knowing at the same time that these words are entirely inadequate to express the sense of their loss.

"For intensity of devotion to the anti-slavery cause, Mr. Phillips must be given the first place among the leaders in that warfare. Other great captains there were, with as much wisdom, patience, and steadiness; but Mr. Phillips was the brilliant and dashing officer, marvellous in skill, and with unquenchable zeal. Yet, in the beginning of his public life, Mr. Phillips knew little or nothing of slavery from personal observation. He had never been shocked by a sight of the brutalities of plantation-life. His knowledge of the negro, and negro character, was confined almost entirely to what he had seen and known of the less than one thousand colored people then living in Boston, and what he could occasionally gather from an escaped slave. But he did know the system of slavery with its attendant evils well. He knew the demoralizing effects of slavery, and its degrading influence. He knew that slavery was wrong, and he abhorred it. The enemies of freedom derisively called the abolitionists negro-lovers. Mr. Phillips did not love the negro as a negro. He loved justice, he hated injustice. He saw that the negro was deprived of his liberty, and was outraged; he saw that society and government were combined against the negro; and he renounced society, rebelled against government, and took his stand against both to defend the negro. At this time Mr. Phillips was well acquainted with the leading intelligent colored men then in Boston: John T. Hilton, Rev. Thomas Paul, Charles Lenox Remond, and William C. Nell, the historian, were all co-workers in the abolition society, which held its meetings in Belknap-street Church (now Joy-street). In this little church Mr. Phillips delivered some of those inspired speeches which unfortunately have never been printed, but are so often referred to latterly. Robert Morris, Lewis Hayden, William Wells Brown, and other colored men, were his co-workers: the relations between Mr. Phillips and his immediate colored constituents were pleasant and mutually agreeable; they thoroughly appreciated his sacrifices for them, and he was well aware of that fact. When danger threatened, or troubles arose, as they often did in the fugitive-slave-law times, the colored man always went to Mr. Phillips for advice and assistance.

"In the eyes of many colored people, Mr. Phillips was the one exceptional white American wholly color blind, and free from race-prejudice. Without saying this, it may be said, that, if he was not the truest, he was among the truest, to the rights and interests of colored people. In his demand for equal rights for colored people, there was no qualification, — absolutely none; the demand covered every relation of life: and when Richard H. Dana, fugitive-slave defender as he was, said, that when he remembered what his race was, and what the negro race was, in an insurrection his sympathy would go with his race, Mr. Phillips, from an infinitely higher plane, replied, in such a case 'My sympathies would go with the right.' His teachings to the colored people were of inestimable value: it was the higher education to them. He taught them their duty to themselves, he encouraged their aspirations, false notions of life were unlearned, he taught them self-reliance and manliness. He once said, 'A slave I pity, a rebellious slave I respect.' The question has been often asked, 'Which had the stronger hold upon the affections of the colored people, Mr. Garrison, or Mr. Phillips?' That question can never be satisfactorily answered; it is beyond the ability of any person to sound the depths of feeling entertained by the colored people for both: but in a general way it may be said, older men gravitated towards Mr. Garrison, while younger men were more demonstrative for Mr. Phillips. And it may be further said, if this distinction is correct, that this feeling had its origin in the discussion between Mr. Garrison and Mr. Phillips, on the dissolution of the Anti-Slavery Society at the close of the war, — Mr. Garrison contending that the slaves were free, the work was done; and Mr. Phillips insisting that the work was not done, but should be continued until the slaves had equal rights.

"Mr. Phillips never failed to give pecuniary assistance to worthy colored students who applied to him for aid. He not only gave himself, but helped the applicant to get assistance elsewhere.

"Wide apart as were Mr. Phillips and his colored friends in race and social position, there was, nevertheless, this community of feeling between them, — they were both under the ban of public disfavor. The negro was despised, and Mr. Phillips was the best-hated man in Boston.

"In his speeches to the colored people, he never lowered himself in style or substance to the level of their capacities. He spoke to them as he did to any other public audience, but at times he was very practical. He talked on the education of children, obtaining homesteads, and learning trades.

"The people of Boston never appreciated Mr. Phillips: it seems to have never occurred to them, that they had in him a most valuable citizen, the brightest ornament to the city. If they did appreciate him, it was not admitted in his lifetime. Small and unworthy men came to the front, and played important parts, while Mr. Phillips lived unnoticed in an unfashionable quarter of the city. Mr. Phillips must have had this in mind when he said, 'I know the back-stairs which lead to the governor's room.'

"The colored people adopted heartily the general principles of the abolitionists, and they manifested their sympathy in various well-known ways. In matters of detail, however, they chose their own methods. The abolitionists were non-resistants. If a fugitive slave was to be rescued, or a body-guard was to go with Mr. Phillips from Belknap-street church to his home, the colored people did not accept that doctrine. The abolitionists did not vote. The colored people always voted, when, by so doing, they thought they could thereby cripple the slave-power; and Mr. Phillips never found fault with them for exercising this discretion. The fact is, that, in political action, the negro has been guided largely by that instinct, based on the first law of nature, — self-preservation. He always voted, and he always voted right.

"The last time Mr. Phillips was with the colored people, socially, was at a dinner given to him by the Wendell Phillips Club, six or seven years ago, at their rooms in Cambridge Street. Mr. Garrison was present, and the banquet lasted until a comparatively late hour of the night. The war was ended; slavery was abolished; the constitutional amendments were adopted; the negro was free and equal before the law. And here were the two veteran abolitionists, covered with honor and glory, sitting at table with colored citizens, to celebrate their victory. Grander sight was never beheld! Reminiscences of the anti-slavery struggle were given with zest, names of departed heroes and scenes passed away were recalled, and the words of wisdom and hope which fell from the lips of Garrison and Phillips that night will never be effaced from the memories of those who were present while life lasts. The abolition movement was the purest and highest movement that was ever carried forward in this country. It was more than philanthropy, morality, or statesmanship. It was all these combined. The abolitionists sought to reach human conscience. They were not heeded, and the great sin of slavery was expiated in rivers of blood. Hail to the abolitionists, dead and living, men and women! Never-dying honor is yours! The freedom for which you contended has triumphed, and your deeds are recorded in the brightest page of your country's history. Illustrious Phillips, hail!

"Ladies and gentlemen, I present to you a gentleman, who, from his name, position, and ability, is the man to deliver the eulogy."

Mr. Grimké's oration was worthy alike of the subject and of the speaker. The following extracts are here given: —

"Freedom and slavery made great advances, from the murder of Lovejoy to the passage of the Fugitive-slave Law. Calhoun had continued that agitation of slavery in and out of Congress, which looked to the union of the South for decisive action. Year by year the circle of his influence widened, and the seeds he had sowed were springing up. And year after year the slave-power grew more aggressive and insolent. The great Nullifier was generating the electrical energies of the irrepressible conflict. At the end of this period, the South had but one policy and passion. To preserve slavery, it trampled, rough-shod, upon the Constitution, and the liberties of the North. Texas it had got. The Mexican war it had precipitated upon the free States. It had finally extorted from the recreant North the infamous Slave Bill. Southern arrogance could go no farther, and Northern servility could crawl to no lower deep of wickedness. The slave-power had again overreached itself.

"The anti-slavery agitation did not remain where the year '37 had left it. It advanced through the North with increasing fervor and numbers. It was arousing and uniting the North. A determined purpose had formed in the free States, to resist the extension of slavery. Northern servility and selfishness were caught in the conflagration which Garrison had kindled, and Phillips fed. They were consuming in 'the penal fire' of the reformation. And out of their ashes was rising the new North, liberty-crowned. And so, while the years from '37 to '50 had united the South, they had also aroused the manhood of the North. The impious enactment of 1850 accelerated the collision of the moral forces of the Republic.

"It is impossible to convey any adequate idea of the earnestness and daring which then caught Phillips up, and bore him on wings of flame to the manhood of the North. He was transported to limits beyond all fear, beyond all regard for wicked laws and slave commissioners, all love of country, all the known methods and safeguards of civil society. He flung himself back upon the 'great primal right of self-protection' as 'the kernel of possible safety' for the fugitive. He shrank from no act, 'however desperate,' to rescue 'a human being hunted by twenty millions of slave-catchers.' At moments of supreme passion he trampled upon the sentiments of his best friends. With what vehemence he stamped upon the non-resistant doctrines of Mr. Garrison! 'If your hearts answered instead of your nerves,' he exclaimed on the anniversary of the rendition of Sims, 'you would rise up, every one of you abolitionists, ready to sacrifice every thing, rather than a man should go back to slavery!' Friends shook their heads, and said his doctrine was bloody. Enemies accused him of spreading anarchical principles. But neither enemies nor friends could frighten or dissuade him. The air which he breathed carried into his blood the monstrous dishonor done the North, and the brutal wrong done the black man. He burst through all the barriers of civil society, and stood face to face with the slave-hounds of the Constitution. He bade the fugitive turn, and smite his pursuer. He declared that the shooting of a Morton, or a Curtis, 'on the Commissioners' Bench, by the hand of him they sought to sacrifice, would have a wholesome effect.' In every speech he made now, there was a possible John Brown.

"From the passage of the Fugitive-slave Law, Garrison was thrown into the background by his great coadjutor. The anti-slavery agitation had passed from the first to the second stage of its growth. Over the first, the pure spirit and uncompromising heart of Garrison had presided. It was the period of beginning, incubation, preparation. It was the stage of investigation, discussion, revelation. It was the seed-time of the struggle. The peace-principles of Garrison were the hovering wings of the movement. Under their shelter and mother-love, truth and justice stirred at the centre of a nation's life. They hatched apathy into feeling, feeling into knowledge, knowledge into repentance, repentance into conviction. Within their shadow, malignity could not reach, and public opinion was impotent. Thus protected, the moral forces of the reformation grew. This period formed, like the clouds, amid the still processes of nature. The sun drinks up the rivers: atmospheric changes come with the winds. The blue sky vanishes, the tempest flies overhead, the imprisoned heat speaks, 'the live thunder' leaps, and rain tumbles upon the thirsty fields. The period of preparation has gone. The time of action has come. 'I must decrease, but thou must increase,' expresses one of the subtle moods of nature. Childhood advances, and then succeeds manhood to all that it brings. To-day stands tiptoe on yesterday, and reaches up to where to-morrow begins. The years from '29 to '50 toiled, and laid up, to furnish Phillips his vantage-ground.

"We make no comparison. None can be made between Garrison and Phillips. We love them both with a love which only those who have received much can give. But, if we wished to describe Mr. Garrison's relations to the struggle, we should perhaps say that he sustained to it the relations of motherhood, and Mr. Phillips those of fatherhood. They are the common parents, under God, of our deliverance. For, without both, our freedom would never have been born.

"But when the year 1850 came, and the slave-power hung with its black bill over the free States, non-resistance had no longer any place in the conflict. The time for argument had passed: the time for arms had arrived. On the first wave of this momentous change, Wendell Phillips mounted to leadership. His speeches were the first billows, breaking in prophetic fury, against the South. They were the first blast of the tempest, the first shock on the utmost verge of civil war. Forcible resistance of the black bill was now obedience to God. It was the dictate of the highest justice. The passage of the bill was the actual opening of hostilities between the two sections. The Union, from that moment, was in a state of war. Of course, there were not then any of the visible signs of war, — no opposite armies, two belligerent governments, two hostile social systems in actual and bloody collision. It was none the less real, however. Such a conflict ends always in an appeal to force.

"The peaceable surrender of a fugitive becomes now treason to freedom. Wendell Phillips comprehended the gravity of the situation. He refused to cry peace where there was no peace. He answered the Southern manifesto with the thunder of his great speech, on the anniversary of the rendition of Sims. Right and wrong has grappled at last in mortal strife. 'Why does the mayor stand there arguing? Why does he not call for the guns?' revealed in '35 the character of the man. Mr. Garrison's non-resistant doctrines in '50 shrank from the consequences of meeting force with force. But this time Phillips is no longer a spectator in the street. He is in command, and has called for the guns. No half-way measure will now do. No mere resort to legal remedies to rescue fugitives can save the North from the basest capitulation. He saw clearly, that the danger of the reform lay in the stupor and indifference which repeated executions under the law would produce. The South was united and highly organized, impelled by a single purpose, and in possession of the whole machinery of government. He saw the North timid, irresolute, sordid, drugged by Whigs and Democrats, and frozen with the fear of disunion, ready to call the crime of yesterday, indifferently bad to-day, and the unavoidable to-morrow. Peace was slavery, and sleep was death. The only hope of freedom lay now in the finger that could pull a trigger. This might beat back the advancing apathy, and save the citadel of liberty. The fate of millions of slaves, the destiny of a free people, hung by a thread, which one bad precedent might sever. It is the glory of Phillips, that he saw this, — saw the peril in its imminency and all its consequences, and smote, with undying eloquence, the myrmidons of slavery. He was an army in himself. His eloquence, poured out month after month, and year after year, became a kind of immanent presence, an elemental influence, an omnipresent curse, an incorporeal spirit of justice and duty throughout the North. The very air of the free States vibrated with the disembodied soul of his mighty invectives. Slave-catching he has made a crime the blackest in the calendar of the republic. The probate judge of Massachusetts, who sat as a commissioner in the case of Burns, he annihilated. His indictment of Judge Loring is a masterpiece worthy to be ranked with Burke's impeachment of Warren Hastings. He became a terror to the kidnapper. The slave-hounds bayed with bated breath at the sound of his magic voice. Black men heard him, and learned to pull the trigger, and swing the bludgeon. White men heard, and learned to sleep upon muskets shotted to the lip for the man-stealer. John Brown heard him, and, with his brave little band, has flung himself upon Virginia, and struck for the freedom of the slave. Harper's Ferry has taken its place with Marathon, Marston Moor, and Lexington; and the gallows on which John Brown died has become more glorious than the throne of the Cæsars.

"Shock after shock has loosened the ice from the conscience and courage of the North. The Republican party is born, and then comes the first political victory of freedom. Abraham Lincoln has entered the White House, and Jeff Davis has turned his back upon Washington forever. The trial-morning is rising gloomily on the Republic. The gray light is haunted with strange voices, winged portents, bloody apparitions. Right and Wrong, Freedom and Slavery, have reached the plains of '60.

"For years Phillips had advocated disunion. To him, as well as to Garrison, the Constitution was a 'covenant with Death and an agreement with Hell.' It was the strong tower of the slave-power, and he longed to see it pulled down. He firmly believed that nothing could save slavery after this crutch, which the Devil had given it, had been broken. To shatter the staff over the head of the Evil, was the solution of the problem. He did not perceive at once all the forces and circumstances which were to effect a consummation he so devoutly labored for. He saw the wrong, and he sought the remedy in dissolution. He thought this could be reached by peaceable secession, a solemn division of the Union in convention, a formal separation of two civilizations, the Fourteenth and Nineteenth centuries, a parting on that great day of the sheep and the goats, — liberty and slavery, — the one on the right, the other on the left — the one to enter into peace, honor, justice, and a more perfect union; the other into outer darkness, to poverty, public distress, financial ruin, masters weeping, and slaves breaking their chains amid the horror of insurrection. He saw but in a glass dimly. The confusion, the wide-spread misery, the lamentation, the thick darkness, and the blood of masters, were indeed to fall upon the South, but not as a consequence of peaceable secession and a possible insurrection of slaves. They were to come to pass amidst the tramp of mighty armies from the North rushing over her white fields and smiling cities, laying waste with the sword of a million freemen her magnificence and institutions, stained with the wrongs of two centuries of oppression. Phillips had become the oracle of Destiny impending. He, too, groped at times amid the thick-falling shadows of fate; but it was always toward justice in the fore-front of the host of freedom. All he wanted was more light; and it came, in the glare of cannon in Charleston Harbor. The God of battle revealed his purpose to the great leader in the smoke and fire of that mad April morning. He saw in a twinkling Emancipation marching in the lurid track of war, — war for the Union. With swift energy and triumphant faith he whirled into line with the majestic figure and under the flag of the Union. Under the flag at last, his divine speech broke loose, and rolled onward, swelling and dashing like the free and glorious ocean. Every throb of his great soul drove the hot blood of patriotism through vast multitudes. He was the eagle of eloquence, bearing on his outspread wings the tumultuous longings, the rising wrath, of nineteen millions to action, — Godlike action.

"To abolish slavery, and arm the blacks, he proclaimed now the supreme duty and demand of the hour. He saw at once, what it took Lincoln and Seward and the Republican party two years to see, that the Rebellion could never be crushed until the slaves were freed, and invoked to strike for their liberties. Any other policy he saw would end in dishonor and defeat. The foul stain of two hundred years must be washed out by an act of sublime justice before victory would smile upon the national banner. Till then our armies would advance only to retreat. The best and bravest of the land would fight only to die. The treasures of the North could not save, the courage of her citizen soldiery could not conquer peace, and restore the Union. One act of justice could. National justice had become a national necessity. The highest wisdom dictated it. It now was his mission to lift or lash the North to a comprehension of the situation. No one escaped the stern scrutiny and rebuke of those eyes, which burned through shams and lies to the innermost and uttermost of motive and conduct, — through the procrastination and irresolution of President and cabinet, general and statesmen, and laid open the faithlessness and shortcomings of all. He who swerved a hair's-breadth from the path of justice to the slave, felt the keen lash of this merciless censor. Not Sumner, nor Lincoln, nor Grant escaped. All regard for the feelings of others, all the strengths and weaknesses of friendship which make one man hesitate before censuring another, were evaporated from his heart, dried up in the fervor and madness of one mighty passion, — justice to the negro. In his great soul, there were no saving clauses for high or low, friend or foe, who did not reach up to the full measure of equal and impartial justice as the policy of the republic. With this sign, his matchless eloquence was stamping public opinion, and impelling the North to rally and conquer by it.

"The public sentiment which Lincoln obeyed, Phillips created. It was not enough to feel it responding to his touch. It was necessary also to tell the administration that the tide had risen. And it happened often, that, if he would be heard, he had to deliver his message in no uncertain tone. 'Free the slaves at once: you can never save the Union until you do,' said Phillips. While Lincoln would reply, 'Not so fast there: I am waiting for public sentiment to ripen for emancipation and colored troops.' And Phillips would rejoin, 'The administration, and not public sentiment, is the laggard in this war. Courage, man! You have only to do justice bravely, and the people will sustain you.' But Mr. Lincoln did not so think. And Mr. Lincoln — with all reverence I say it — was troubled with that same disease which he said McClellan had, — the *slows*. The martyr President had it, and that very bad, during the first two years of the war. Phillips was vigilant, and Lincoln was tardy: that is all. Justice long deferred came at last. The Emancipation Proclamation transfigured the flag of the Union, and verified the predictions of Phillips. The colored troops at Wagner, Olustee, and Petersburg proved by their blood and heroism the race's title to liberty. After the war Mr. Phillips abated nothing of zeal and vigilance in our behalf. For the freedmen he demanded the ballot, and every right of American citizenship. To Sumner in the Senate, and Phillips on the platform, the one acting upon government, the other upon public opinion, we owe, under God, more than to any other means, the political rights which we now possess.

"The great struggle for freedom may be divided into three parts: The first beginning with the imprisonment of Garrison in 1829, and ending with the passage of the Fugitive-slave Law in 1850, — the period of pure moral agitation, of which Garrison was the leader. The second extends from 1850 to the close of the war, — the period of decisive action, during which Phillips was the pre-eminent figure. And the last, opening in 1865, is not yet finished. The labors of the first two are to be permanently secured in this, the third, by law, and the social changes which come with national growth. To the day of his death, Sumner's was the towering character of this the concluding act of the great drama.

"Sumner and Garrison are not, for God has taken them. And to-night we are standing by the open grave of the greatest of the three. But not in yonder burial-ground are we to look for a life so inspired and inspiring. Dust to dust was never spoken of a soul so luminous with the light of immortal living and doing. Justice, faith, love of liberty, were the great qualities which distinguished the man. Whoever had a wrong to redress could appeal with confidence to him. The needy Irishwoman, or the distressed colored man, who sought his aid, was never turned away uncomforted. He was the fast friend of woman, of Ireland, temperance, the Indian, of every good cause and true, the world over. Around his bier, rich and poor, learned and unlearned, met, and mingled their tears. Whoever saw him on these streets during the last years of his life, whose hearts did not pour out, at the sight of him, the homage of unspeakable trust, admiration, and love? In his soul, there was no guile. He walked among us, the incarnation of honor, purity, righteousness. True, brave, generous, marvellous man, — as he spoke, so he lived, the paragon of eloquence and the exemplar of the noblest virtues of the husband, citizen, and uncrowned king of public opinion. Such a life does not die in the heart of the world. It lives on, a sweet constraint, wherever the poor prays for bread; a stern compulsion wherever the slave clanks his chains, and liberty struggles with power.

"Whoever mistook appearance for reality, and preferred the temporal and visible to the eternal and invisible verities of mind and God, *he never*. He saw this great country, her ships sailing upon the sea, her cities shining in the plain, labor toiling at the loom, capital flowing into vaults, — he saw all the glory of this republic, its opulence and power, — and he looked, and beheld that all was vanity. For, under all this splendor and laughing prosperity, sin was at work. He knew that a lie was strong enough to overthrow and crumble all this worldly power and grandeur. Truth, justice, righteousness, are the only permanent forces in the universe. All else must fail and perish, like the grass which to-day is, and to-morrow rots where it once flourished. Ideas, character, goodness, — the emotions are all that we really possess. They pass over the huge, sensuous world, and empires rise and fall, races endure or vanish. They alone are worth striving for. All else is dust. Put justice at the centre of life, keep truth pure in the heart of a nation, bind about it love for all mankind. These are the only forces which make for it permanent peace and advancing greatness. We hear this voice now sounding in our ears. We feel this light now breaking in our hearts. They come to us from the open grave of our fallen leader, from the air breathing, burning with the eloquence of his life and death, saying, 'Boston, Massachusetts, my country, love righteousness, be just!'

"And now, fellow-citizens of the same race, this loss comes to us with peculiar grief. He was our own, our beautiful, our strong, our devoted one. The sentinel has fallen at his post. Take a last look, and the eternal blessing of those mute lips. They speak to us words of hope and duty. They bid us finish what yet waits to be done. The message to us is FAITH, LABOR. Let us gird ourselves with the spirit of our great friend. The work to be done now, is to be done by our own hands. The battle against caste-prejudice, the battle for the civil and political liberties of our race in the South, the battle against moral foes within, against the mastery of the appetites, against idleness, intemperance, and ignorance, are now to be fought. Over these obstacles let us march to equality under the law, to domestic happiness, to temperate, industrious, and educated manhood. Great lights are above us. Sumner, Garrison, Phillips, and the innumerable company of anti-slavery saints and martyrs, watch us from the skies. Night and day are full of their glory. They gleam now from the firmament. They beam now upon our faces. They implore us by the chains which we wore two hundred years; by the struggles, sufferings, and triumphs of liberty; by our duties, our rights and wrongs; for ourselves, posterity, and country, — to be faithful to the high trust of FREEMEN."

Shortly after the funeral, Frederick Douglass, a life-long friend of Mr. Phillips, delivered an address before an audience at Washington, D.C. From the manuscript of this eulogy, which the orator has kindly loaned us for the purpose, we select the following passages: —

"We are here to commemorate the virtues, and commend the example, of Wendell Phillips, — a man of rare endowments, and of rare devotion to the cause of justice, liberty, and humanity.

"Death has been very busy during the last few years, in thinning out the ranks of such men. The list of those who have departed is longer and more brilliant than that which remains. We cannot think of the anti-slavery movement without remembering such names as John Quincy Adams, William Slade, John P. Hale, Salmon P. Chase, Charles Sumner, William H. Seward, Horace Greeley, Benjamin F. Wade, Thaddeus Stevens, William Lloyd Garrison, Samuel J. May, William Goodell, Gerrit Smith, and many others who might as worthily be named. These have all disappeared behind that curtain which veils the living present from the mysteries of death and eternity; and now the most brilliant and eloquent of them all, has laid aside his shining armor, and passed on to his eternal rest.

"I was among those who travelled many miles to attend his funeral services. This simple act was a better expression of the love and reverence felt for this man, and a higher tribute to his many virtues, than any words of mine, however well chosen, can render. The ties that bound me to Wendell Phillips were closer and stronger than ties between most men. They were both general and special, public and personal. He was among the first of those noble anti-slavery men in Massachusetts, who, more than five and forty years ago, gave me a heart-felt welcome to a home of freedom and a life of usefulness. I went to his funeral as to that of one of my own household; as to that of a life-long friend, an affectionate brother, one to whom I was indebted for offices the highest and best that a great man can bestow upon his humble brother. It was his to give me generous sympathy, wise counsel, and a noble example. His funeral was an occasion long to be remembered. It was not so much a season of tears as a season of calm resignation. The grief that he was gone was subdued by a sense of gratitude that he had been spared so long. Lament we may and must when a friend has departed, and when a great champion of liberty has fallen. But our grief is not without consolation: for when the full measure of human life has been evenly filled up with good works, as in this case; when all the great purposes of individual human existence have been fairly accomplished; when a blameless and beautiful career amid all the sweet consolations of home, family, and friends, has been calmly ended; when sin, the poisonous sting of death, has lost its power to inflame the wounds of the living, or to disturb the repose of the dead; when a life that began in conflict, clouds, and darkness, ends in peace, victory, and glory, — there is no permanent lodgement for pain and sorrow.

"The place of his funeral service was strikingly appropriate and suggestive. It was the old Hollis-street Unitarian Church, famous for the marvellous ministry of John Pierpont, a man who added to his high qualities as a teacher, writer, and preacher, those of poet, scholar, patriot, statesman, and reformer. This edifice is one of the oldest in the city of Boston. To those who knew its history, there were sermons in its very walls. Looking up to its lofty pulpit, high above its high-backed, old-fashioned pews, my mind was carried back to the time when John Pierpont spoke his brave, scorching, and incisive words against those twin monsters, the liquor-power and the slave-power of our country, and thereby brought down upon himself the bitter and persistent hostility of the common enemies of human welfare and happiness. It was here, too, that Starr King, king of pulpit orators in his time, poured forth his soul for truth, justice, and liberty. It was here, too, worshipped Francis Jackson, the brave man who welcomed to his house an anti-slavery prayer-meeting, in the face of a howling mob that threatened to tear it down if he gave such welcome. The very atmosphere of the place seemed pervaded with the principles that inspired the energies, moulded the life, and fashioned the eloquence, of Wendell Phillips.

"As was the place, so was the conduct of the funeral. It was made impressive by its very simplicity. There were no sombre weeds of mourning festooning pillars, pulpit, or chancel, no floral decorations, no solemn pomp, no high-sounding ceremony, no ostentatious symbols of grief to be seen anywhere; but all was like the great man whose funeral it was, unstrained, modest, natural, simple, and consistent. A few well-chosen scriptural quotations, a prayer, more of thanks than of supplication, a hymn of joy rather than a dirge of sorrow, and all was over; and the corpse of Wendell Phillips, on the arms of those who had loved and honored him in life, was silently and reverently borne away to old Faneuil Hall, to lie in state, where for nearly fifty years the same noble form often stood up to reprove and denounce the errors, prejudices, and wrong-doings of his fellow-citizens, and where I have often seen him hooted down by the infuriated populace, because of his fidelity to the claims of justice and liberty.

"The contrast between then and now is conspicuous, striking, and impressive, — Wendell Phillips, reviled while alive, reverenced and adored when dead; unpopular when he spoke, applauded now that he was silent.

"The hold this man had upon the people of Boston and Massachusetts was well illustrated by the thousands wading through mud and rain to Faneuil Hall, to take one last look at the tranquil features of him they had so often seen and heard in life. Not more significant was this grand procession as to numbers, than was its composition and representative character. Rich men, poor men, learned men, simple men, Englishmen, and Irishmen, reverently gathered around the corpse of this, the friend of all men.

"Until I made one of this vast throng, and looked into the casket that held all that was mortal of Wendell Phillips, I could hardly realize that my friend and co-laborer of five and forty years was indeed dead, and the great loss the cause of humanity had sustained in his death.

"Of all the multitudes now doing honor to the memory of Wendell Phillips, none have a better right to engage in such manifestations than the colored people of the United States. It is true that Mr. Phillips was a friend to temperance, to the cause of the working-classes, and to Ireland. Wherever the tyrant reared his head, he was ready, like O'Connell, to deal his bolts upon it. But he was primarily and pre-eminently the colored man's friend, not because the colored man was colored, not because he was of a different variety of the human family from himself, but because he was a man, and fully entitled to enjoy all the rights and immunities of manhood. The cause of the slave was his first love; and from it he never wavered, but was true and steadfast through life.

"It was for him the theme of themes, the one that touched his heart, aroused his soul, and fired his eloquence. Great and powerful as he was as a speaker on all other subjects that engaged his wondrous faculties, he was incomparably greater when he spoke for the rights of the American slave. Other subjects stirred his intellect; but this touched the deepest chords of his heart, and engaged the whole man more completely than all else. Only a part of his weapons were employed elsewhere: here he brought to his help his whole mental and moral artillery. Not only the cruelty and wickedness of slavery, but its superlative meanness, stirred his soul, and kindled his moral indignation. He gave no quarter to its defenders at any point, but poured the living coals of truth, and his boundless wealth of scorn and execration, upon the system, and the men who upheld it. He was the most uncompromising man I ever saw. Nothing that stood in the way of the slave's freedom, secured respect or exemption. He spared neither church nor state, priest nor politician, high nor low, friend nor foe. Especially was he severe upon a half-hearted and halting support of anti-slavery principles. The lash and sting of his fierce invective often fell mercilessly upon men who thought they were serving the cause of emancipation not less well and faithfully than himself. Hale, Chase, Giddings, Seward, Lincoln, Mann, and even Charles Sumner, were sharply criticised by him. It need not be pretended that Mr. Phillips was always just in his criticisms and invectives. He made no pretensions to infallibility, but his sincerity and devotion to principle were utterly beyond question.

"He was universally popular as a lyceum lecturer, and often received calls to lecture by associations bitterly hostile to his anti-slavery opinions. He had more calls to fill such appointments than he could possibly comply with. To such invitations he usually replied, 'One hundred dollars and expenses if upon a literary subject; free of charge if upon slavery.' To this cause he gave his time, his money, and his eloquence, without reserve, and without fee or reward.

"In measuring this man's worth, we must not view him in the sunlight of the present. We must go back to the time when he first gave his support to the anti-slavery cause, and reflect what was the condition of the public mind on that subject at that time.

"Daniel Webster, you know, once said, 'Any man can do an agreeable duty, but not every man can do a disagreeable duty.' After slavery struck at the life of the nation, after it had crippled and killed thousands of our sons and brothers on the battle-field, after it had rent asunder the nation at the centre, and imperilled the existence of the republic, it was easy to be an anti-slavery man: but when slavery ruled both the State and the Church, when it commanded the support of both press and pulpit, and wielded the purse and the sword of the nation; when he who dared to speak in favor of the abolition of slavery, lost caste in society, made himself of no reputation, and exposed his person and property to violence and peril, — to espouse this cause at such a time was not an agreeable duty, but one that required the noblest qualities of head and heart.

"A few facts only need to be stated, to show how dark and terrible was the moral atmosphere of the republic when young Phillips gave his heart to the anti-slavery movement. In 1831 Nathaniel Turner headed an insurrection in Southampton County, Va. The excitement caused by this act was tremendous, and kindled against the negro the fiercest hate. In the same year Mr. Garrison established 'The Liberator,' in Boston. In 1835 he was mobbed, and dragged through the streets of that city with a rope around his neck. In 1837 Lovejoy was murdered at Alton, Ill., for advocating emancipation in his paper. In 1838 Pennsylvania Hall was burned down in Philadelphia by a pro-slavery mob. In 1842 a slave-holding mob burned down several colored churches and halls in Philadelphia, and held sway in that city for several days without check or hinderance. In the South, at this time, abolitionist was but another name for a negro thief and a cut-throat. In the North, it stood for a disorganizer and a fanatic. Both the great political parties, Whig and Democratic, were pledged to the suppression of anti-slavery literature; and Congress adopted what was known as the gag-rule, suppressing all papers in any way relating to slavery. Gov. Everett of Massachusetts recommended the passing of a law making the discussion of slavery an offence punishable at common law. The great Methodist-Episcopal Church, at its General Conference, held in Cincinnati in 1836, issued the following resolution: '*Resolved*, By the delegates of the annual conferences in general conference assembled, that they are decidedly opposed to modern abolitionism, and wholly disclaim any right, wish, or intention to interfere in the civil and political relation between master and slave, as it exists in the slave-holding States of the Union.

"The position of the four leading religious denominations were in harmony with the position of this resolution. The sentiment of the time was, Down with abolitionism! Suppress the agitation! The common arguments against anti-slavery men were, 'You had better mind your own business.' 'You are meddling with what does not concern you.' 'You are only making the condition of the slave worse.' 'You have put back their cause fifty years.' 'You should leave slavery where the wisdom of the fathers left it.' You will never put down slavery by this agitation.' 'What have we to do with slavery?' 'What would you do with the negroes if you had them all?' 'The North is no better than the South.' 'You would not associate with negroes.' 'You want the negroes to cut their masters' throats.' 'If you turn them loose, they will all come North.' 'If you want them free, why don't you pay for them?' 'The negro will not work without a master.' 'The slaves are contented and happy.' 'The Bible sanctions slavery.' 'England forced slavery upon the colonies.' 'Slavery is guaranteed by the Constitution.' 'The early Christians said nothing against slavery.' 'Are you wiser than the Fathers?' 'The slaves are the happiest peasantry in the world.' 'You dare not go South, and preach your abolition.' 'They could not take care of themselves.' 'They are not prepared for freedom.' 'You are just making trouble.' 'If God wants slavery abolished, he will do it in his own good time.'

"These sentiments reflect the public opinion of the time when Wendell Phillips bravely stepped into the anti-slavery ranks, and took his place with the lowly and despised, nearly fifty years ago.

"It is said that the redeemer always comes from above. Whatever may be the truth in respect to this, as a general rule, there is no question that Wendell Phillips, in a very important sense, came from above. He belonged to the upper circle of American society. He had ancestry, birth, wealth, talents, influential friends, and the best education which wealth and opportunity could give him. Office and honors were before him. Power and fame were within his reach. He laid them all aside, and cast his lot with the slave and the men everywhere spoken against.

> "Then to side with Truth is noble
>   When we share her wretched crust,
> Ere her cause bring fame and profit,
>   And 'tis prosperous to be just;
> Then it is the brave man chooses,
>   While the coward stands aside,
> Doubting in his abject spirit,
>   Till his Lord is crucified,
> And the multitude make virtue
>   Of the faith they had denied.
>   .   .   .   .   .   .

> For Humanity sweeps onward:
>   Where to-day the martyr stands,
> On the morrow crouches Judas
>   With the silver in his hands;
> Far in front the cross stands ready
>   And the crackling fagots burn,
> While the hooting mob of yesterday
>   In silent awe return
> To glean up the scattered ashes
>   Into History's golden urn."

Among all the noble men in Massachusetts who early came to the support of William Lloyd Garrison, in his war upon slavery, none came from a higher social plane, or parted with brighter prospects, or brought to the cause more brilliant abilities, than did Wendell Phillips. He might have been congressman, governor, senator, of the United States, and, possibly, have risen higher still, had he allied himself to either of the great political parties. In the Senate, had he reached that body, he would have ranked with Sumner and Conkling as an orator, and with Fessenden, Grimes, Douglas, and O. P. Morton as a debater.

"Eloquent as he was as a lecturer, he was far more effective as a debater. Debate was for him the flint and steel which brought out all his fire.

"The memory of Mr. Phillips was something wonderful. He would listen to an elaborate speech for hours, and, without a single note of what had been said, in writing, reply to every part of it as fully and completely as if the speech were written out before him. Those who heard him only on the platform, and when not confronted by an opponent, have a very limited comprehension of his wonderful resources as a speaker.

"In his style as a debater, he resembled Sir Robert Peel, in grace and courtliness of manner, and in the fluency and copiousness of his diction. He never hesitated for a word, or failed to employ the word best fitted to express his thought on the point under discussion.

"It may be said, that, on the subject of slavery, it was easy to do all this; since one might have a full command of all the facts and arguments, and be ready at any moment to employ them against an opponent. But this was not so. The anti-slavery platform in Massachusetts was not confined to the bare subject of chattel slavery. The whole circle of human interests came up for discussion.

"Legal, political, ethical, social, and religious questions claimed attention and debate. As the whole man was struck down by slavery, so the whole man was considered by the friends of liberty in advocating his claims to liberty. In all these discussions Mr. Phillips bore his full share.

"His oratory, like the oratory of all men, had its period of youth, its middle age, and its old age. When young, his style was ornate, and abounded in word-pictures. More than forty years ago, when he had just returned from a tour in Europe, where he witnessed the disgraceful position this republic had been made to occupy by Gen. Cass, our minister to France, in refusing to sign the quintuple treaty for the abolition of the slave-trade, he made a speech in the Tabernacle in New York, which illustrated this youthful quality of his oratory. 'As I stood,' said he, 'on the shores of Genoa, and saw our beautiful American ship, the "Ohio," floating on the placid Mediterranean, with her masts tapering proportionally aloft, her pennon flying, and an Eastern sun reflecting her graceful form upon the sparkling waters, attracting the gaze of the multitude on the shore, I thought the scene one to pride any American to think himself an American; but when I thought, that, in all probability, the first time that gallant ship should gird on her gorgeous apparel, and wake from beneath her sides her dormant thunder, it would be in defence of the African slave-trade, I could but blush, and hang my head, to think myself an American.'

"On another occasion, after tracing the progress of liberty, under the symbol of the eagle, from Greece to Rome, and from Rome to Western Europe, and thence to America, he made an impressive pause in his rapid sketch; and, while his audience were yet under the spell of his matchless eloquence, he exclaimed, 'Did God send that eagle here to die? Did he form the Mississippi valley for its grave? Did he pile up the Rocky Mountains for its monument? Did he pour out Niagara's thunders for its requiem?' This florid style of the young orator was early laid aside for a more direct and dignified one, which grew more and more chaste with his advancing years.

"Perfect as Mr. Phillips was as a speaker, he lacked one element of a perfect orator. He could make men think, make them angry, make them wince under his scathing denunciations; he could make them smile; but he could not bring young tears from mature eyes. His mission was, to point out the defects in the thoughts, speech, and action of others; to expose the short-comings of men, — and he did this unsparingly and thoroughly. He would not occupy official position himself, and sharply criticised all who did. When asked to come and fill their positions better, his answer implied, that, were he in office, he would be compelled to do as others did, or do nothing. At any time within the last twenty years, he might have been sent to Congress had he wished it; but he did not wish it, because, in that case, he would have to forsake his vocation as a critic, and become an actor, and, of course, open to criticism. I cannot but think this was a mistake; for Mr. Phillips was not only a speaker, but a man of affairs, and was marvellously well fitted to manage affairs.

"The true nobility of this man was shown in his tender regard for the feelings of the lowly and proscribed. In this he touched the point of supererogation. For instance, after delivering a lecture to the New-Bedford Lyceum before a highly cultivated audience, and when brought to the railroad station, as I was not allowed to travel in a first-class car, but was compelled to ride in a filthy box called the Jim Crow car, he would step to my side in the presence of his aristocratic friends, and walk with me straight into this miserable dog-car, saying, 'Douglass, if you cannot ride with me, I can ride with you.' On the Sound, between New York and Newport, in those dark days, a colored passenger was not allowed abaft the wheels of the steamer, and had to spend his nights on the forward deck, with horses, sheep, and swine. On such trips, when I was a passenger, Wendell Phillips preferred to walk the naked deck with me, to taking a state-room. I could not persuade him to leave me to bear the burden of insult and outrage alone. Acts like these gave me a peep into this man's soul, and taught me to love and respect him, even when afterwards he made me, at times, the object of his sharpest criticism.

"Wendell Phillips had reached that point where he respected neither race nor color, but honored manhood wherever he found it. He had no word to say in favor of race-pride or race-prejudice, but everywhere evinced his high respect for a common manhood; and in this he set an example for men of every shade and color.

"When I first essayed to speak in public, I often left the platform feeling depressed with the thought that my effort had been a failure; but I never felt thus in the presence of Mr. Phillips, that he did not give me some cheering word. When I was going to England, and expected to do some speaking there, he said to me, 'Douglass, you will find many speakers in England inferior to ours, but you will find some who are superior to any of our speakers. But have no fear: speak there as you do here. Be yourself, and you will succeed.'

"Perhaps there was no one act in the life of Wendell Phillips that showed what manner of man he was, and better illustrated his dauntless courage, than his prompt vindication of the character and motives of John Brown, immediately after his raid upon Harper's Ferry. For the moment, the blood of the nation stood still, and the boldest held his breath. Murderer, assassin, cut-throat, incendiary, traitor, were the best names that the nation could apply to Capt. John Brown. A fierce scream for his blood came up from all the land. Anti-slavery men made haste to free themselves from all complicity with him by condemning both the man and his methods. It was at this time, in the midst of a reign of terror such as the country had never before seen, that Wendell Phillips dared to step forward, and demand a hearing for John Brown. He stood alone. No voice but his was raised. Men were stunned by his temerity. By many he was deemed as mad as the men at Harper's Ferry. But his isolation was of brief duration. His words from Beecher's Brooklyn pulpit were contagious. They sounded over the land like a voice from heaven. Wise men heard them as Saul heard on his way to Damascus, and soon John Brown vaulted in the hearts of the loyal North to the dignity of hero and martyr. He spoke the word for which millions were listening, and which became at last the watchword of the loyal nation, and to which the armies of the nation were to time their high footsteps to Union, law, and liberty.

"The cause of the slave had many advocates, many of them very able and very eloquent; but it had only one Wendell Phillips.

"He was the Wilberforce of America; and as Lamartine once said of that great English philanthropist, so we may say of Wendell Phillips, that he went up to heaven with a million broken fetters in his arms, as evidence of a life well spent."

The memorial services in honor of Mr. Phillips, under the auspices of the city government of Boston, were held in Tremont Temple on the afternoon of April 18. Admission to the hall was by tickets; and so eager were the fortunate holders of them to secure their seats, that when the doors were opened at two o'clock, one hour before the time announced for the exercises to begin, a crowd of people was waiting to enter.

The exercises were introduced by an organ voluntary by Mr. Howard M. Dow. Promptly at three o'clock the Temple Quartet, upon a signal from Mayor Martin, who presided on the occasion, stepped to the front of the platform, and sang to the tune "Loyal to the end," a hymn written by C. J. Sprague, beginning, —

> "Freedom dwells throughout our own beloved land:
> Up to heaven its voice is swelling."

The Rev. M. J. Savage then delivered a prayer, in which he spoke of Mr. Phillips as one of the prophets of God, who was sent to rouse the heart and conscience of the world. After the prayer, the quartet sang a hymn, written for the occasion by Mr. Savage. Then followed the reading of a poem by Mrs. Mary E. Blake.

In introducing the orator of the occasion, Mayor Martin spoke briefly. George William Curtis, on rising, was received with prolonged applause. He succeeded in holding the closest attention of the audience.

No one in the audience who ever heard Mr. Phillips could fail to be impressed with the marked resemblance between the two men in their oratorical style.

Mr. Curtis began his oration by remarking that Mr. Phillips was not the treasure of the city or of the State alone, but he was the nation's possession. He occupied a place of national eminence, and presented the strange anomaly of a man, who, while a private citizen, was yet a public leader. The homage paid him was a tribute to personal character. His early life was briefly sketched; and, after a rapid glance at his youth and his college-course, Mr. Curtis came to the time when, sitting in his law-office waiting for a client, Mr. Phillips witnessed the exciting scenes of the Garrison mob. The long-awaited client came to him that day: it was "wronged and degraded humanity." A detailed account of the circumstances of Mr. Phillips's first speech in Faneuil Hall was then given, and the old, familiar story gained new beauty and significance from the fascinating and inspiring manner in which it was told. Having thus introduced him upon the rostrum, Mr. Curtis then proceeded to speak of Mr. Phillips as the orator of the anti-slavery cause. He brought out the full force of the fact, that Mr. Phillips stood alone, against parties and established order and old traditions. The country needed to be aroused: agitation was the duty of the hour, and to this task Mr. Phillips devoted himself. How well he performed it, and by what methods, Mr. Curtis showed by a careful analysis of his subject's oratorical powers. Then, changing his theme, Mr. Curtis unfolded before the audience the growth of slavery till it became a mighty giant, grappling in deadly conflict with liberty. A quarter of a century passed, and "liberty arose unbruised and unharmed." Returning again to Mr. Phillips, Mr. Curtis sketched rapidly the events of his later years, and closed by a careful summing up of his work, and presentation of the principles which ruled his life. The orator finished his manuscript amid the enthusiastic applause of the audience. A pleasing episode, at this point, was the calling upon Dr. Smith, the author of "America," — the singing of which closed the exercises, — by the mayor, to rise in his place upon the platform, that the audience might honor him. He was greeted with prolonged applause. After singing with spirit the familiar hymn, the audience received the benediction, and then dispersed.

I cannot better close this chapter than by reproducing, with the author's kind permission, the following beautiful poem by Mr. John Boyle O'Reilly of Boston: —

WENDELL PHILLIPS.

What shall we mourn? For the prostrate tree that sheltered the young green wood?
For the fallen cliff that fronted the sea, and guarded the fields from the flood?
For the eagle that died in the tempest, afar from its eyry's brood?

Nay, not for these shall we weep; for the silver cord must be
   worn,
And the golden fillet shrink back at last, and the dust to its earth
   return;
And tears are never for those who die with their face to the duty
   done;
But we mourn for the fledglings left on the waste, and the fields
   where the wild waves run.

From the midst of the flock he defended, the brave one has gone
   to his rest;
And the tears of the poor he befriended, their wealth of affliction
   attest.
From the midst of the people is stricken a symbol they daily saw,
Set over against the law-books, of a higher than human law;
For his life was a ceaseless protest, and his voice was a prophet's
   cry,
To be true to the truth, and faithful, though the world were arrayed
   for the lie.

From the hearing of those who hated, a threatening voice has
   past;
But the lives of men who believe and die, are not blown like a leaf
   on the blast.
A sower of infinite seed was he, a woodman that hewed to the
   light,
Who dared to be traitor to Union when Union was traitor to right!

"Fanatic!" the insects hissed, till he taught them to understand
That the highest crime may be written in the highest law of the
   land.

"Disturber" and "Dreamer" the Philistines cried, when he preached an ideal creed,
Till they learned that the men who have changed the world, with the world have disagreed;
That the remnant is right, when the masses are led like sheep to the pen;
For the instinct of equity slumbers till roused by instinctive men.

It is not enough to win rights from a king, and write them down in a book:
New men, new lights; and the fathers' code the sons may never brook.
What is liberty now, were license then; their freedom our yoke would be:
And each new decade must have new men to determine its liberty.
Mankind is a marching army, with a broadening front the while:
Shall it crowd its bulk on the farm-paths, or clear to the outward file?
Its pioneers are the dreamers, who heed neither tongue nor pen
Of the human spiders, whose silk is wove from the lives of toiling men.

Come, brothers, here to the burial! But weep not, rather rejoice,
For his fearless life and his fearless death; for his true, unequalled voice,
Like a silver trumpet, sounding the note of human right;
For his brave heart, always ready to enter the weak one's fight;
For his soul, unmoved by the mob's wild shout, or the social sneer's disgrace;
For his free-born spirit, that drew no line between class or creed or race.

Come, workers! here was a teacher, and the lesson he taught was good:
There are no classes or races, but one human brotherhood;
There are no creeds to be outlawed, no colors of skin debarred;
Mankind is one in its rights and wrongs, — one right, one hope, one guard.
By his life he taught, by his death we learn, the great reformer's creed, —
The right to be free, and the hope to be just, and the guard against selfish greed.
And richest of all are the unseen wreaths on his coffin-lid, laid down
By the toil-stained hands of workmen, — their sob, their kiss, and their crown.